HOW 'BOUT THEM
COWBOYS?

ALSO BY GARY MYERS

My First Coach
Brady vs Manning
The Catch
Coaching Confidential

HOW 'BOUT THEM
COWBOYS?

Inside the Huddle with the Stars and
Legends of America's Team

GARY MYERS

GRAND CENTRAL
PUBLISHING

NEW YORK   BOSTON

Grand Central Publishing
Hachette Book Group
1290 Avenue of the Americas, New York, NY 10104
grandcentralpublishing.com
twitter.com/grandcentralpub

First Edition: October 2018

Grand Central Publishing is a division of Hachette Book Group, Inc. The
Grand Central Publishing name and logo is a trademark of Hachette Book
Group, Inc.

The publisher is not responsible for websites (or their content) that are not
owned by the publisher.

The Hachette Speakers Bureau provides a wide range of authors for
speaking events. To find out more, go to www.hachettespeakersbureau.com
or call (866) 376-6591.

Library of Congress Control Number: 2018943208

ISBNs: 978-1-5387-6234-9 (hardcover), 978-1-5387-6422-0 (B & N signed
hardcover), 978-1-5387-6231-8 (ebook)

Printed in the United States of America

LSC-H

10 9 8 7 6 5 4 3 2 1

To Allison, Michelle, Emily, and Andrew

CONTENTS

HOW 'BOUT THEM
COWBOYS?

INTRODUCTION

Welcome to Dallas

The rock star owner of the Dallas Cowboys, the most popular, famous, and valuable team in the world, opened the door to his suite on the eleventh floor of the elegant St. Regis Hotel just off Fifth Avenue in midtown Manhattan.

Welcome to Jerry's World.

The view was spectacular and the day almost clear enough for Jerry Jones to see back to all those years ago in Dallas when he bought the Cowboys and the lease to Texas Stadium in 1989 from financially strapped banker, real estate, and oil-and-gas magnate Bum Bright for $154 million. At the time, it was the most money ever spent for a sports franchise, the first to crack the $100 million plateau, which fit right into Jones's business model: If you are going to do it, do it big. The Arkansas wheeler-dealer had been one of seventy-five investors who contacted Bright. He made the cut to fifteen and then five and then the team was his.

Jones paid 60 percent in cash that tapped out his liquidity, and the remaining 40 percent was financed with loans using his personal assets as collateral. In return, Jones bought himself a down-on-their-luck America's Team, coming off a 3-13 season, a debt-ridden operation that was losing $1 million per month. He had to buy 13 percent of the team in foreclosure—it was in the possession of the FDIC—and another 40 percent would be headed to the courthouse if the team wasn't sold ASAP.

It wasn't as if the Jones family was left wondering where the next meal was coming from after Jerry finished writing the checks, but the lifestyle he and his wife, Gene, and their children, Stephen, Charlotte, and Jerry Jr., were accustomed to could not be supported if the football team drained them as it had Bright and Clint Murchison before him, especially with the Dallas economy in ruins.

"Gene wouldn't have had to go to work waiting tables," Jones said with a grin in his luxurious suite. "But it sure was not going to be a lie if you had lost all that you'd have to start over, and I was forty-six. I certainly knew those consequences. I had not taken any risks like that in my oil-and-gas business. You have to remember people were saying the NFL was flat and the NBA was taking over. Of course, you know what Dallas was. Dallas looked like a nuclear bomb had gone off in it."

Once Jones finished negotiating all but the final millions with Bright on a Saturday morning at Bright's office on Stemmons Freeway, a few miles from downtown Dallas, they announced the sale. Bright was out after just five years as the owner; Murchison had guided the Cowboys through their first twenty-four years. The announcement was premature by months. It was made before Jones had been vetted by the NFL finance committee and before owners would vote to approve him. A press conference was planned for 8 p.m. that evening, but Jones and soon-to-be former Cowboys president and general manager Tex Schramm first flew on Jones's private plane to Austin so Jones could tell coach Tom Landry he was fired. It was an time the Cowboys returned from training camp in 2016, they had moved again, this time to "The Star," in suburban Frisco, which was the practice center equivalent in glitz to AT&T Stadium, which opened in 2009. The stadium and the practice facility are only thirty-nine miles apart, but with Dallas traffic, it takes a little more than an hour by land. Jones often has the need to shuttle back and forth but doesn't have the time to go by car. He purchased the perfect solution to bypassing the traffic: He became the proud owner of a helicopter that had reserved parking spots at the $1.3 billion stadium and on the practice field at the Dallas Cowboys World Headquarters, which sits on ninety-one acres the Cowboys are developing with a final price tag of $1.5 billion. Of course it's called The Star. What else? Why not? The blue star on the Cowboys silver helmet is the equivalent to the New York Yankees pinstripes. The Star is not just home to the Cowboys. It has an Omni hotel, health club, sports medical center, multiple restaurants, and stores. The low-rise building where the Cowboys operate also has office space in a separate tower for outside businesses, many of whom partner with the football team.

* * *

How 'Bout Them Cowboys? will take you along for a wildly entertaining ride. I spent a lot of time with the Jones family. This really is a Mom-Pop-and-Kids operation. Stephen, the oldest, is his father's conscience and has been forced to play good cop–bad cop when his dad acts out on his many whims. His play-by-play of talking Jerry out of drafting Johnny Manziel in 2014 is compelling and quite funny.

Charlotte Jones Anderson is the most powerful woman in the NFL and was thrust into the middle of the Cowboys' de-

I took the train from New York to Baltimore the night before the Cowboys-Colts game. The Cowboys easily beat the Colts, who would finish with a 2-14 record. I then took the train back to New York, finished packing up my stuff, and flew to Dallas that Tuesday. By Wednesday, I was in the locker room trying to develop sources and break stories. The Cowboys clinched the NFC East the next week with a victory at home against the Eagles, then lost in overtime in New York to the Giants to finish the regular season, which also gave Big Blue its first playoff berth since 1963.

I asked maybe the dumbest question of my career in the Cowboys locker room after the game. Perhaps caught up in my New York upbringing and actually being a Giants fan before I started my journalism career in 1976 and became completely neutral, I was curious if Cowboys veteran safety Charlie Waters felt good about the Giants finally making the playoffs after all those years of ineptitude. The game was meaningless for Dallas, which had already locked up the number 2 seed.

Waters, busy zipping up his bag by his locker, raised his head for a second.

"No," he said.

He meant to say: *Are you out of your mind?*

Then he turned away.

In the coming weeks, I worked the locker room trying to learn faces to attach to the names. My first trip to the Cowboys "facility" on Forest Lane, a few blocks off Central Expressway, was a shock. It was a blue metal shack that lacked for amenities and cleanliness. It was run-down and roach-infested and, quite frankly, not at all what I expected from America's Team.

High schools in football-crazed Texas had nicer locker rooms. High schools in New York that didn't even have a football team had nicer locker rooms. Cowboys players went across the street to the Tom Thumb supermarket to pick up lunch and sat on

My personal journey with the Cowboys began in December 1981 when I was hired to cover them for the *Dallas Morning News*. The plan of executive sports editor Dave Smith was for me to be the backup writer for the rest of the season, using the next six to eight weeks to get to know the players and Landry and Schramm and personnel director Gil Brandt and the assistant coaches, then take over as the main beat writer as soon as the season was over.

That sounded great, also giving me time to adjust to my move from New York to Dallas, dump my Queens accent, learn how to say y'all, realize football was the predominant religion, and step into the middle of one of the greatest newspaper wars in the history of American journalism between the *Morning News* and the *Dallas Times Herald*. The Cowboys were the most important story in town, and the Cowboys were the battleground on which the winner would be declared. That was appealing to any journalist who enjoyed the competition.

Two weeks before I was to meet the Cowboys and my new *Morning News* teammates in Baltimore for a game against the Baltimore Colts, Smith called and told me they'd had a change in plans. He had decided to remove the incumbent beat writer starting with the game in Baltimore.

"You're it," he said.

"Sounds good," I said. I was actually thinking, *Oh crap.*

The only Cowboys player I had ever spoken to was Tony Dorsett, when he was at the University of Pittsburgh and I was a student at Syracuse covering a game for the *Daily Orange*. We hardly forged a relationship in the visitor's locker room at old Archbold Stadium on the Syracuse campus, but I did bring my story with me to Dallas to show Dorsett and break the ice. It worked. Dorsett and I quickly formed a great player-writer bond.

have to drop them off by a back door like concert promoters had to do with the Beatles to keep them away from their adoring fans. Their mere presence prompts "Cowboys Suck" chants on the road just as quickly as loud cheers that make the home team feel like they are playing a road game. Even at a crucial showdown at the end of the 1993 season against the New York Giants at Giants Stadium that would decide the NFC East and the number 1 seed, Cowboys fans drowned out Giants fans with "moooooose" calls for fullback Daryl "Moose" Johnston. The fans in Dallas don't travel around the country like Pittsburgh Steelers or Philadelphia Eagles fans to see their team play, but they don't need to. They are already well represented in every NFL city.

Their brand is worldwide, and they have the most creative marketers. They took their direction from Jones, the ringleader of a three-ring circus, who learned it on the fly. Marketing was not his background—he was an oilman—but he sure taught himself how to transform the Cowboys into a moneymaking machine. Jones had to fight the NFL off in court when he brazenly signed lucrative deals in the midnineties to break away from the league's all-for-one-and-one-for-all revenue-sharing sponsorship rules and negotiated contracts with Nike, Pepsi, and American Express at Texas Stadium. The NFL sued him for $300 million. Jones countersued for $750 million. They settled, with future commissioner Roger Goodell playing peacemaker. Jones won over other owners who at first shrieked that he was ruining the league and then rejoiced when he showed the way to turn their franchises into ATM machines with no cash limits. That is why Jones is in the Hall of Fame. He changed the way the NFL does business. He turned multimillionaires into multibillionaires.

* * *

was so extravagant the estimate in the media went as high as $16 million, but not even Jones was willing to spend quite that much to celebrate himself.

* * *

Troy Aikman, Michael Irvin, and Emmitt Smith came and went with the Cowboys following careers that put them in the Hall of Fame, Jimmy Johnson left Dallas halfway through his ten-year contract, and even former adversary Bill Parcells of the New York Giants stopped by to say hello and coach the team for four years. They were shooting stars in the Cowboys' galaxy.

Jones has been the consistent face of the franchise, but this was not a start-up operation he purchased. Long before he arrived, the powerhouse brand was established by nearly three decades of Tex, Tom, and Gil, five Super Bowl appearances, great television ratings, and the coveted late afternoon television spot on Sunday doubleheaders.

NFL Films is officially credited with coining the America's Team nickname. It was the title of the Cowboys' 1978 highlight video, a pat on the back that Landry, by the way, despised. Now it can be told: Doug Todd, the Cowboys' public relations director at the time, went to his grave claiming he was the one who came up with America's Team.

Jones inherited a franchise that was hemorrhaging more than $30,000 a day in cash, but it still had tradition and the Landry Legacy and, of course, the world-famous Dallas Cowboys Cheerleaders, so popular they were the subject of a parody in the immensely popular porn film *Debbie Does Dallas*.

There was an awful lot to build on.

Love 'em or hate 'em a lot, ambivalence is not on the menu. The Cowboys pack hotel lobbies on the road and the team buses to buy the Cowboys and how it still gave him anxiety. His eyes got red and moist, and his voice cracked.

Yes, there is crying in football. It was an emotional time in Jones's life with the Hall of Fame voting imminent, the sadness he felt that his parents had passed and were not around to share the moment, and the flashback to risking his fortune when he was worrying so much he went from perfect health to being diagnosed with arrhythmia, an irregular heartbeat. He had what doctors told him was a "good-time heart," which he said was most common among medical students studying for endless hours and not sleeping enough and using caffeine or alcohol to stay awake.

"When your body says stop, you don't stop," Jones said.

The anxiety that was so paralyzing in 1989 paid off with three Super Bowl titles, recognition among the greats in the game with a bust in Canton, and a franchise valued by *Forbes* at $4.8 billion, the most in the world and just about $700 million more than the runner-up Manchester United. The Patriots were the next NFL team at $307 billion.

"I didn't have the answers financially," he said. "I really stuck it out there to buy the team. I had walked with the financial devil to buy these Cowboys."

Jones went to his doctor to find out why he had been having these episodes of uncontrollable tears while telling stories of how he gambled it all to buy the Cowboys.

"You had a traumatic experience back then," his doc said.

The tears didn't stop in the hotel room. He cried right up until the day before his August 5, 2017, induction, which he topped off with an A-list party of one thousand of his dearest friends at the Glenmoor Country Club in Canton. The party cost $8 million—that included a hometown discount from Justin Timberlake for his two-hour performance. The event extraordinary turn of events, considering Jones did not even officially own the team, at least as far as the NFL was concerned.

Thus began one of the wildest and most entertaining eras in NFL history. Jerry Does Dallas, indeed.

Jones pulled Landry off the golf course in the middle of a round at Hidden Hills Country Club near Landry's vacation home in the exclusive Lakeway section of Austin—on a day he was playing well and smacking his drives right down the middle of the fairway, no less—and fired him. Hours later, Jones held the press conference that became known as the Saturday Night Massacre that enraged all of Dallas, even the hypocritical Cowboys fans who had been pleading with Schramm for years to fire Landry. The difference: They had wanted Tex to do it; instead, some unknown bumpkin from the wrong side of the Red River in Arkansas decided the end had come for Saint Tom, with a $1 million golden parachute settling the final year of his contract.

"This is like Lombardi's death," Commissioner Pete Rozelle, who three months later would announce his own retirement, said with deep regret.

It was inconceivable back then that in 2017 Jones would join Rozelle, Landry, and Schramm in the Pro Football Hall of Fame.

At the St. Regis, Jones was dressed immaculately in a suit and tie. He learned early the value of dressing nicely when his mom had him wear a bow tie to greet customers in his father Pat's grocery store. On this day, he had just returned from a meeting at the NFL offices on Park Avenue and been recognized on his ten-minute walk back every step of the way. No team had more fans in enemy territory than the Cowboys.

Jones was now holding a cup of hot tea in his right hand, and the spoon inside it clanged against the mug as his hand began to shake. He paused, then began a story about the risks he took cision to sign Greg Hardy and to stick by Ezekiel Elliott, both allegedly involved in ugly domestic violence incidents. Jerry Jr., by his father's account, is most like his old man. He has the lowest profile of the Jones kids but had major input on the building plans for the stadium and The Star. Jerry and his wife, Gene, were married in 1963, much to the initial chagrin of her father.

The patriarch of the Jones family himself challenged Goodell in an epic power struggle in 2017 that led to whispers the NFL would try to force Jones out of the league.

Jones's response? Literally laughter.

Jason Witten, the future Hall of Fame tight end, was handed the torch from Bob Lilly as Mr. Cowboy and displayed the grace and dignity that made him one of the franchise's most beloved figures. His experience growing up in a home with domestic violence led to his charitable endeavors centered on providing help to children in abusive homes. Moving away at a young age with his mother and brothers from his destructive father in Virginia to his grandparents' home in Tennessee changed his life. Witten and Tony Romo met before a rookie minicamp in 2003, and they have been inseparable ever since. Romo retired in 2017 to accept the lead NFL analyst role on CBS. One year later, Witten was preparing for his sixteenth season, with plans to play until he was forty years old, when he was presented with an opportunity he could not refuse: ESPN offered him the coveted analyst position on *Monday Night Football*, a job first held by former Cowboys quarterback Don Meredith when the series debuted in 1970 on ABC. Witten hung 'em up in early May 2018, a few days shy of his thirty-sixth birthday. It gave former Cowboys three of the number one NFL analyst jobs on network television with Witten joining Romo and Aikman, who is on Fox. You will learn about the incredible Romo-Witten bond.

Dorsett, Dennis Thurman, Springs, and Robert Newhouse shared a dorm suite at training camp in Thousand Oaks for four summers. They were the heartbeat of the fun-loving team. Newhouse was trying to squeeze as many years as possible out of his career, while Dorsett, Thurman, and Springs were young and full of life and talkative. They were my guys. Springs was gone at fifty-four, Newhouse was dead three years later at sixty-four, and Dorsett, by his early sixties, was suffering from severe memory loss. Their bond lives on. As does the bond between Troy Aikman and Michael Irvin. And between Emmitt Smith and Daryl Johnston.

After Jones and Jimmy Johnson couldn't find a way to share the credit and divorced after five years, what led Jones to hire an equally strong-willed Bill Parcells ten years later?

There are many turns to the Cowboys reality show, so hang on to your Cowboys hats and buckle up your boots.

* * *

Back to my journey in Dallas. Back to 1981.

The Cowboys easily eliminated the overmatched Bucs 38–0 in the divisional round of the playoffs a few weeks after my arrival. My first big game for the *Morning News* was the following week in San Francisco for the NFC Championship Game, which became known as the Dwight Clark "Catch" game. I had not even unpacked all my bags or purchased my first pair of cowboy boots (full disclosure: I never did buy a pair in my eight years in Dallas) and was covering what would go down as one of the most iconic games in NFL history. Landry was awful with names but I felt proud that by the San Francisco 49ers game he knew mine.

I spent the off-season developing contacts and writing stories. That was the easy part. The newspapers in Dallas had historically covered the team as if the writers had to first clear their stories with Tex, Tom, and Gil. The media loved being associated with the organization and were sensitive about being put on an enemies list and being frozen out of information. As a result, there was a lot of meat on the bone or, to put it in Texas terms, lots of guacamole in the bowl for me to gobble up. There were so many stories that needed to be reported. A few weeks after the Cowboys lost to the 49ers, I published a story with a chart detailing the salaries of the Cowboys players and how underpaid most of them had been in comparison to the rest of the league. It was splashed across the top of the *Morning News* sports section.

It also prompted a phone call from Doug Todd, the Cowboys' public relations director.

"How could you do that?" he said.

"Do what?" I said.

"We are a family here. You hurt my family with that story," he said.

Not one player complained except Drew Pearson. The numbers I had been provided by the NFL Players Association did not have Pearson's updated salary, and it showed him making less than Butch Johnson.

"You think I'm stupid?" Pearson shouted. "You think I'd be making less than my backup?"

The players liked the concept of publishing their salaries. It exposed Schramm and Brandt as being cheap, and I began to give the players a forum to express their unhappiness with the Cowboys' negotiating tactics, which had never been done in Dallas with any consistency by previous beat writers.

That summer, on the first night of training camp in Thousand Oaks, Todd and the beat writer for the *Times Herald* had a few too many cocktails and stood outside my dorm room at California Lutheran University at 3 a.m. chanting my name.

They had decided that "Myers Sucks" was the professional way to respond to my hurting Todd's family and breaking stories ahead of the *Times Herald*. Once Todd realized I worked for the *Morning News* and not the Dallas Cowboys, we got along fine, and he was much more understanding of my approach of doing my job and not cutting the team slack, which by then I realized was a novel approach to covering America's Team.

Landry was much more civil. He was the best to cover. Straightforward and honest. "Call me at home if you have a question," he told me. "I don't want you to be wrong." I was there to cover the beginning and the end of his football demise, and it wasn't pretty. Only his first year with the expansion Cowboys in 1960 was worse than his last year with a roster depleted of talent.

He told the players in the opening evening team meeting at my first camp to be careful, "because we have a New York writer covering us now." By 8 a.m. the next morning, several players pulled me aside on their way to breakfast to tell me about Landry's warning.

I laughed. "That's respect."

Those Cowboys teams were the most quotable locker rooms of all time: Dorsett, Everson Walls, Too Tall, Pearson, Harvey Martin, Tony Hill, Johnson, Doug Cosbie, Thurman, Springs, Bob Breunig, Danny White, Randy White, John Dutton, Timmy Newsome, Anthony Dickerson, Mike Hegman, Tom Rafferty, Howard Richards, Billy Joe DuPree, Gary Hogeboom, Dextor Clinkscale, and Ron Fellows. I had an up-and-down relationship with Danny White, but on the rare days he felt like talking to me, he was always insightful. Those guys were fun to be around; they were great talkers, and they won a lot of games.

Schramm was Pete Rozelle's right-hand man and his former boss with the Los Angeles Rams. Having daily access to the de facto commissioner made my job so much easier. Schramm was a great man and accessible. When he was completely out of football in the last years of his life, and his beloved wife, Marty, had passed, I used to call him every six weeks or so to talk football. After all the help he had given me over the years, I thought I was doing a mitzvah by making sure he still felt involved. Brandt was a wealth of knowledge and information, even if he would now and again intentionally hand me bad draft information, hoping I would call my friend Giants GM George Young to mislead him as to what the Cowboys were thinking.

My last Cowboys game for the *Morning News* was the final game of the 1988 season, when the 'Boys lost to the Eagles to finish 3-13, which, combined with the Green Bay Packers' victory two hours later in Arizona, clinched the number 1 pick in the 1989 draft for Dallas, setting them up to draft Aikman.

I worked in Dallas for nearly eight years but unfortunately covered only the final few games of Waters's career. He was such an especially smart player, compromised at the end by knees ravaged by playing such a brutal sport. He retired after the loss to the 49ers in the NFC title game in 1981. He was used to being pampered by the Dallas media, but twenty-five years after he retired, he told me, "You changed the way this team is covered. That's a good thing."

* * *

At the Bengals-49ers Super Bowl in Miami after the 1988 season, Brandt invited University of Miami coach Jimmy Johnson to watch the game from the Cowboys suite. One month and three days later, Jones bought the Cowboys. Landry was immediately out of a job. Schramm and Brandt would soon follow. The Cowboys hierarchy had no idea at the Super Bowl what Jones was up to, and Johnson insists he didn't know Jones was going to buy the team and hire him to replace Landry when he sat with the Cowboys brain trust in Miami.

The Saturday Night Massacre press conference was brutal. Jones was so excited he could hardly control himself. He said buying the Cowboys was like Christmas and he would be involved in everything from the "socks to the jocks." He had his entire family around him soaking in the moment. The hostile media treated it like a death in the family. Schramm, knowing he was about to be marginalized and eventually pushed out, stood off to the side, morose. There was not even a chair for him. Brandt was out of town. Landry was having dinner with his wife and son in Austin.

"Tom Landry is the Cowboys," Jones said, a remark that did nothing to calm a media that acted like a lynch mob in the next morning's editions of the three area newspapers.

The race was on in Dallas to find Landry. The winner got a potentially exclusive interview. There would be no farewell press conference. The first place to stake out on Sunday morning was Addison Airport in North Dallas, which accommodated smaller jets similar to what Landry was flying. Landry piloted his own plane back and forth to Austin. He had flown thirty missions as a bomber pilot in World War II and survived a crash landing in Belgium when his plane ran out of fuel. His brother Robert, three years older and also a bomber pilot, died when his B-17 exploded near Iceland and disappeared into the Greenland Sea. A quick trip to the state capital on Landry Airlines to him was as easy as a drive around his beautiful neighborhood in the Preston Hollow section of Dallas.

It was quiet at the airport with not many takeoffs or landings that morning. I figured Landry first would attend church in Austin and then return to Dallas to clean out his office.

By noon, no sign of Landry.

Next stop: his home in Dallas, set on a hilltop cul-de-sac at 5336 Rock Cliff Place overlooking Bachman Creek. There was no indication of activity in the house and no car in the driveway. Was Landry still in Austin? Did he go right from Addison Airport to Valley Ranch?

David Moore of the *Fort Worth Star-Telegram* drove up about thirty minutes into my Landry Watch. We staked out the house for another hour and decided to head to Fuddruckers at North Park Mall for lunch. Stakeouts can make you hungry. Nothing changed at Landry's house after lunch.

There was just one other place to look: Valley Ranch.

His car was parked in his reserved spot. This seemed too good to be true. Could he be here? Maybe his son Tom Jr. had come by to pack up his father's office.

In those days, the media were given the access code to get in the front door and the various wings of the building. It changed after the Landry regime, and now at The Star there are security guards strategically placed throughout the building. The press room is not even on the same floor as the locker room. As Moore and I approached Landry's office, his door was slightly open, and we could see him sitting behind his desk inside. His assistant, Barbara Goodman, told us the coach was not available.

Landry heard our voices and peered out through the crack in his door.

"It's okay. They can come in," Landry said.

I was observing and living through an important piece of NFL history. Landry was the only coach the Cowboys had ever had, and he had held the job for twenty-nine years. He was one of the most respected men in NFL history, and Moore and I were invited by him to sit down and watch him pack so many years of memories into cardboard boxes. That openness will never happen again on any level in professional sports. Saint Tom was revered in Dallas, never more than this moment when he became a sympathetic figure, virtually a martyr, after being unceremoniously dumped. Suddenly this mysterious man of few words, whose public image was the suit and tie and fedora and scowl on the sidelines, was feeling the pain of losing a job he still desperately wanted, even at the advanced coaching age of sixty-four. He was like any other worker who had been laid off by a new boss who wanted change or just wanted his own people.

He sat there on a Sunday afternoon going through his desk drawers and placing trophies into boxes that he would load into the trunk of his car. He was dressed in a plaid shirt and a pair of checked slacks. No trademark fedora. No familiar sideline scowl. A smile. The pictures were off the walls. Papers were scattered across his desk. His custom-made office door with his two Super Bowl trophies chiseled in, given to him as a gift, would soon be coming down.

"Once the owner came in and expressed his sentiment, I was through," Landry said. "There was no place for me. It was just a matter of whether the deal came to a conclusion. Once it did, I was out of a job."

He paused.

"I'm not bitter," he said.

For all these years, Landry had designated one of his lower-level assistants as "the Turk," to knock on doors at training camp and say, "Coach Landry wants to see you. Bring your playbook."

Now it was Jones, a man Landry could not pick out of a lineup, telling him to turn in his playbook, his code to the building, his pass to the washroom, and his company car. "Amazing how much you accumulate for that many years," Landry said as the boxes piled up. "You wonder why you never cleaned your files out before."

Landry was not a heartless man. He just didn't want to show his emotions in public. He tried hard to hide his feelings that day, but it was evident he was hurting.

"People based their judgments just on what they saw on the sideline," he told me one month after he was fired. "The way I trained myself to concentrate, I blanked everything else out. You can't show emotion. I trained from watching Ben Hogan. He never let his concentration break. The image never bothered me. My friends know me."

His players never doubted he cared about them but also wondered why he never allowed himself to become too close to them. His answer was simple: He didn't want personal feelings getting in the way of personnel decisions.

"People say you have to know when to retire, which is a dumb thing to say," Landry said in his office that day. "If people want to go out on top, yeah. It becomes important when you quit if you're afraid to get into the situation we've been in the last two or three years. But I'm not afraid of that situation and I'm not afraid to be fired, either. That doesn't bother me."

The next day he said good-bye to his players in the team meeting room. He cried in front of them for the first time.

"He told us we'll forget about him in two weeks," Walls said.

* * *

On that Tuesday, Jones brought Johnson back to town for his introductory press conference. Johnson had been with Jones in the final stages of the negotiations with Bright, and then Jones

19

sent him to Miami for a few days to let things in Dallas calm down. Johnson was an accomplished coach. He had won a national championship at Miami and nearly won another. Yet, by the end of the press conference, which was more like a court-martial, Johnson was pleading for the media and Cowboys fans to give him a chance.

They did. Thus began the adventures of Jerry and Jimmy on a bicycle built for two. After five years and back-to-back Super Bowl titles, Jimmy jumped off/was tossed to the curb, and Jerry paid him $2 million to leave Dallas. The Cowboys won the Super Bowl again two years later with Johnson's players coached by Barry Switzer.

I left Dallas three months after Jones and Johnson arrived. They were fun to write about in those very early days and I left knowing I had set the foundation for a good relationship. One night back in New York I called Landry's old office line and Johnson picked up himself. I was working for HBO's *Inside the NFL* and had a segment on the show devoted to news around the league. I knew from my dealings with Johnson in Dallas that he enjoyed the gossip and rumors and that first phone call yielded a few items that I used on the show. "Whatcha got?" Johnson would say.

To get something I had to give something, so I made sure I had a few things to share with Jimmy. We talked every Tuesday night during the season and Johnson became invaluable in my news gathering for *Inside the NFL*. Of course, our agreement was that I would never use his name. After Johnson split with Jones, he took two years off from coaching and we became teammates when he joined the cast of *Inside the NFL*. He would occasionally come to New York for the taping, always joining us the handful of times we took the show on the road during the season, and the rest of the time he appeared via a remote setup in front of his fish tank at his home in Tavernier, Florida.

Jones was easy to get to know. He loved to do interviews. I kept in touch with him, especially in the early years. After Jones won his third Super Bowl in four years, with the last one coming after Johnson was gone, he felt he would just keep winning championships.

Then came the drought. By the end of the 2017 season, the Cowboys had gone a franchise-record twenty-two seasons without playing in the Super Bowl. Even as an expansion team in 1960, it took them just eleven seasons to get to their first Super Bowl, and that came after two heartbreaking losses in the NFL Championship Games to Green Bay. Dallas has not even been to an NFC title game since its last Super Bowl.

"I almost can't even recognize it," Jones said. "It made me appreciate even more the early years when I came into the NFL and got to be a part of three Super Bowl teams."

That has not prevented Jones from growing the NFL game, his Cowboys brand, and his bank account as the league's preeminent businessman. For sure, Gene will never have to work waiting tables. The Jones Way of doing business was validated by his selection to the Hall of Fame, which he viewed as a family accomplishment.

"It was a celebration of the way we've been involved," he said.

By the end of our talk at the St. Regis, the tears were gone.

"Sure did enjoy our visit," he said.

Even after I returned to New York after nearly eight years in Texas, I've always had a special place in my heart for Dallas and my experience covering America's Team.

As Jimmy Johnson shouted with such passion, "How 'bout them Cowboys!"

CHAPTER ONE

Let's Party

The odd couple of Warren Buffett and Paul Anka finished their salute to the Pro Football Hall of Fame Class of 2017 with a cringe-inducing version of "My Way," with the words tailored for each of the eight inductees who were standing right behind them. They had literary license to mangle the words as they pleased, because Anka wrote the classic song for Frank Sinatra and because Buffett has more money than he knows what to do with and who is going to tell him no.

The crowd at the Canton Civic Center for the Gold Jacket Dinner on the Friday night of Hall of Fame weekend did its best to act entertained as the duo crooned, and the applause at the end was just as much for its finally being over as for any appreciation of the updated lyrics that even at their most clever struggled to prompt a smile.

Jerry Jones had made it to pro football's ultimate insiders club, joining colleagues who once sued him, but there was at least one prominent candidate wondering how and why.

"How does Jerry get in the Hall of Fame before me?" he complained.

Jones and Buffett struck up a friendship at the Super Bowl

one year, and Buffett is a big football fan, so it was no surprise he traveled to Canton and after the dinner attended the $8 million party Jones's wife, Gene, and their daughter, Charlotte, were throwing twenty minutes away at the Glenmoor Country Club to celebrate Jones's induction the following evening. It's now a tradition for the newest members of the Hall of Fame to each host and pay for a party in their honor, but it's usually held on Saturday night after the ceremony. The endless induction speeches have pushed the party start times back to after 11 p.m., so Jones followed the lead of his friend and former 49ers owner Ed DeBartolo Jr. and scheduled his party for immediately after the Gold Jacket Dinner at the country club Eddie D had his extravaganza in 2016.

Buffett arrived at the party dressed in the same understated attire he was wearing at the Gold Jacket Dinner: a sport shirt and tie and baseball warmup jacket with a Pro Football Hall of Fame patch. The jacket was gold, of course. If you didn't know Buffett was worth $87.5 billion, making him the third-richest person in the world, his appearance was not going to give it away. He was able to blend right into what had to be the most star-studded event in the history of Canton. Guests valet parked near the main entrance to the club and were transported by golf cart down a winding road to the party tent that was constructed just for this special event. *Tent* is not really an accurate description. It would take a pretty good tee shot to cover the area from one end of the party room to the other. There was enough space to fit Jones's private plane and his helicopter, and still have plenty of room for whatever aeronautical toys Buffett might have had at his disposal in Canton or back home in Omaha.

When Jones arrived, the party was well under way. He walked to a short set of stairs that took him up to a private area for his family and for the most elite of his elite guests. Just about all those on the invitation list were VIPs, so to be invited up the steps was literally a different level. When his family had settled into their area, Jones stood by the railing of his private box and looked down on the sea of people beneath him.

"That was not a meeting of a lot of people. That was a roomful of my private relationships," Jones said later. "When I was looking out over the group, I did not look at it as a crowd. I could see and know everyone who was in there. Even the Hall of Famers, I felt like I knew them because of my love for the NFL and football. I knew every one of them and knew the background of everybody in there that had a gold jacket."

He grabbed a microphone. The music from the DJ stopped. Everybody stood still and looked up to where Jones was about to make an uncharacteristically short speech.

He closed with, "It's great to be with you tonight."

Loud cheers.

Then he shouted:

"Now, let's have a party."

The guests followed his instructions.

The man knows how to make money. The man knows how to party. The man knows how to drink.

If the NFL had any doubt that Jones liked to have a good time, it was answered at one of his first league meetings in the spring of 1989 in New Orleans. He entered one of the renowned joints in the French Quarter and immediately established himself as the life of the party. He was forty-six and part of the new wave of younger owners coming into the league but still outnumbered by the likes of Wellington Mara, Dan Rooney, Art Modell, and Ralph Wilson. By the end of that evening in New Orleans, it was determined that a new era had arrived in Dallas and most likely in the NFL. In a city with an enclave as vibrant as the French Quarter, the night didn't end for Jones with dinner and bedtime. There was some drinking to get done.

Back to Canton: Buffett's presence guaranteed that Jones would be no better than the second-richest man in the room. New Jersey governor Chris Christie, a huge Cowboys fan, much to the dismay of his constituency, was talking with Tony Dorsett. Jon Bon Jovi, better known for his close relationship with the Patriots and Bill Belichick and Robert Kraft, was there as well. Cowboys icons Roger Staubach and Troy Aikman, who combined to win all five of Dallas's Super Bowl titles, were among the A-listers. There was a handful of media, including a few who spanned the eras of Clint Murchison, Bum Bright, and Jones, such as longtime radio play-by-play man Brad Sham.

Jones made it a priority to invite all living Hall of Famers and all of his 2017 classmates. Fifty past Hall of Famers honored Jones with their presence: Dan Marino, Jim Kelly, Charles Haley, Mel Renfro, Joe Greene, and Bob Lilly, among many others. Ten or so NFL owners attended, including Redskins owner Daniel Snyder, a longtime Jones wannabe.

Stan Kroenke of the Rams and Mark Davis of the Raiders also showed up to pay tribute. Jones championed the moves of the Rams from St. Louis to Los Angeles and the Raiders from Oakland to Las Vegas. It's probably not a coincidence that Legends Hospitality, owned by Jones and the New York Yankees, is managing the suite sales and sponsorship deals in the new stadiums in Los Angeles and Las Vegas. As Kroenke was in the final stages of edging ahead of the Chargers and Raiders to become the NFL's first priority while all three teams competed to get to Los Angeles, the numbers were getting silly. The relocation fee was $600 million. Kroenke's new stadium was expected to cost $2.8 billion, but by early 2018 the number was up to $5 billion. As the cost kept going up, Jones kept encouraging Kroenke to stick with it. "Now Stan, don't let a little old $100 million stand in the way here," Jones said. "You get this Los Angeles franchise." Kroenke, who is worth $8.3 billion, told Jones he wanted to choke him.

Jones spared no expense for the party.

"The idea of wanting to demonstrate or show just how much it meant to me and our family for me to get to go in the Hall of Fame I think will be clearly evidenced by the party tonight," he said hours before it kicked off. "I'm not going to disappoint. I know that."

Each tabletop was designed with images of Cowboys stars, big moments in team history, or the Jones family. The menu was ballpark chic with sliders, small chicken sandwiches and French fries, and an open bar. The black cocktail napkins were creative. Jones is known for having his own language and set of expressions to describe a situation when trying to make a point. They are known as Jerry-isms. The napkins, with gold "JJ" letters in the corner, were uniquely designed:

Jerry-ism

Jer-ee-iz-uhm/noun, phrase, who knows?

1. An excerpt from an interview, press conference, or dialogue with the Dallas Cowboys owner, Jerry Jones; causes confusion by the audience, friends, and family; holds a deeper meaning that very few people understand.

2. See also: circumcision of a mosquito; crippled cricket's ass.

Tony Fay, who has his own public relations firm in Dallas, worked closely with Charlotte Jones Anderson to provide a hilarious video tribute to Jones that highlighted many of the Jerry-isms.

"It's so messed up, the owls are fucking the chickens."

"I want me some Glory Hole."

"He's got one of those bubble butts."

"He's sharper than a skeeter's peter."

"I'm looking up on my back and all I see is ass."

"You don't have to spend a lot of time kind of circumcising the mosquito."

Jones is the only one who knows the true meaning of any of his pet expressions, and the video didn't even attempt to explain. The lineup of celebrities interviewed on the video was impressive, including two former presidents of the United States. In order of appearance: Joe Buck, Savannah Guthrie, Matt Lauer, Tony Romo, Jimmy Kimmel, Jamie Foxx, Al Michaels, Chris Paul, Bill Clinton, Bon Jovi, Ezekiel Elliott, George W. Bush, Aikman, Irvin, Gene Jones, Jason Witten, Dak Prescott, Emmitt Smith, and Randall Stephenson (AT&T's big boss).

Jones's guest list included a couple of his adversaries. After winning two Super Bowls together in the first five years after he bought the team, Jones could no longer stand the sight of Jimmy Johnson. The feeling was mutual. Johnson was at Jones's party.

But if Jones knew then what he found out one week later, he might have reconsidered inviting Roger Goodell, the NFL's $40-million-per-year commissioner who was not even the third-richest man in the room. Goodell called Jones once Jones returned from Canton to Cowboys training camp in Oxnard, California, to inform him he was suspending running back Ezekiel Elliott six games for domestic violence, which Jones insists was contrary to what Goodell had told him earlier.

That set off a season-long toe-to-toe battle between Jones and

Goodell that finally boiled over in December at a winter owners meeting in Jones's backyard at the ritzy Four Seasons in Irving, Texas, when Goodell's five-year contract extension, valued at $200 million if he hit all the incentives, was officially announced. Jones had been arguing for Goodell's compensation to be more closely tied to his performance, and Jones was able to push through a protocol change on the standards Goodell would be judged by and which of the owners would make the determination if he was doing a good job.

The feud quickly heated back up again when NFL and team owners became intent on recouping $2 million spent on legal fees it said it used to defend itself against Jones in the Elliott case and Jones's challenge of Goodell's contract. The fine was the greatest ever levied against an NFL owner. The other owners made the claim to be reimbursed even though Jones never sued the NFL in the Elliott case and never brought anything to court regarding Goodell's contract.

Make no mistake, Jones was incensed with the Elliott suspension and threatened to take the NFL to court to stop Goodell's new contract, even hiring lawyer David Boies, who had represented the NFL in the 2011 lockout of the players. The NFL's first response was to threaten to take away Jones's franchise and throw him out of the league.

"It was laughable to think there would be a discussion," Stephen Jones said. "It was never taken seriously in any shape, form, or fashion. Because you have an opinion that is contrary to what people think you ought to have, it doesn't mean, as far as we're concerned, that there should be anything. It's one team's opinion and you're allowed to have that."

Goodell stopped by where Jones was holding court upstairs in the private area of the party to congratulate him and chat. He then found a comfortable spot in the back of the room on the main level away from the stage where Justin Timberlake was performing. The optics were fascinating. Down on the main level, Elliott was walking twenty-five feet from Goodell seemingly without a care in the world.

Goodell and Elliott did not cross paths at the party. Goodell surely had already made up his mind after a thirteen-month investigation that he was going to suspend Elliott for six games, but he elected to wait to announce it so he would not ruin Jones's party and his induction weekend. When it was suggested to Jones by a member of the media that Goodell was partying on his nickel having already decided he was going to exile Jones's best player, Jones quickly agreed.

"You are right on it," he said. "You are right."

Goodell refused to confirm if he attended Jones's party knowing that just a few days later he would be placing the phone call to him that essentially ruined the Cowboys' season. "I'm not getting into that," he said.

Jones and Patriots owner Robert Kraft had been Goodell's most influential allies since he was named commissioner to succeed Paul Tagliabue on the fifth ballot at a special owners meeting outside Chicago in the summer of 2006. Jones was among the Chicago 11 in 1989 who blocked the election of longtime Bears and New Orleans Saints general manager Jim Finks to succeed Pete Rozelle. Jones and DeBartolo and other younger owners felt they were getting pushed around by the Maras, Modells, and Rooneys when they had paid more than any of them to buy into the NFL—Wellington Mara's father, Jack, founded the New York Giants in 1925 for $500—and the new guard wanted more of a say in how the league was going to function.

It turned out that Jones and Tagliabue were two trains going 100 mph on the same track heading right toward each other.

Jones always felt Jones was the smartest man in the room. Tagliabue always felt Tagliabue was the smartest man in the room. But it was Jones who helped lead the revolt when Modell and Tagliabue wanted to give a refund to the network partners crying about their financial losses, and that led to Fox winning the bidding for the NFC package in 1993 and TV revenues exploding. Jones had developed a relationship with Fox boss Rupert Murdoch, and once he guaranteed Murdoch that Fox would not be used just to drive up the price on the other networks, it created the path for network contracts to reach $5.5 billion per year.

Kraft had become closer to Goodell than any of the other owners, as his business-savvy, engaging personality, and frequent business trips to New York (where he owned an apartment in the Plaza Hotel on Central Park West) made it easy to confide in him. Relationships count for Goodell, but business is business. Pittsburgh's Dan Rooney was the owner who knocked on Goodell's hotel room door to inform him he was elected as commissioner, but Goodell fined Rooney $25,000 two months into the job for criticizing the officiating.

Goodell is an NFL lifer and his mantra is to protect the shield. The NFL is the only place he ever worked other than when he was a bartender while attending college at Washington and Lee University in Pennsylvania. When he went back for homecoming shortly after he was named commissioner, they put him to work behind the bar. He didn't have the little book he used to carry in his pocket that served as a cheat sheet on how to mix drinks, so he poured them from memory.

He once told his father, Charles, a congressman in New York who was later named a United States senator by Governor Nelson Rockefeller after Robert Kennedy was assassinated in 1968, that he one day wanted to be NFL commissioner. He inundated the league office with résumés and letters while he was in college and was finally hired as an intern in the public relations department after he graduated. He never left as the NFL offices moved twice up and down Park Avenue and he worked his way up to the very top rung.

He learned a lot about principles and integrity from his father, but it has not protected him from an avalanche of criticism as he has dealt with sensitive topics like domestic violence and concussions and the Spygate, Bountygate, and Deflategate scandals.

Charles Goodell was an outspoken Republican who opposed the Vietnam War. His stance upset the Richard Nixon administration and eventually ended his political career.

Vice President Spiro Agnew called Charles the Christine Jorgensen of the Republican Party, which upset Roger Goodell and his brothers. Jorgensen was the first American to have sex reassignment surgery. "We're five boys, we're a pretty tight-knit group," he said. "Somebody attacks your father, you're upset. The five of us were ready to go. My father would always laugh it off. It never got under his skin. He would understand that he was being attacked politically, but he never took it personally. The Goodell boys did."

The stance of Agnew, who was doing Nixon's dirty work, cost Goodell his Senate seat to Conservative Party candidate Charles Buckley in 1970 when Goodell split the liberal vote with Democrat Richard Ottinger. "It was difficult on one level, but it was educational and important from a principle standpoint," Roger Goodell said. "He stood up for what he believed in, regardless of the consequences. He knew what the consequences were going to be."

Goodell wasn't old enough to fully appreciate the pressure his father faced with his antiwar position or the repercussions it had on his political career, but he learned about it and learned from it. Do what you believe is right and you'll never have an issue with defending your position or integrity, regardless of the backlash. As a result, Goodell has become the most unpopular commissioner in the history of sports. He is loudly booed at the draft every year, to the extent that some owners would like him to relinquish the job of announcing the picks, because having the commissioner subjected to such anger is a bad look for the league. But the owners wanted him back, and they rewarded him with a new contract in December 2017 because he'd inherited a $6-billion-a-year enterprise when he took over in 2006, and it was then up to $14 billion.

The Goodell booing reached a new level at the 2018 draft, which was held in Jones's stadium in Arlington. Prior to announcing the first pick on opening night, Goodell came onstage accompanied by Cowboys greats Aikman, Bob Lilly, and Witten. They did not provide a buffer. It was the first opportunity for Cowboys fans to let Goodell know they didn't appreciate his suspension of Elliott. The booing kept getting louder, which led Goodell to joke to the crowd that they shouldn't be booing the Cowboys.

* * *

On the afternoon of the Gold Jacket Dinner and his starstudded party, Jones and the other Hall of Fame inductees held individual yet simultaneous media sessions in Canton McKinley High School adjacent to Tom Benson Stadium. The largest group of media surrounded Jones, the headliner in the class. He detailed his path from ostracized owner to Hall of Famer that was preceded by a flirtation with buying the San Diego Chargers for $5.8 million in 1966 when he was just twenty-three years old. His father talked him out of it.

He shed tears as he got caught up in the 1989 moment again. He was introspective and informative and entertaining unless the serious subject of potential punishment for Elliott, the best player on his team, was raised. All along, Jones had been adamant that he was aware of all the facts regarding the interaction between Elliott and his girlfriend in Columbus, Ohio, two months after the Cowboys had made him the fourth overall pick in the 2016 draft. Police did not charge him, and the NFL's lead investigator didn't find the woman credible and recommended Elliott not be suspended.

Cowboys training camp in Oxnard had been going on for two weeks by the time they all left for Canton for the Pro Football Hall of Fame preseason game against the Cardinals and the induction ceremonies, and Jones was planning for Elliott to be available the entire season. Dallas had signed running back Alfred Morris as a free agent in 2016 after he rushed for at least 1,000 yards in three different seasons with the Redskins. They still had veteran Darren McFadden, who had been a 1,000-yard rusher with Oakland and the previous season with the Cowboys, and Rod Smith, the brother of Cowboys linebacker Jaylon Smith and Elliott's backup at Ohio State in 2014.

Even though the Cowboys had reinforcements in the event they had to play part of the 2017 season without Elliott, who had rushed for 1,631 yards and 15 touchdowns as a rookie, Jones was clearly not anticipating a suspension. "No. No, I'm not," he said. "I don't want to be too proactive about how I feel, because that's not going to make any difference here at all. What I don't want to do is hurt things. That's that. I think that when you look at everything that I am aware of, then I'm not anticipating a suspension. All I've made my comments based on is all the knowledge that I have. I have everything."

Goodell's imminent decision did not prevent him from enjoying the festivities and food and drink at the most elaborate Hall of Fame party of all time. On the way out, just to make sure the guests didn't forget who their host for the evening was, they were handed little boxes with the initials "JJ" with two doughnuts inside. Golf carts took the partygoers back up the hill to the valet stand, where thick hamburgers wrapped in aluminum foil and a bottle of water were handed out for the ride back to the area hotels.

The Hall of Fame events were over for Jones on Sunday morning, and he returned to Cowboys training camp in Oxnard knowing he would be hearing from Goodell in the coming days.

The first phone call came that Wednesday, August 9. Goodell informed Jones that it was his intention to announce that Elliott was going to be suspended six games. The decision was not yet final, but that was the plan. "Don't do that," Jones implored.

Goodell's decision also led to this response from Jones, according to a story posted on ESPN's website three months later: "I'm gonna come after you with everything I have." Then, referencing how Kraft was critical of Goodell after the Deflategate discipline, he told Goodell that was tame compared to the fight he was about to wage.

Goodell was not going to back down to Jones, just as he did not back down to Kraft. Goodell's contract, which was due to expire in March 2020, was the pressure point Jones needed to make Goodell squirm. Even though Jones had previously supported Goodell in his fight against Kraft, now Goodell had given him the opening to question the power granted to the commissioner by the owners—he was sure to have the NFL Players Association as a partner on this issue—as well as the commissioner's compensation.

Elliott actually won a series of court battles that put his

suspension on hold and allowed him to play the first eight games of the 2017 season. He was not the dominant force he was in his rookie year, with the suspension looming over him. The Cowboys were just 5-3 when Elliott lost in the Second Circuit Court of Appeals in lower Manhattan and he had run out of realistic legal options. The week-to-week uncertainty was over. He had to serve the six-game suspension. The Cowboys lost their first three without Elliott and fell out of the playoff race.

It began as a season when Dallas had legitimate Super Bowl aspirations. They had a breakthrough 13-3 season in 2016 led by rookies Prescott and Elliott. Jones has been looking for vindication for two decades for the decision to end his partnership with Johnson. Once Johnson was gone, Jones was truly the general manager. In the Johnson years, Jones had the title of GM, but it was Johnson who devised the extraordinary Herschel Walker trade in 1989 for the greatest draft choice haul in NFL history. He then wheeled and dealed those picks into three Super Bowl titles. Once the Cowboys beat the Steelers in Super Bowl XXX following the 1995 season, they continued to be hit hard by free agency, but without Johnson making the personnel decisions, Jones could not replenish the roster. At the time, it seemed like the right thing to do when he passed on selecting wide receiver Randy Moss with the eighth overall pick in 1998, but that turned out to be a costly blunder. Moss came with baggage and a long list of off-the-field problems. The Cowboys had also been through hell with Michael Irvin and had been humiliated by the discovery of their own White House, a two-story brick house at 115 Dorsett Drive in Valley Ranch, a couple of punts from the team offices. The players rented the house—receiver Alvin Harper's name was on the lease—and brought their ladies to the five-bedroom, three-bathroom palace, having turned it into their house of pleasure.

The drop-off following Jones's third Super Bowl was sharp, with no end in sight. Beginning with the 1996 season, the Cowboys made the playoffs just nine times in twenty-two years and won only three playoff games, never more than one in any season. They did not make it past the divisional round of the playoffs in any season. In those twenty-two years, a total of nineteen teams made it to at least one Super Bowl, with the Patriots making it to nine. The Saints, Cardinals, Bucs, Titans, Falcons, Seahawks, Panthers, and Ravens all made the Super Bowl for the first time during Dallas's absence. Still, their five Super Bowl titles are just one fewer than the Steelers', the all-time leader, and tied with the Patriots and 49ers for second place.

It was against this backdrop that Jones put his full support behind Elliott as he fought his suspension. Jones had presented Michael Irvin, Emmitt Smith, and Larry Allen when they made it to the Hall of Fame, and in his own speech he went out of his way to praise Goodell.

"As a young man, I always knew why this game was great and why it had such value, certainly individually, for me," Jones said. "As someone who owned a team, I was always thinking how we could go to the next level, how do we make it better. We have a leader today in Roger Goodell who really does live by that standard."

Until, well, Jones thinks he doesn't.

Jones says his challenge of Goodell's contract structure predated Goodell's decision to suspend Elliott. But he still feels Goodell betrayed him by promising him Elliott would not be suspended and then suspending him. Goodell vehemently denied even hinting to Jones that he was letting Elliott off the hook. "N. O. No," Goodell said in the hallway outside a conference room at the conclusion of the NFL owners meetings in

Orlando in March 2018. "Do you understand that? Would you like me to write it out for you?"

When Jones bought the Cowboys, fans and maybe even some league people thought they were getting Jed Clampett, played by Buddy Ebsen on the TV show *The Beverly Hillbillies*. (In the show, Clampett was a poor hillbilly from Limestone, Tennessee, who struck oil on his property, then packed his family and belongings into a truck and moved to California.) Two days after the sale was announced, Jeff Rohrer, the Cowboys linebacker from Yale, walked around the Cowboys locker room singing the *Beverly Hillbillies* theme song. He was cut before the season.

The NFL instead got itself J. R. Ewing, the character played by Larry Hagman on the *Dallas* television show, which opened with an overhead view of Texas Stadium. Ewing was a ruthless, conniving, underhanded power broker whose every move was designed to benefit himself. *Underhanded* is too strong to describe Jones, but *ruthless* and *conniving* are not. Every decision was based on two things: *How will it help the Cowboys win? How much money will it put in my pocket?*

Jones cut receiver Dez Bryant two weeks before the 2018 draft, proving he could distance himself from his emotions, much as he had when he released Tony Romo one year earlier. He truly liked Bryant, who came from a tough upbringing to succeed in Dallas. He dropped to the Cowboys, who picked him twenty-fourth in the first round in 2010, and Jones thought enough of him that Bryant was assigned treasured uniform number 88, most recently worn by Drew Pearson and Irvin. It appeared that Bryant was the next Irvin, with his physical style of play and ability to fight for the ball. Bryant became one of the top handful of wideouts in the league by his second year and then exploded in years three through five with a total of 273 catches for 3,935 yards and 41 touchdowns. That earned him a five-year $70 million contract with $45 million guaranteed in 2015. But his numbers took a nosedive, beginning when a foot injury limited him to just nine games in the first year of his new deal. He never established the same chemistry in his last two years in Dallas with Prescott that he had with Romo. His fading production, reduced speed, inability to get separation from defensive backs, and emotional sideline behavior, which was a distraction, convinced Jones he wasn't getting his money's worth; Bryant was scheduled to make $12.5 million. Shocking? Not in the NFL. If the 49ers can cut Jerry Rice, then the Cowboys can cut Dez Bryant. Even so, if the Cowboys were certain that tight end Jason Witten would retire weeks later, perhaps they might have negotiated a pay cut with Bryant to squeeze one more year out of his career.

If Jones was trying to buy Elliott a slap on the wrist and a hefty fine with kind words about Goodell in his Hall of Fame speech, it did not work. "What I had gotten indicated was he would need to express and show contriteness," Jones said. "He would then get the equivalent of a scolding."

Instead, Goodell called Jones back on August 10 and informed him the decision was final. The NFL announced the suspension the next day.

"Stunned" was how Jones described his reaction.

Misled, too? "The answer is more so than not," he said.

He said he was given just a brief heads-up that the NFL would be releasing a statement. "Yes," he said. "Like hours. Just taken aback. We're not talking about evidence here. It was circumstantial. There was no new evidence from what I had known for a year."

He was upset it took thirteen months to investigate. The criminal system and the judicial system, he said, do not drag things out publicly. "Just by the very nature of it, it shows one of the flaws in our system," he said. "That's a major part of my criticism."

Goodell's decision to suspend Elliott began the most tumultuous year of Jones's time in the NFL. Instead of building on the euphoria of being number 307 in the Hall of Fame and hoping to end the season in the Super Bowl, he began an all-out attack on Goodell and the league's six-owner compensation committee. He was also the only owner who threatened to bench players who did not stand for the National Anthem.

Jones took a hard stance against the peaceful protests, but he supported Elliott and signed former Carolina Panthers defensive end Greg Hardy, who had been punished by the NFL for domestic violence. The two stances might have been unrelated but also incongruous. Jones backed Elliott every step of the way during his court battles—just as Kraft had done with Brady in Deflategate—that went from a home-court advantage in Texas to Louisiana and finally up to New York.

Although Jones was among the owners who voted 32–0 to give the compensation committee, chaired by Atlanta's Arthur Blank, the full authority to enter into contract negotiations and complete a deal with Goodell, it was not long after the Elliott decision that Jones began to publicly attack the exclusive nature of the process. Jones had been asked to serve on the compensation committee, but he preferred to be an ad hoc member and represent all the other owners not on the committee. He claims Goodell's contract and Elliott's suspension were mutually exclusive issues and he was not trying to institute a new pay structure for Goodell as retribution.

Once Jones hired David Boies, a high-powered attorney, and threatened to sue to prevent Goodell's extension, the gloves were off. This was a heavyweight battle between the most powerful owner in sports and the most powerful commissioner in sports. Blank removed Jones as an ad hoc member. When the Cowboys played the Atlanta Falcons in Blank's sparkling new Mercedes-Benz Stadium in the first game of Elliott's suspension, Blank and Jones stood on the field during warmups and did not speak. Jones was fed up with the Falcons owner, who he felt was giving Goodell a blank check. Blank was thrilled the Falcons crushed the Cowboys. Jones was quick to remind anyone who would listen that the commissioner worked for the owners, not the other way around.

"I can show you many positives that this commissioner Roger has done and is doing," Jones said on his KRLD radio show in Dallas. "I can show you things he wants to take back. [The Elliott decision] is a very example of it. I'm sure he would like to take back his initial Ray Rice ruling and a few others. He's in the process of trying to correct and in doing so Zeke is the victim of an overcorrection."

Jones's attack on the league and his fellow owners was not the first time he clashed with his partners. In 1995, he signed sponsorship deals with Pepsi, American Express, and Nike that permitted their products to be marketed at Texas Stadium without any of the revenue being shared with the other teams. Jones felt he shouldn't have to be limited by the deals the NFL negotiated and make the same money as the Cincinnati Bengals, who didn't even sell naming rights to their stadium. The NFL sued Jones and Jones countersued and they wound up settling. The end result was that the other teams now had the opportunity to sign their own stadium sponsorship deals.

"I understand why they were reluctant early," Jones said. "First of all, some things, marketing being one of them, one and one is three, not two. That's kind of got some art to it."

Jones once stood up in front of the owners at a league

41

meeting to present his ideas on sponsorship. Jones can be long-winded, and he often gets so excited with his ideas and concepts that he is hard to follow. At times, it seems like he's filibustering or double-talking. There is always an underlying message with a lot of wisdom in what he says. Bud Adams, who owned the Houston Oilers from the first day of the old American Football League in 1960, was an old-guard owner totally on board with the way the NFL had always done business. He approached Jones after one of these meetings.

"Dammit, Jerry," Adams said. "I didn't really understand what you were saying, but whatever you were saying, I want some of it. You got me fired up. I'm going along with you."

Jones didn't make the Hall of Fame in the contributor category because the Cowboys were the first team to win three Super Bowls in a four-year period. He was elected because he's a visionary, a cutting-edge, out-of-the-box thinker who taught a bunch of rich people new tricks.

Even traditional old-guard owner Wellington Mara came to appreciate Jones's business acumen. In the early '60s, the Giants saved the NFL when they agreed that all network television revenue should be shared equally among the fourteen teams. That allowed the small-market Green Bay Packers to compete with the New York Giants and Chicago Bears. Revenue sharing is the lifeline of the NFL. In 2016, the thirty-two teams shared $7.8 billion in national revenue, which worked out to $244 million per team.

When Jones decided to venture outside the structure, Mara was livid. Jones made it worse by parading Nike chairman Phil Knight across the field at Giants Stadium right before kickoff at the 1995 season opener, timing it just as a news release was handed out in the press box announcing that the Cowboys and Nike had entered into an agreement. It became a beautiful and profitable relationship between Jones and Knight that was highlighted by Knight's designing a custom-made pair of gold sneakers to match Jones's gold jacket. Jones showed off the sneakers on his feet during his induction.

By the time Mara passed away in 2005, he and Jones had become friends. But the day after Jones showed up Mara with his grand entrance with Knight, the Giants patriarch displayed a passive-aggressive side of his personality that was rarely seen.

"I think I feel a little different about Jerry Jones than I ought to and how most people do," he said. "I feel kind of sorry for the guy. I don't think he's got the concept of what it means to be a member of a team. Jerry's like the guy who runs a great leg on a mile relay team and refuses to give up the baton to the next guy. I think it's an example of being penny-wise and pound foolish."

Jones taught the Giants that they could run a family business but still be big business. He showed Mara how to cash in on the Giants brand. "Even my father at the end had come to enjoy him," his son John said. "When Jerry got up to speak at a league meeting, my father would always perk up and give him a big greeting. He enjoyed Jerry. At the beginning, he didn't."

He was embraced by the old guard and the new guard, and he had come to be embraced as the ultimate league man until the summer of 2017, when he decided to go at it with Goodell. He said Goodell was being overpaid with "layup" incentives in his contract, and he wanted to make him earn it in light of the league's declining television ratings and National Anthem crisis that year, which turned off a lot of fans. Jones's induction into the Hall of Fame seemed to empower him to speak his mind and put him back on an island by himself, where he'd been in 1995. What were they going to do? Take away his gold jacket?

"Eight years before Al Davis died, he told me when Park Avenue starts running this game, we are going to have more trouble than you can count," said Bill Parcells, the Hall of Famer who coached the Cowboys for Jones from 2003 to 2006. "He turned out to be 100 percent prophetic. I'm telling you, they ruined the goddamn officiating. They got more lawyers and doctors involved in this game. It's ridiculous. It's fucking ridiculous, some of the things they are doing."

Jones first brought up his concerns about Goodell's contract at the 2017 spring meetings in Chicago. At that time he had already been elected to the Hall of Fame but had not yet been inducted. However, he still voted to give the compensation committee the go-ahead. "There was a need for change in many areas," Jones said. "My position was not necessarily to replace Roger but was to basically address those subjects as we addressed his extension. I had been on record on individual aspects of it, whether it be behavior, whether it be the investigation process, the punishment process, some of the issues regarding substance [abuse]. Some of those issues, I had really spoke to those the last several years."

By the time the owners arrived for the league meetings at the Four Seasons in December, Jones had managed to get his point across, but he backed off any litigation attempting to delay or eliminate Goodell's extension. When the one-day meetings of the owners concluded, they hustled to the front of the hotel, where their limos waited to take them to their private planes.

Jones's driver was waiting for him out front for the twenty-minute ride home. But first Jones stopped off to address the media in a press conference setting. In most cases, only Goodell holds a press conference to conclude a league meeting. Goodell was first to the microphone, with Jones standing off to the side. Their relationship was a bigger topic than Goodell's new contract.

As Goodell spoke, Jones listened intently.

"My relationship with Jerry has been great," he said. "We don't always agree. I'm not paid to agree and he's not paid to agree with me. That is, again, what the strength of our league is. As a league, we are stronger when thirty-two teams are together. We have our differences, but we work together to try to solve those differences and address them in a way that is responsible. I think we have done that."

One of the final questions Goodell was asked was whether he took the pushback from Jones personally.

"Do I look like I take it personally?" he said.

Then he looked to his left where Jones was standing.

"Jerry, do I look like I take it personally?" he said. "No, to answer your question. As I said before, I think people disagreeing, people having the ability to do that within the context of our structure, is something that makes us stronger."

When he was done, Goodell shook hands with Jones, and they briefly shared an uncomfortable hug. Before Jones began his press conference, Goodell was out the door.

Jones then quickly broke the ice with a quip about the huge numbers attached to Goodell's new contract.

"I know how much Roger Goodell loves the National Football League," Jones said. "And he should love it even more right now."

Just like every holiday season, Jones sent a Christmas card and a Christmas tree ornament to every NFL owner. Just like every holiday season, Roger Goodell was on the list.

The league responded two months later by sending Jones a bill for over $2 million to cover its legal costs as it fought off his challenges to Goodell's contract, even though it never went to court, and his challenges in the Elliott case, even though it was the NFLPA that was handling the case for Elliott. Jones felt he got his $2 million worth, because he was able to convince the other owners to dispense with the committee selected by the commissioner and instead act themselves on a rotating basis to decide commissioner compensation. Allowing the commissioner to pick the owners who would then decide his pay made little sense. It was almost as if they were allowing Goodell to fill in the amount.

Jones wrote his master's thesis on the role of communication in football. He got his point across. He chose not to fight anymore. He wrote the check and moved on. It was worth it to rewrite the parameters on what had been a one-sided contract in favor of the employee—the commissioner.

"Owners don't want to give you credit for being a pain in the ass," Jones said. "That's what makes it change is the pain in the ass. It would have never changed."

"Our relationship is the same as it was before. Productive," Goodell said. "I have great respect for him. He brings a really unique perspective to the issues we deal with and really helps us find great solutions. He is incredibly important. He's critical to the league. Obviously, his recognition as a Hall of Famer shows the contributions he's made to the game. He understands the game from a football standpoint as well as from a business standpoint."

* * *

Can it really be America's Team if there is not an American flag in the house? It's hard to ignore the hypocrisy.

Jerry Jones took the harshest stance with his players over the National Anthem controversy during the 2017 season. If they didn't stand, they wouldn't play. The anthem protest began during the preseason in 2016 when Colin Kaepernick played for the 49ers. He sat and then kneeled for the anthem as a way to raise awareness about racial inequality, social injustice, and police brutality against African-Americans.

A handful of players followed his lead, and although Kaepernick became a lightning rod for criticism—and was essentially blackballed from the league when, despite a paucity of quality backup quarterbacks, no team would sign him after he became a free agent—the issue had pretty much subsided by the time the 2017 season was under way. Fewer than ten players took a knee during the anthem in the second week of games.

Then on the Friday night prior to the third week of the season, President Donald J. Trump stirred things up during a speech in Huntsville, Alabama: "Wouldn't you love to see one of these NFL owners, when somebody disrespects the flag, to say, 'Get that son of a bitch off the field right now. Out! He's fired. He's fired!'"

Two days later, approximately 250 players responded by kneeling for the anthem. Just about every player and coach locked arms on the sidelines. Several owners came down to the field and locked arms with their players as a show of support. Three teams elected to remain in the locker room during the playing of the anthem.

Trump ignited a firestorm that only began to let up toward the middle of the season.

"I have so many friends that are owners," Trump said on *Fox and Friends*. "And they're in a box. I mean I've spoken to a couple of them. They say, 'We are in a situation where we have to do something.' I think they're afraid of their players, if you want to know the truth, and I think it's disgraceful."

Trump and the NFL have a contentious history, and he

clearly holds a grudge. As the owner of the New Jersey Generals of the United States Football League, Trump funded a $1.69 billion antitrust lawsuit against the NFL in 1986 that was designed to force a merger. When the NFL was found guilty on the most serious of the nine charges, operating as a monopoly, Trump's eyes got wide as he sat in Room 318 in U.S. District Court in Foley Square in lower Manhattan.

He anxiously awaited the damage award. He was already making plans to build a stadium in Manhattan for the Generals to compete with the Giants and Jets in New Jersey if the USFL hit the jackpot. Then the jury foreman read the damages: $1. One stinking dollar. Trebled under antitrust law, it became $3. Trump stood up, walked to the back of the courtroom, and was in his waiting limousine before the verdict on the other eight charges were read: not guilty eight times over. NFL attorney Frank Rothman, doing the equivalent of a touchdown dance in front of Judge Peter Leisure, opened his wallet and offered to pay up right away. Days later, the USFL not only ditched its plan to move from the spring to the fall, which was Trump's idea, but it folded. All of its players were free to sign with NFL teams.

Trump's dream of taking the Generals into the NFL, with Herschel Walker and Jim Kelly as his stars, was over, too. The Cowboys had invested a fifth-round pick in Walker in 1985 with an eye toward signing him when his contract expired or the USFL folded. Trump and Walker had become extremely close friends, and the quirky Walker said he would actually flip a coin to determine whether he would sign with Dallas or retire. Not surprisingly, when the Cowboys offered a five-year $5 million contract, the largest in history for a running back, Walker decided to put his retirement plans on hold. Three years later, Jones bought the Cowboys, and not even halfway through the season, Jimmy Johnson traded Walker to the Minnesota Vikings. Jones and Trump later became good friends, and Trump called Jones incessantly during the anthem controversy he ignited and begged for his support.

Jones was called to testify during Kaepernick's collusion grievance against NFL owners after he claimed his anthem stance led to him not being signed. Kaepernick attended Jones's testimony at The Star. The *Wall Street Journal* reported that in his testimony, Jones related a conversation with the president in which Trump told him regarding the anthem, "This is a very winning, strong issue for me. Tell everybody you can't win this one. This one lifts me."

By the end of the 2017 season, the anthem issue had faded. The NFL pledged $89 million in midseason to be spent over seven years on social justice causes. Yet, the owners went into the off-season intent on avoiding any more confrontations with Trump, fearing it could once again lead to declining television ratings and sponsor pushback.

In a league meeting in May 2018 in Atlanta, the owners voted in a new rule: Any player who didn't want to stand for the anthem should remain in the locker room until it was over. If they came out for the anthem and took a knee, the team would be fined and the team could fine the player. Just as training camps opened, the policy was put on hold. Trump tweeted: "The NFL National Anthem Debate is alive and well again— can't believe it! Isn't it in contract that players must stand at attention, hand on heart? The $40,000,000 Commissioner must now make a stand. First time kneeling, out for game. Second time kneeling, out for season/no pay!"

Trump's crushing loss to the NFL in the antitrust trial was not the first or the last time he made a run at owning a team in the NFL. In 1982, he backed away from buying the Baltimore

Colts because he felt the price was too high. He was involved in the bidding for the New England Patriots in 1988 but passed because he deemed the $104 million debt a deal breaker. Then in 2014, he offered $1 billion for the Buffalo Bills but was outbid by Terry and Kim Pegula, who bought the team for $1.4 billion. Even if the estate of the late, great Bills owner Ralph Wilson had chosen Trump, there was serious doubt regarding whether he would have received the 75 percent needed in a vote of the thirty-two owners to approve the deal. Fifteen of the teams were still owned by the same persons or families from the days of the USFL trial to remember how Trump tried to take them down.

If Trump had been successful in his bid for the Bills, he said he would not have run for president. On the campaign trail, he said he was glad he didn't get the team because running for president was "much more important."

Trump's comments in Huntsville created a bond among the players, black and white, veterans and rookies, stars and end-of-the-roster players. Nine NFL owners had contributed a total of $7 million to Trump's campaign or inauguration, which created a tug-of-war. Do they support their president or their players? Jones and Patriots owner Robert Kraft were the owners especially close to Trump and each contributed $1 million to his inaugural committee. Neither was part of the NFL when Trump sued it for nearly $2 billion. Kraft said he was deeply disappointed by Trump's remarks in Alabama, and he supported his players' efforts to peacefully effect social change. About twelve Patriots knelt that weekend before their game against the Houston Texans and were booed by the fans in Foxborough. The next week, all the Patriots were on their feet for the anthem.

Kraft, otherwise a lifelong Democrat who was one of the largest contributors to Barack Obama's campaign, admitted his allegiance to Trump escalated after his wife, Myra, died of ovarian cancer in the summer of 2011. They had attended Trump's wedding to his third wife, Melania, at Mar-a-Lago in Florida on January 22, 2005, just before the Patriots won their third Super Bowl in four years.

"When Myra died, Melania and Donald came up to the funeral in our synagogue, then they came for a memorial week to visit with me," Kraft said. "Then he called me once a week for the whole year, the most depressing year of my life when I was down and out. He called me every week to see how I was doing, invited me to things, tried to lift my spirits. He was one of five or six people that were like that. I remember that."

The Cowboys and the Arizona Cardinals were the final teams to play on the third weekend of the 2017 season in a Monday night game in Glendale, Arizona. The anthem controversy had been the major story around the league one day earlier. The anthem prior to the game Dallas and Arizona played was more anticipated than the game itself. How would the Cowboys handle it? This was America's Team. The NFL Network reported: "Jerry Jones, before the Cowboys took the field on Monday night, was in the locker room. He got four separate calls from Donald Trump imploring him: 'Please do not have America's Team kneel during the anthem.'" Jones met with his players and staff, and a compromise was reached. The entire team, including Jones and his daughter, Charlotte, and sons Stephen and Jerry Jr., and the players and coaches, walked off the sideline together prior to the anthem, locked arms, and took a knee together. Then they retreated to the sideline, and all stood for the anthem with arms locked.

Jones was praised for finding a way to appeal to the players and also his own belief that players should stand.

He received a call from Trump two days later, which the

president made sure to point out on Twitter: "Spoke to Jerry Jones of the Dallas Cowboys yesterday. Jerry is a winner who knows how to get things done. Players will stand for Country!"

Jones acknowledged the phone call and that Trump complimented him on how the Cowboys behaved in Arizona—which, Jones said on KRLD, "doesn't mean that in any way we acquiesced to what he was implying. What we did was exclusive from that. What we wanted to do was basically make a statement and certainly not dishonor the flag.

"Anybody in the United States, for the most part, I'm talking the great majority of people, it's madness to think that somebody would dishonor the flag. The debate is whether you are dishonoring or not. That is where people get their case. So just to stand up there and say a group such as the NFL and our players are doing anything that doesn't respect the flag is just not something that could be accepted. Our effort specifically said it's different when the flag is out and we're going to stand and honor the flag than when it is not out."

Jones was sensitive to not making it appear he was a puppet for Trump. "I've known him for several years," he said. "There are many things we don't agree on."

Instead, aware of his own constituency and customers in Dallas and the state of Texas, he knew from feedback he was receiving that it was not good for business if his players took a knee for the anthem. He did not want sponsors dropping out. He didn't want Cowboys fans skipping games. Jones was protecting his brand. Two weeks later, following a disheartening loss to the Packers, Jones took it a step further. Although none of his players took a knee the previous week against the Rams, he issued a warning: If any player did not stand, he would not play. He emphasized that respecting the anthem and the flag had been in the NFL's operating manual for thirty years. The

Dallas Morning News reported that prior to the Green Bay game, defensive ends David Irving and Damontre Moore raised their fists at the end of the anthem. Jones claimed he was not aware of that until he was told after the game.

"The policy and my actions are going to be if you don't honor and stand for the flag in a way a lot of our fans feel that you should, if that's not the case, then you won't play," he said on his radio show.

Would he actually bench a player? "I would just ask anybody to look at my record relative to what I say I'm going to do and go from there."

Trump supported Jones's stance of no stand, no play: "A big salute to Jerry Jones, owner of the Dallas Cowboys, who will BENCH players who disrespect our Flag. Stand for anthem or sit for game!"

Jones's $154 million investment in the Cowboys is approaching $5 billion. His hard-line stance on the anthem did not catch anyone by surprise. Jones spared not one penny when he built Cowboys Stadium, now called AT&T Stadium, in Arlington. He needed to keep filling the seats.

The stadium is spectacular. But one detail was missing when it opened in 2009. There was not one American flag hanging in the building. Not one.

The stadium has a twenty-five-thousand-square-foot high-definition video board, 160 feet long by 72 feet high, that hangs 90 feet above the field and runs from about one 25-yard line to the other. It has smaller screens that face each of the end zones. There are also ribbon video boards that run around the perimeter inside the stadium. The picture on the video boards is so clear that fans often watch the screen instead of the action on the field in front of them. Jerry Sr. was inspired and impressed after seeing a massive video board at a Celine Dion concert in

Las Vegas that he wanted one of those HD toys for Jerry World. Done.

Jones made the decision that for the National Anthem, an image of the American flag would be shown on the huge video boards; the red, white, and blue would be on the ribbon boards; and the actual flag would be paraded onto the field, at times covering the entire field.

Despite the enormity of the building, Jones reasoned there was no good place to hang the flag. It did not become an issue until there was a high school game played in the stadium later in the inaugural season, and there was pushback because there was no American flag hanging inside. When Arlington mayor Bob Cluck complained, Jones fired back that there were two flags on stadium grounds outside. "He can go out there and take a look at the flag there on Randol Mill [Road] and Legends Way," Jones said. "They're waving there every day."

By late November 2009, Jones gave in to the criticism. One flag was placed on either side inside the stadium high up behind each end zone. The initial lack of a flag was not an oversight by Jones, but a conscious decision. "We had it on the screen. We had it in the ceremony," he said. "People called up and said they needed a flag. We were always going to bring the flag out for all events, kind of a ceremony aspect to it. When I realized that people wanted to have a permanent flag hanging up, we immediately put it up."

Not initially having the flag inside his palace is a direct contradiction to the strong stance Jones took for the anthem. Having a flag flying inside the stadium is a tradition as old as the game itself. It took complaining for the Cowboys to get it right. "And that was a hell of a point and we fixed it immediately, we corrected it ASAP," Stephen Jones said.

It was a forgotten issue until eight years later when the

anthem controversy hit the NFL. Kaepernick got it started and Trump made sure it didn't go away. Even when the Cowboys have an off year on the field—their 9-7 record, impacted by Elliott's six-game absence, was thoroughly unfulfilling—Jones managed to be in many of the NFL headlines.

The Cowboys were a microcosm of all the NFL's problems. It was not an easy year in 2017: It covered the Elliott suspension that brought attention to the league's domestic violence issue; the battle with Goodell that accentuated how unpopular he was; the anthem controversy that Jones handled differently from any other owner; the disappointing season in Dallas; the league-wide stark downturn in television ratings and the game's appeal; Jones owing the league $2 million for speaking his mind.

It could not have started off any sweeter for Jones than the Hall of Fame party and induction. He was comforted knowing that those who were closest to him would stick by him. Jones phased out Tony Romo, but that led to his second career at CBS. Romo expressed his gratitude with a Twitter post from Jones's party. "Jerry, you have no idea how many dreams you've made come true in this life. Your drive, vision, loyalty, and love you've shown me all these years will never be forgotten. Tonight, I got to see your dream come true. You will never be replaced. Your QB."

Justin Timberlake, who came to know Jones on visits to Cowboys training camp, held up a plastic cup during a break in his Grammy-quality performance and toasted Jones. "The greatest owner in the history of professional sports being honored here," he shouted.

Jones raised his glass. Then he partied some more.

CHAPTER TWO

Cowboys, Inc.

After so many years of working together on the Cowboys' annual highlight film, Doug Todd and Bob Ryan had their routine figured out down to the last detail. The heavy lifting was done, and now they were in Ryan's car driving from Philadelphia to Atlantic City for dinner and a night of gambling.

In 1979, Todd was the Cowboys' public relations director and had arrived in enemy NFC East territory to work on the movie with Ryan, the best producer, writer, and director on the NFL Films roster, who had the title of vice president and editor in chief. They would spend the day reviewing the film and spend the night celebrating another masterpiece. Once Todd signed off on Ryan's work at the NFL Films office in Philly, Ryan would need another week or two to make any changes Todd suggested, insert the iconic music and John Facenda's mesmerizing narration, and ship the final product to Todd in Dallas.

The Cowboys would then have a grand premiere for the media, send the film to Rotary clubs, provide copies to players making appearances around Texas, Arkansas, and Oklahoma, and have a video yearbook to preserve for posterity.

For good reason, Todd and Ryan always got together on a

Friday with no work the following day. The first stop was dinner at the Knife and Fork Inn in AC. They ate and drank a lot before moving on to the casinos, which had opened the previous year in New Jersey. Ryan had a home in Margate on the Jersey Shore, not even six miles from Atlantic City, so when they called it quits, it was a quick trip to navigate home. Good thing.

"By the end of the evening, we were quite inebriated," Ryan said.

A pretty good indication: "One night when we finished dinner, Doug stood up in front of all these people and did a speech by Errol Flynn from *Captain Blood*. He did just look like Errol Flynn with his hands on his hips and his chest thrown out," Ryan said. "All these people were agog. Doug was absolutely one of the funniest, most charming people I met in my life."

Todd had joined the Cowboys as assistant public relations director in 1971 and was promoted to the top job in 1976. Ryan had been producing the Cowboys' highlight film since the midsixties and had been collaborating with Todd for many years.

When they got together after the 1978 season, the Cowboys were coming off a heartbreaking loss to the Pittsburgh Steelers in Super Bowl XIII, having nearly repeated as Super Bowl champions. They lost 35–31; the game turned on two plays. The first was tight end Jackie Smith's drop of a Roger Staubach pass when Smith was wide open in the end zone that would have tied the score in the third quarter, prompting Cowboys radio announcer Verne Lundquist's memorable call, "Oh, bless his heart. He's got to be the sickest man in America." The second was a crucial and controversial pass interference on Dallas cornerback Benny Barnes in the fourth quarter.

The Cowboys had by then won two Super Bowls, against the

Dolphins and Broncos, but had also suffered a handful of the most excruciating losses in NFL history. They lost to the Packers in back-to-back NFL Championship Games in 1966 and 1967. First, in Dallas, Don Meredith's desperation pass into the end zone was intercepted, preventing the Cowboys from tying the game in the final minute. The following year they lost in the famed Ice Bowl in Green Bay on Bart Starr's quarterback sneak in the closing seconds. They lost Super Bowl V to the Colts on a last-second field goal despite Baltimore committing seven turnovers. The Cowboys had four. They suffered a disheartening loss to the Steelers in Super Bowl X, after Dallas became the first wild card team to make it to the big game.

By the time Ryan sat down after the 1978 season to brainstorm ideas for the Cowboys' highlight film, he was tired of doing the traditional game-by-game recount. He noticed from the endless reels of footage he had viewed for more than a decade that so many fans around the country were adorned in Cowboys jerseys no matter where the game was played. Even in New York, Philadelphia, and Washington, fans wore Cowboys colors when Dallas played their hated rivals. The Cowboys had hosted a Thanksgiving game every year except one since 1966. Tex Schramm saw it as an avenue for his team to become more visible. They were invariably on *Monday Night Football* and frequently the high-profile late-afternoon slot on Sunday doubleheaders, and they always captured the highest ratings.

"I had a lot of good titles in the past," Ryan said.

Possible titles included:

> *Like a Mighty River . . .*
> *Team on a Tightrope*
> *The Decline and Rise of the Dallas Cowboys*

According to the Cowboys, Ryan's first suggestion for the title of the '78 film was *Champions Die Hard*. Todd rejected it. He didn't like the idea of the Cowboys dying. It was football, not war.

Ryan decided he wanted to play off the Cowboys' unique universal popularity.

Here's where the story takes a controversial turn, with two versions of who was ultimately responsible for titling the Cowboys' 1978 highlight film *America's Team*, a name they embraced and that has been their calling card for more than three decades.

Should Ryan or Todd be credited?

"I came up with two titles," Ryan said. "One I didn't like. One I loved. Of course, the one was *America's Team*. The other one was *The Dallas Cowboys: America's National Team*. Or *The New National Team*."

The Cowboys had reached the level of and perhaps surpassed the New York Yankees, the Boston Celtics, and Notre Dame's Fighting Irish as a love-them-or-hate-them team.

Ryan says he presented the options to Todd.

"Doug loved *America's Team*," Ryan said. "The Cowboys loved *America's Team*. We went with it."

At their meeting in Philadelphia, Todd had some other business to take care of in addition to meeting with Ryan. He was in need of a new number two person for his department. His former assistant, George Heddleston, had been hired as the public relations director of the San Francisco 49ers. Ed Croke, the New York Giants' public relations director, recommended Greg Aiello, who had been covering the Giants and the NFL for United Press International. Aiello traveled from New York to Philadelphia to meet with Todd, and they hit it off right away. By April, Aiello was working for Todd and the Cowboys.

Aiello was not in the meeting with Todd and Ryan, but he

was in Dallas when the Cowboys' 1978 highlight film was released. Todd told Aiello that it was Ryan's idea to base the title on the Cowboys' popularity and Ryan had suggested *The National Team* and the *U.S. Cowboys*.

"Doug claims, and I believe him, that he was the one who turned the phrase 'America's Team,'" Aiello said. "That sounds like Doug. He was a very clever, creative guy. He was a big patriot; he loved John Wayne and that kind of thing. It sort of fit Doug's sensibility and the way he thought."

Regardless of the inconsistency in the stories of Ryan, and Todd through Aiello, Ryan once said that when he handed the script to Facenda, he looked it over and said, "Bobby, you've given me a great horse to ride. I hope I can." Schramm, the Cowboys' master showman, ran with *America's Team*. Aiello said the Cowboys knew how self-serving and pompous it would sound if they told people they came up with the name themselves. "We were able to lay it off on NFL Films," he said. "In other words, not to sound arrogant that we were calling ourselves America's Team, it was 'No, it was NFL Films that came up with that.' It was the way we could promote ourselves as America's Team and claim that we weren't doing it. But we were."

Todd was fired by Jerry Jones shortly after he bought the team in 1989, and he moved to Illinois and had several jobs, including in public relations at Arlington Park racetrack. Todd died in 1997 at the age of fifty-four, after suffering a heart attack due to complications from a lung biopsy. Aiello was promoted by Jones to take Todd's position. He left Dallas after the 1989 season when he was hired to run the NFL's public relations department at the league's Park Avenue office in New York. Aiello said that Todd was so adamant he came up with the name that after he left the Cowboys he put on his résumé that he was the creator of the term "America's Team."

Ryan is retired from NFL Films, and although he never profited financially from *America's Team*, he is proud to say he was the originator. "If doesn't matter to me if Doug wants to take equal credit," Ryan said. He is emphatic, however, that he came up with the name. "Well, it's going to be on my gravestone," he said. "I'm serious about that. It will be kind of cool, although I think I'm going to be put in a mausoleum instead of buried with a headstone. That's sort of morbid and hopefully I have many more years left, but it's something I am really proud of."

He does regret not cashing in. "I put out a highlight film like I had done for years and years, never knowing it would be anything more than a highlight film," Ryan said. "The thing blew up. I wish I had marketed it myself like Pat Riley did with 'three-peat.' I never knew it would get that kind of national recognition."

The nickname caught on quickly. Newspaper stories were published. NFL Properties produced an "America's Team" calendar—which likely was not as popular as the Dallas Cowboys Cheerleaders calendar, but it was catering to a slightly different audience.

The highlight film opened with the *America's Team* title on the screen in red-and-blue lettering and white stars and stripes. The name was established. The brand was recognized worldwide.

Schramm loved "America's Team." Predictably, Tom Landry hated it. So did the team.

"If the players were asked about it, they said they didn't consider themselves America's Team," Aiello said. "They were trying to be humble, and they didn't like that it put a target on their back with other teams and fans. But so be it."

Schramm and Landry worked well together for twenty-nine

years because they rarely ventured into each other's territory. Schramm's genius was in the marketing of the franchise. Landry was a football savant. Their personalities were so different. Schramm was outgoing. Landry was all business. It was Schramm who decided to have cheerleaders and dress them in short shorts and revealing tops. They became world famous. Landry considered Schramm's showmanship a distraction.

As part of the NFL's merger with the AFL in 1966 that was to be implemented for the 1970 season, the teams would be split into two conferences, the NFC and the AFC. The Pittsburgh Steelers, Cleveland Browns, and Baltimore Colts agreed to switch to the AFC to join the eleven AFL teams to give each conference fourteen teams. The Cowboys had no desire to switch to the AFC and insisted on being placed in the newly formed NFC East, although geographically it was out of whack.

Schramm wanted the Cowboys playing in the big Northeast markets of New York, Washington, and Philadelphia for ultimate exposure. When the NFL had some minor realignment in 2002 and became a thirty-two-team league with four divisions of four in each conference, it was the Cardinals, who had moved from St. Louis to Phoenix in 1988, who were switched out of the NFC East to the NFC West. It was never a consideration for Dallas.

The star on the helmet. The sleek uniforms. The two Super Bowl trophies. The gorgeous cheerleaders.

When Jerry Jones bought the Cowboys, he didn't inherit a winning football team or a moneymaking team; he inherited America's Team. Now he had the chance to grow the business with the sky the limit, and the view was clear through the famous hole in the roof at Texas Stadium, which the Cowboys boasted was designed so God could watch His football team.

* * *

"This could be a really bad idea," Jerry Jones said.

He had gone to Washington to visit his daughter, Charlotte, his middle child who was working for Arkansas congressman Tommy Robinson, and his youngest, Jerry Jr., who was a student at Georgetown, to fill them in on his latest potential business enterprise: buying the Dallas Cowboys. The three of them gathered around a table at Charlotte's apartment in Washington Harbour, at the foot of the Georgetown section of the nation's capital.

"What do you think about this deal?" Jerry asked his kids.

"The deal is terrible. It's not really about the deal. You're going to put everything that we have on this idea of what you are most passionate about," Charlotte said.

Oldest son Stephen was already working with his father in the oil-and-gas business. "He laid it all out. He wanted us to understand the financial challenge that it was," Charlotte said.

He looked his kids in the eye and uttered what turned out to be one of the few understatements he's ever made in his life: "If we do this, it just might change our life a little," he said.

He took note of Charlotte's beautiful apartment. He told her if he lost it all on the Cowboys, she would be moving out and renting a room at the Marriott. At least he didn't say Days Inn or Motel 6. Charlotte said he should close the deal. "If he's got that kind of crazy passion, you got to go with it and believe in it," she said.

Texas Stadium needed to be spruced up. Fortunately, Schramm had moved them out of the roach-infested metal shack on Forest Lane in North Dallas in 1985 into a state-of-the-art facility in Valley Ranch in Irving, twenty minutes from the stadium. It was a sprawling one-story building with huge heating bills and a lot of debt, and after briefly flirting with moving the entire operation to the stadium, Jones elected to stay put.

Nearly thirty years after Jones signed the final papers with Bright, the Cowboys were valued by *Forbes* at $4.8 billion, which is thirty times what Jones paid for the team.

The Cowboys are the most popular team in American sports history, and Jones turned them into the most valuable. He has made plenty of football mistakes, especially parting with Johnson and stubbornly holding on tight to the general manager's job rather than hiring an experienced football man to run that side of the building, but when it comes to the business side and making money, Jones is in another league.

The Cowboys are not so much a football team as they are a multi-interest corporation leveraging the brand to venture into business opportunities that go way beyond the field. They play four preseason games and sixteen regular-season games each year and hope to play two or three playoff games to get them to the Super Bowl. That means at most they will be on the field twenty-four times from August through early February. Unlike just about every other sports franchise in America, the Cowboys are a business that is up and running and selling their brand 24/7/365. The Patriots are the only team that even attempts to expand this far beyond football, with Kraft developing the land in the parking lot at Gillette Stadium in Foxborough into an outdoor mall called Patriot Place.

Jerry Jones Jr. likes the suggestion of what the Cowboys' enterprise has become.

"Cowboys, Inc.," he repeated.

Jerry Jones's prefootball life once included an office in midtown Manhattan at 362 Fifth Avenue across the street from the Empire State Building. He was thirty-two years old and selling wholesale oil products. Back in Arkansas, he was entertaining oil industry wheeler-dealers from Venezuela in a huge maroon limousine with a gold derrick on the hood. When Jones wasn't booking the car to facilitate closing business deals, Governor Bill Clinton and Arkansas First Lady Hillary Clinton would use the limo.

Jones was a millionaire many times over again when he bought the Cowboys. He learned how to market them as he went along. He made sure Stephen, Charlotte, and Jerry Jr. were paying attention.

"When we started, as big as the Dallas Cowboys were, I don't want to say we were a mom-and-dad-shop operation, but we were a very small operation, especially relative to where we are today," Jerry Jr. said. "There is no question we are working with an incredible brand with the history and tradition and arguably everything else the Dallas Cowboys represent."

Jerry has given his three children major responsibility and accountability. Stephen is the executive vice president, CEO, and director of player personnel, and he concentrates on the football side. Charlotte is the executive vice president and chief brand officer, and Jerry Jr. is the executive vice president and chief sales and marketing officer.

So much of the Cowboys' business is centered around their stadium in Arlington, which opened as Cowboys Stadium in 2009 before naming rights were sold to AT&T in 2013 for about $19 million per year over twenty years. AT&T's corporate headquarters are located in Dallas. Later, the Cowboys built The Star in Frisco, a lavish training facility, hotel, sports medicine, and shopping complex.

When Jones made it known that the Cowboys had outgrown Texas Stadium, which opened in October 1971 as a grand palace but had become run-down and unsightly, the first plan was to move to the Fair Park section of Dallas near the Cotton

Bowl, where the team played its games from its inception in 1960 until they moved to Texas Stadium in Irving. Negotiations with the city of Dallas broke down in 2004, and Jones opted for Arlington, across the parking lot from the Texas Rangers baseball stadium. Arlington was also interested in developing a training facility for the Cowboys at the time Jones decided to move them out of Valley Ranch, which was located about fifteen minutes from Texas Stadium. Frisco blew Arlington away with its proposal, as well as Irving, which hoped Jones would agree to stay in town and build a new facility at the site of Texas Stadium. The stadium had been imploded but the land remained undeveloped, and it was an eyesore for drivers passing by at the intersection of State Highways 114 and 183.

Jerry Jr. was the point man for his father in the developments of Cowboys Stadium and The Star. After he graduated SMU Dedman School of Law, he worked for a law firm for a couple of years but always had his mind set to join the family football business. He moved around, from the team's general counsel to a job in player programs to internet director to media director to ticket sales director and suite director to chief marketing officer.

"I've worn a lot of hats and seen a lot along the way," he said.

That allowed him to develop relationships in every facet of the business world. At his Hall of Fame speech in Canton, Jerry said that Jerry Jr. was most like him. "You can tell that because I want to grab him by the throat every other day," he said. "He's my namesake. He's my baby. He's a pit bull. The third apple did fall the closest to the tree. And why I get so frustrated is he's creating new ways to out–Jerry Jones Jerry Jones."

Jerry named his second son Jerry Jr. Stephen remembered his father once told him he wasn't named after him because he would have been called Junior, which Jerry didn't like. That's why Stephen, whose name is actually John Stephen, was not named Jerry. "By the time Jerry came along, I saw that I regretted not naming Stephen a junior," Jerry said. "So I made Jerry the junior."

Junior set out to meet with teams and tour stadiums and arenas to find out what was working and what wasn't, then incorporate and refine the best ideas into Cowboys Stadium. It turned out to be a fascinating mixture that Aiello laughingly calls "Texas Stadium on steroids."

It has a retractable roof, but when it's open it looks like the hole in the roof at Texas Stadium. The shape of the stadium is similar. There are the blue stars on the walls. It's much bigger, better, and cleaner, and much more profitable. "The pageantry we learned from Texas Stadium," Jerry Jr. said. "What we were about to do, which was create the highest revenue-generating venue in the history of sports, you know the product was there, you know the content was there, but you had to have the fan experience, too. *Experience* is a very big buzzword for our family."

The process started in 2006, three years before the stadium opened. Jerry Jr. admired how the NBA was conducting its business. He especially admired things the Detroit Pistons were accomplishing on the business side. "The NBA is doing a fantastic job, so I flew up and met with the Pistons president, with the marketing team, and really studied what they were doing," he said. "Everybody always used to ask: What was the biggest challenge building the stadium? If you ask any of us, the biggest challenge was meeting the expectation of our fans and what our brand means. We knew we had to do it first-class and have the bar as high as possible, as you could imagine."

He studied the Tampa Bay Lightning of the National Hockey League. He went to visit the NHL Phoenix Coyotes and noted how close the fans came to the players behind the scenes. "They showed us this club when the players were leaving the locker room and walking past the club as they were walking towards the ice," he said. "We looked at that and said, 'Boy, that's cool and that's neat and that's a great idea.'"

He envisioned the Cowboys walking out of the locker room, through a tunnel with fans behind glass on either side, and right out onto the field. Now when the Cowboys are on television, the cameras follow them through the gauntlet with fans giving them high fives right before they emerge from a tunnel and take the field. "That's how the clubs down on the field got put in place," Jerry Jr. said.

He loved the end zone decks at Raymond James Stadium in Tampa. "You saw what a great job they had done with that pirate ship and all those fans down there and all that commotion and excitement going on," he said. "That's great. But how do you expand on that?"

Everything is bigger in Texas, y'all, so the Cowboys have three decks in each end zone and even a platform where women employed by the team dance in what appears to be a cage. Tampa didn't have that. On another trip, Jones Jr. asked a ticket sales manager for one team that if a customer came in and said money was no object and he's going to be sitting with his son and says he wants the best seat in the house, what would he show him? "We'll take him up to the club seats and show him here's how you buy it," he was told.

That scenario actually had happened a day or two earlier, but the fan said the seats were great with a nice view, and the club was terrific with great food, but sitting in the 300 level was too far away. He wanted to be in the 100 or 200 level closer to the field. "We just ended up selling him a reserved seat," the sales manager told Jones Jr. "It was on the 50-yard line, but he didn't buy a club seat. He bought a cheaper product."

The Cowboys were already in the design phase for their new stadium and breaking ground for construction when Jerry Jr. returned from his trip. "A lot of the ideas that look like fantastic ideas, the basis of them really are copycats," he said.

He arrived in Dallas and called a family meeting. "I came back to Dad and said, 'I think we need to take all these club seats all the way down, not just the 300 level, but the 200 and 100 level,'" he said. "That was going to take your club seats from 7,500 to 15,000 and double your club seats and impact your seat option revenue hugely, impact your game ticket hugely."

Jerry Jr. told them of the story he'd just heard. The Cowboys' seat options, known around the NFL as personal seat licenses, charge a one-time fee; in Dallas's case the payments can be spread over thirty years, giving the fan the right to buy the same season tickets every year. The Cowboys benefitted financially by increasing the number of club seats. Instead of the options being $5,000, $6,000, or $12,000 for reserved seats, the club seats were priced at $16,000, $34,000, and $50,000, with some at $150,000 or $250,000, which obviously were intended for anybody lucky enough to strike oil.

"That's where we really started reinventing ourselves as a family [in] how to run our company," Jerry Jr. said. "It's really when we started running like a corporation. Stephen, Charlotte, Dad, and myself are extremely hands-on."

The Cowboys have been sold out on season tickets every year in the new stadium. Gene and Charlotte put together an art advisory board that comprised accomplished people in the field in North Texas. They helped identify up-and-coming artists who did big pieces of art for public places. The works are displayed in the stadium.

The Cowboys dove headfirst into the stadium entertainment

business. They hosted the Super Bowl after the 2010 season, but the entire week, including game day, turned into a disaster. Dallas was paralyzed by an ice-and-snow storm, one of the worst in the city's history, canceling many Super Bowl events. Six people were injured two days before the game when massive chucks of ice came flying off the roof of the stadium and struck them. Things went from bad to chaos on game day when it was discovered that 1,250 of the 13,000 temporary seats installed for the game had not been cleared by the fire marshals, with construction not complete. Eight hundred of the displaced fans were given new seat locations, and four hundred fans were able to watch the game in stadium clubs.

Massive lawsuits followed. Jones and the NFL were criticized for being greedy by attempting to squeeze in every last seat.

This was not how the Jones family wanted to show off their new stadium.

"I do, along with the NFL, take responsibility for the seating issue and some of the things that we would like to improve on regarding the seating issues," Jerry Jones said at the scouting combine a few weeks after the Super Bowl fiasco. "The informing of the fans that were involved, the NFL and I take responsibility for. You always like to look at areas you can do better, get better. We certainly intend to and will get much better in terms of the seating and how that is handled."

Jerry World, as it soon became known after it opened, was able to squeeze in more than one hundred thousand fans for NFL games, concerts, and other events. The 2010 NBA All-Star Game holds the stadium record with 108,731 fans, followed by the Cowboys' first regular-season game against the Giants in 2009, when 105,121 fans were in attendance. It has also hosted the NCAA Final Four; the college football national

championship game; the Cotton Bowl; a George Strait concert in 2014, which drew 104,793; and Wrestlemania, which
brought in 101,763 in 2016. All the high-profile events have
turned the stadium into Jones's personal oil well. The NFL
even gave him a second chance hosting at a big event by
holding the three-day 2018 NFL draft, the league's glamour
off-season extravaganza, at AT&T Stadium. For each of the
first two nights, there were 20,000 people inside the stadium
and 80,000 outside at the 900,000-square-foot NFL Experience.

Arlington kicked in $325 million for the stadium that was
supposed to cost $650 million, with Jones picking up the other
half. The final bill was $1.3 billion. The city was capped at
$325 million, so the balance was on Jones to cover the over-
runs. "Dad tells the story, and I can hear it in my sleep, of
buying the Dallas Cowboys and risking everything he worked
for. He just believed in being part of the Dallas Cowboys,"
Jerry Jr. said. "He said, 'I danced with the devil and I never
want to do it again.' Of course, when the stadium came along,
he ended up dancing with the devil a second time. They were
fifty feet in the ground and 2008 hits and the greatest reces-
sion in the history of our country. We were spending a million
bucks a day and he's dancing with the devil again."

* * *

Jerry Jones might not have had the stomach to dance with the
devil again, but he was all for dancing with The Star.

That was what he named the Cowboys' $1.5 billion project
in Frisco, so far north of downtown Dallas that twenty years
earlier it was considered part of Oklahoma. There were miles
and miles of undeveloped land in Frisco. In the '90s, Jerry
Jones worked with the city of Frisco on real estate projects,

and by the time he was ready to move the Cowboys out of Valley Ranch, it became a viable option for the relocation of his team.

Frisco had set aside funds to build a $90 million high school stadium to be used by all the schools in the district. Texas Stadium, an NFL stadium seating 65,000, cost $35 million. "Only in Texas are high schools putting that kind of money towards it," Jerry Jr. said. "It's truly unbelievable." The city of Allen built a $60 million, eighteen-thousand-seat high school stadium that opened in 2012. "That was the beginning of the high school arms race," Jerry Jr. said. Two years later, cracks in the concrete forced the shutdown of the Allen stadium for eighteen months.

The city of Frisco had a ninety-one-acre tract of land that was reserved for the Nebraska Furniture Mart, a sprawling multi-level store owned by Warren Buffett. At the "midnight hour," Jerry Jr. said, "they went down the street" and made a deal with The Colony, a neighboring town. Frisco still had the land, they still had $90 million burning a hole in their taxpayers' pockets to build a high school stadium, and they had the Dallas Cowboys looking for a new home.

Frisco turned the land over to the Cowboys to develop, along with a $25 million relocation fee and the $90 million for the stadium, with the stipulation that it be used by the Frisco schools for football, cheerleader and band competitions, lacrosse, and every high school sport and school graduation. "They gave us the keys to the venue and we built it for them," Jerry Jr. said.

The Cowboys constructed a twelve-thousand-seat indoor stadium for Frisco that cost $170 million. "They got about a $170 million high school stadium sitting there for the price of $90 million," Jerry Jr. said. "That's a little bit of how Texas operates. You give a little incentive, you get people and developers, or businesspeople and their families doing more aggressive things because they're not operating on one hundred cents on the dollar. That's what happened in Arlington. They did a $325 million referendum on the stadium that at the beginning was going to be $650 million. We made a commitment that we would spend at least $650 million. The city was capped at $325 million and we built a $1.2 billion stadium."

The Ford Motor Company and the North Texas Ford Dealers signed a ten-year naming rights deal to have it called the Ford Center. As long as it's nailed down and can't move, Jerry Jones and his family will find a way to cash in through sponsorships, which they prefer to call partnerships. At Valley Ranch, they had a $2 million MRI machine that was very convenient for the team, but it was hard to justify the cost of the equipment just for use by the players on Monday mornings after they were banged up on Sunday. "We figured out how to take the MRI and make it an outpatient service," Jerry Jr. said.

They understood doctors loved referring their patients in need of an MRI to the Cowboys' very own MRI machine. "No one likes going to the doctor and no one likes getting an MRI, but if I can walk through something that has a lot of Cowboys touch and feel, it became an experience," Jerry Jr. said. "We had success with that."

Come right in and slide into the same machine that diagnosed Tony Romo's broken collarbone! Let's see if we can find a torn ACL just like Sean Lee's! The Cowboys made it sound like it was almost worth getting injured just to brag to friends you had used the same MRI machine as Jason Witten. Imagine that.

The Cowboys were able to monetize more than an MRI machine on all that land in Frisco that now belonged to them. "I don't know if it was his contrarian approach or a mad scientist approach, but Dad was very challenging to me, Stephen, and

Charlotte about doing this," Jerry Jr. said. "He said there had to be an ROI [return on investment] with everything about The Star. Early on, he really didn't have an appetite to dance with the devil again."

The Cowboys got into the sports medicine business through a partnership with the Baylor Scott and White health-care system, the largest not-for-profit health-care system in Texas. The Cowboys team doctors now do their surgeries at The Star. The sports medicine care piece is a huge part of The Star, as health and safety in the NFL has become a hot-button issue with the concussion crisis. Stephen and Jerry Jr. each played football in college—Stephen at the University of Arkansas and Jerry Jr. at Georgetown. Stephen's son, John Stephen, accepted a scholarship in 2018 to play quarterback at Arkansas. The challenge for the NFL is to keep kids playing football at the youth and high school level, which feeds into college and eventually into the pros. If parents decide it's too risky for their kids to play football, it will eventually impact the NFL.

"My kids play and I'd like to think I know a lot about the game," Stephen said. "I've always said if they weren't playing football, they'd be driving a truck eighty miles per hour down some road or they'd be jumping creeks on a motorcycle. These alpha kids—they want to do something that is fast and dangerous. I just think football is the ultimate team sport and it teaches a lot of life lessons and leadership and supporting one another."

The flip side is if the Joneses spent less time trying to devise ways to make money and more time trying to end their two-decade absence from the Super Bowl, perhaps the sixth Lombardi Trophy would be in the lobby. The Cowboys believe these are mutually exclusive goals. Winning will bring more money in and doesn't get in the way of the Super Bowl goal, but the Cowboys' record over the past two decades has proven that bringing in record amounts of revenue doesn't lead to winning. As much time as Jerry Jones might spend on the business side as the team's owner and president, it takes away from his job as general manager. Even if he delegates and trusts his personnel staff, the Cowboys do not have a full-time general manager to compete with the teams that employ one person to be responsible for the entire football operation.

"For them, this is the way to do business," a former longtime general manager in the NFL said. "When Clint Murchison owned the Cowboys, I thought they did the best job of selling their brand without putting the team in competition with it. Jerry doesn't have a feel for that. He sees the bottom line, and it's not the goal line. Whatever way he has something presented to monetize the brand, he's going to do."

As long as that doesn't interfere with giving his team the best chance to win, then what's the issue? "What kind of culture is he creating? Culture is subjective," the former GM said. "It permeates within the building. That's why everybody looks for leaders. The leaders are the ones that set the culture. Usually that is the identity of what the team is on and off the field. I think Jerry has no feel for that, either. He's P. T. Barnum. He knows how to promote. If he has to stop and create a mentality that we are in the football business and we don't want players to misconstrue who we are, he would never do that. That to him is nonsense."

The assessment is harsh, but it's backed up by just three playoff victories since the last Super Bowl in the midnineties. "If Jerry were a real football guy, he would not want to send a message to players and coaches that we are a circus act," the former GM said.

The Cowboys partnered with Omni and own 50 percent of the sixteen-floor hotel attached to their offices. "Everything

Dad taught us, how you can leverage the Cowboys brand and do something unique in the heartbeat of the growth in North Texas, we got to do what has now become The Star," Jerry Jr. said.

The final cost of The Star development will be $200 million more than the stadium. By 2018, the Cowboys were already $750 million into the project.

The Cowboys own 50 percent of ninety-six Papa John's pizza stores in North Texas. When John Schnatter, the founder of Papa John's International, blamed sagging business sales in 2017 on the National Anthem protest by NFL players, many thought he was a mouthpiece for his good friend Jerry Jones. Schnatter was forced to step down as CEO and later resigned as chairman of the board after he used a racial slur. Papa John's had been the official pizza of the NFL, but that partnership ended in 2018.

Monetize. Monetize. Monetize.

The Cowboys draft room is so technologically advanced NASA was thinking of launching the next man to the moon using the war room as mission control. (That's just a slight exaggeration.) But it does have an interactive media wall of three rows, each with five 55-inch HD televisions, two 98-inch televisions side by side allowing for player comparisons, and more supersecret phones than Batman had to reach Commissioner Gordon of Gotham City. Of course, if the Cowboys pick the wrong players, they might as well have been doing it back at the old blue tin shack on Forest Lane. The working conditions are invigorating, but it's the information that comes into the meetings that translates into wins and losses.

"We can do it just as good in the old war room at Valley Ranch," Jerry Jr. said.

So why bother? Is it really worth the money for scouts to gather at The Star for the month leading up to the draft, and then on the three days of the draft, in such opulent accommodations?

"When Pepsi wants to run a promotion in town to win a chance to draft your fantasy football team with you and your closest friends and use the Dallas Cowboys draft room—here is the experience again," Jerry Jr. said. "We spent millions of dollars to create that room. How do you justify it? You sit there and have corporations have events in it. You have sponsors do promotions to have fantasy football drafts. Come August, that is a busy place for people having fantasy football drafts."

Can you imagine Bill Belichick ever allowing fans into the Patriots draft room?

On the walls of the Cowboys team meeting room, furnished with eleven rows of plush leather seats, is the slogan, THE TEAM, THE TEAM, THE TEAM, which the Cowboys may or may not have stolen from the University of Michigan Wolverines, but the room is about much more than Jones's football team. It was built with the idea of companies bringing their employees in to watch the Cowboys' highlight film. "This is the place for AT&T to have a corporate executive retreat, have a meeting, come in here, do a presentation, do their year-in-review on the screen, tie in with Dallas Cowboys production, audio and visual, make it come to life, and give them an experience that they haven't had," Jones Jr. said. "Well, that team meeting room was built for that."

The Cowboys don't consider it a team meeting room as much as a theater that their team happens to meet in a few times each week. Jerry told his kids the way to get a nice team meeting room was to create a return on investment and suck revenue out of it. Jones and his family are not just in the football business to win games. They have made things as elaborate and comfortable for their players as possible by renting out pieces of their building to sponsors to help cover the cost.

* * *

What is any NFL team facility without its own health club?

Jones Jr. met with Harvey Spevak, the CEO of Equinox, a health club with gyms all over the country. They got together at Super Bowl XLVIII in New York in 2014, and Jones's plan was to ask him to put an Equinox at The Star "for the culture of our people," basically giving the Cowboys' employees a place they could work out and socialize on their lunch break or after work.

"Harvey said the gym business is great," Jones Jr. said. "He told me Equinox does a billion dollars in revenue and makes $350 million. Boy, a 35-percent-margin business. So I went back and said, 'I don't think we want to just sign a tenant lease. I think we want to be in the gym business. We got to figure out how to run a gym.' If it's in the 35-percent-margin business, I learned enough from my dad, that's a good business."

He enlisted the help of Mark Mastrov, chairman of New Evolution Ventures and the founder of 24 Hour Fitness, to develop Cowboys Fit, a three-story, sixty-thousand-square-foot facility that advertises to potential members that they can work out on the same equipment as the Dallas Cowboys. On a very special day, they might even bump into one of them on the treadmill. On the third level is a lap pool. Imagine splashing around with Dak Prescott and Demarcus Lawrence, or even coach Jason Garrett, and playing Marco Polo.

The Cowboys' lunchtime has come a long way from Too Tall Jones and his chicken wings. The lunchroom might be the nicest eating establishment in Frisco. But the Cowboys decided it was not going to be just for the players. After a visit to the NFL offices in New York, Jones Jr. took note of two things: 345 Park Avenue was the offices of many more businesses than just the NFL; and, the NFL ran its own cafeteria that had a way of bringing everybody together. He was able to say hello to so many league executives just while he was having lunch on the sixth floor that it would have taken days to make the rounds if he had to set up an appointment to see them all.

"We have to build a cafeteria like that for our offices," he said.

His family was skeptical that players would want to share their training table with the marketing and sales department. More pushback came from people who thought the players would pack their lunches into plastic containers and eat at their lockers.

"What we learned is not only does it work, it works better than we ever dreamed," Jones Jr. said.

The players are eating and chatting with other members of the organization. "Players get tired of looking at each other," he said.

The major piece of the nonfootball puzzle before construction began was Jones Jr.'s biggest takeaway from his visit to New York: If the NFL could share building space with accountants and lawyers, why couldn't the Cowboys? "It was just going to be the one building," he said. "I said, 'We are missing a great opportunity.'"

Of course, they decided to go with the second building. The Cowboys-themed lobby makes it seem as if accountants and lawyers are sharing an office with Jerry Jones and the players. Super Bowl trophies and Cowboys memorabilia in the atrium lobby are hard to miss. So is the sculpture of lights created by Leo Villareal, the artist who came up with the lighting on the Bay Bridge that connects San Francisco to Oakland. There are 160 rods hanging 40 feet from the ceiling that hold a total of 19,200 LED lights.

Walk to the right, and on the ground floor are the coaches'

offices and position group meeting rooms. The executive offices are upstairs. Take the elevator down one level to the Field Level floor, which features the locker room, the weight room, the lunchroom, and the exit to the practice field. The players have their own parking lot near the locker room entrance. The elevator on the left side of the lobby takes tenants to their offices. There is no interaction between the people who work on the left side of the building and the players who work on the right side, but at least they can say they work in the same building as their heroes, for whatever that is worth.

If the Cowboys are establishing a blueprint by turning a football facility into a moneymaking venture, then it will be evident in 2020 when Stan Kroenke opens the headquarters for the Los Angeles Rams in their new stadium and Mark Davis brings the Raiders to Las Vegas. So far, the Cowboys embrace letting the public come a bit closer on days other than Sunday with tours of AT&T Stadium (VIP $32; self-guided $22) and The Star ($32.50, but you get special access to the war room and Super Bowl memorabilia). It allows fans who are not among the ninety thousand who attend games a glimpse of the operation.

"Jerry says less than 10 percent of our Cowboys fans ever get the opportunity to go watch a game live at AT&T Stadium or any other stadium," Stephen said. "So your other 90 percent of your fans are experiencing it through television, merchandising."

Charlotte designed the retail space outside the office buildings at The Star that's being leased to restaurants and retail stores. Inside The Star, the "Lake Landry" nickname for the hot tub has been carried over from Valley Ranch. The football-shaped locker room looks like the lobby of the Ritz-Carlton. With jocks and socks, of course. It all seems much too nice for football players.

"A lot of people said that about our stadium," Charlotte said. "Our goal here was obviously to inspire our own athletes, but it was to create an area, a place of aspiration, really a destination for high school football, for students, for the community to be part of something bigger. This is really our Disney World. It's not imaginary. It's based on reality and it's authentic. This is really what it means to pursue excellence every day."

Why are the Cowboys ahead of the pack on this?

"We've all just seen Dad get enshrined into the Pro Football Hall of Fame," Jerry Jr. said. "It was about everything he was about and had been teaching me and Stephen and Charlotte for twenty-five years."

The Jones family siblings feed off their father's energy for his team.

"Dad, you would rather make $1 off the Cowboys than $100 in another business," Stephen said.

"You're right," Jerry said.

Jerry Jones's worth in 2018 was valued at $5.6 billion by *Forbes*, placing him number 321 on their list of the richest people in the world. Some other interesting numbers from *Forbes*: AT&T Stadium generates more than $100 million a year in premium seat revenue (luxury suites and club seats), and $150 million from sponsors, including at The Star. This does not take into account the millions brought in by concerts and non-NFL sporting events.

America's Team sells. If not for Bob Ryan—or Doug Todd—having a clever idea before they had dinner and a drunken night at the Atlantic City casinos in 1979, maybe much of Cowboys Inc. wouldn't have even happened.

CHAPTER THREE

Mr. Cowboy

The car was loaded up and the Wittens were on the way from their home in Vienna, Virginia, just outside Washington, to Kings Dominion, an amusement park in Doswell that was seventy-five miles away. The ride started off with the anticipation of a fun time and turned into the breaking up of a family.

Jason Witten was seated in the back with his older brothers, Ryan and Shawn. Their father, Eddie, a six-nine, three-hundred-pound mountain of a man, was driving, and their mother, Kim, was next to him in the passenger seat. It was 1993; Jason was just eleven years old and had already seen way too much for such a young boy. He was only six years old when something snapped with Eddie; his father developed a drug and alcohol problem and became abusive toward Jason's mother and brothers. Jason was the youngest and his father didn't touch him, but the emotional pain of seeing the family he loved being torn apart was more scarring than any physical pain he was spared.

"It was tough to watch," he said.

His father would send him to his room and then would hit his mother and brothers. Or, Jason said, his father would hit his mother right in front of him. Ryan is five years older than Jason,

Shawn two years older. The police were called to their condo on several occasions. Eddie would later go to jail for six months for physically abusing his seventy-four-year-old mother. By that time, Kim and her three kids had moved out. Eddie Witten also spent time in a rehab center.

Despite all the turmoil and confusion resulting from growing up in a house with domestic violence, the boys were looking forward to a few days at the amusement park. It was a blast when Eddie took them to an Orioles or a Redskins game, so maybe this would be the time their dad would set aside whatever problems he was having and take care of his family the right way.

Eddie once played high school football for Kim's father in Elizabethton, Tennessee, and now he was working for the postal service as a mailman. "He was a big, large, athletic guy and he kind of got caught up in some drugs and alcohol," Jason Witten said. "By the time I got old enough to know what the heck was going on, it was this torn relationship, because I was the youngest and really loved this guy a lot. He's my dad. He loves sports. We'd go play together. He's just kind of a tale of two lives. He came home and after he'd been drinking, he got very abusive to my mother, and my older brothers experienced some of that."

The car was traveling south on I-95 to Kings Dominion when Witten's parents began to argue. "They got into a scuffle and he dropped us off on the interstate," Witten said.

Literally, the Witten family had come to a "crossroads in our life," he said.

Eddie Witten pulled the car onto the shoulder of the highway and ordered his wife out of the car. She has said that his intention was to speed off with the three boys, but Ryan, the oldest, sensed what was happening, opened the car door, and he and his brothers escaped. They started walking down the highway to the next exit, and Kim was able to get in touch with a family friend to pick them up and take them home. Ryan had already been living for the past year with Kim's parents in Tennessee as a way to escape his father and get more diligent with his schoolwork. Now Kim's plan for herself and her two younger sons was to join Ryan and her parents.

"Enough. That's it," she said. "We're leaving."

Jason Witten's journey—from the little boy abandoned on the side of the road by the father he loved, to being the fourth-leading receiver in NFL history, and finally to when he ended plans to play a sixteenth season with the Cowboys and retired on May 3, 2018, to accept the prestigious and coveted *Monday Night Football* analyst position on ESPN—is one of the greatest stories of perseverance. Witten has done great work with his SCORE Foundation, which matches male role models with children who have been victims of domestic violence. His foundation's "Coaching Boys Into Men" program in Arlington, Texas, trains coaches to educate their players on the dangers of domestic violence and abusive relationships. He has helped thousands of abused children in Texas and Tennessee. He won the prestigious Bart Starr Award and Walter Payton Man of the Year Award in 2012, the only player to win both citizenship awards in the same year.

"I always said if I had an opportunity and if I ever made it, it would always be important to me that I wanted to use that platform to try and help in the community," Witten said.

Kim Witten knew she could not go the rest of her life being abused or sit and hope as a stay-at-home mom that one day her husband would come home and apologize and swear on the lives of his children that he would never touch any of them again. "I see that cycle in the community when we try to help out that these women are overwhelmed because it's the same person they love and care about and there are good memories, too," Witten said. "So they're scared. My mom wasn't perfect by any means but had the will and strength to endure that and come out on the other side."

That was the dangerous cycle his mother found herself in. Then, Eddie forced her out of the car and "literally dropped us on the side of the interstate," Jason Witten said. She decided it was time to take charge of her life. "You never knew what was going to come home," Kim told *Sports Illustrated*. "If he was drinking, he was mean. If he was using something else, the house could burn down around him and he wouldn't care."

The magazine did a feature on Witten, and author S. L. Price described this horrific scene:

At 12, Ryan was pushed into adulthood: shepherding his brothers upstairs when things got heated, getting between his parents, taking blows. More than once Ryan called the police to their Vienna home. One time while driving, Eddie launched a backhand that broke Kim's nose. She says it was because one boy had forgotten his shoes; Eddie says it was because he was angry over getting lost. "I asked her to read a map, and she didn't want to do it," Eddie says, "so I slapped her right there." From the backseat, the older boys saw blood. "Jason was screaming, but he was so young he didn't know," Kim says. "He was screaming because Ryan and Shawn were screaming."

After the I-95 drop-off, Kim waited for her husband to go to work one day and packed up all the important belongings, summoned Shawn and Jason to the car, and drove to re-join Ryan and live with her parents, Dave and Deanna Rider, in Elizabethton. It was the best decision Kim ever made. It changed her life. It changed her sons' lives.

"If it weren't for my mom making the decision to live with my grandma and grandpa, I wouldn't be sitting here today," Witten said. "Any forty-year-old lady making the decision to move back in with her parents, that's not always easy. I'm so appreciative she was able to seek help and drop her pride, if you will, to be able to go do that. There was a lot of hurt and a lot of tough times."

Kim's father became the male role model the three boys needed. They all played football for him at Elizabethton High School, and he insisted on the toughness needed on the field that turned Jason into an NFL ironman who missed one game his entire career. Jason became an outstanding two-way high school player as a tight end and outside linebacker, Shawn played wide receiver at Virginia Tech, and Ryan played one year of college football at Clinch Valley College in Virginia. Their grandfather became the most important man in their world. "He was a ball coach for forty years," Witten said. "I experienced family really for the first true time and my mom was able to get back on track."

Football was the outlet the Witten boys needed. His brothers told him to make sure he called his grandfather "Coach" around the field. "Football became an out for me and a place where I could go chase my dreams," he said.

Shawn later became the head football coach at Elizabethton, and Ryan assisted him. Their grandparents' home provided the boys with the peace of mind they didn't have in Virginia. "So we lived with my grandparents and my life forever changed," Jason said. "This was a southern lady and man, and there's rules. This is how you treat people. This is how you look people in the eye. This is how you open a car door for a woman. This is how you eat dinner together as a family."

Jason developed into a top recruit playing for his grandfather. He went on to play tight end at the University of Tennessee, then elected to leave school and enter the 2003 NFL draft after his junior year. He was disappointed and felt misled by NFL teams when he lasted until the third round. If he knew he wouldn't be drafted earlier, he would have returned to Knoxville for his senior year. But it could not have worked out better. He began his career playing for Bill Parcells. He met free agent quarterback Tony Romo, and they formed a bond that will never be broken. His mother remarried a few years after Jason joined the Cowboys.

Witten was only twenty years old when he was drafted. Parcells was in his first year of coaching the Cowboys. He was exactly the tough-love coach Witten and younger players need early in their career, although he had gotten that from his grandfather, too. Witten was exactly the player Parcells needed. Parcells might have lost battles in the draft room with the Joneses and scouts during his four years in Dallas, but he pushed for the Cowboys to take Witten and won out when others wanted UCLA tight end Mike Seidman.

It didn't take long for Witten to become one of the inner-circle "Parcells Guys." In the fourth game of his rookie year, he broke his jaw in a game against the Cardinals. His face was all swollen. Parcells visited him in the training room in the days after the injury. He told him to suck it up by relating a story about Mark Bavaro, an All-Pro tight end who played for Parcells with the Giants. He told Witten that Bavaro once broke his jaw and didn't miss any games. He advised Witten to maintain his weight by eating sweet-potato baby food. He had three plates in his jaw and was dropping pounds without being able to eat solid food. Witten missed one game and made weight the next week by stuffing coins in his sweatpants pocket. It was the only game of his fifteen-year career that he missed. He remembered the advice Parcells had given him that summer in training camp: "I'm just telling you, the best ones, they find a way," Parcells said. "Durability and dependability are invaluable."

Witten finished his career having played in 235 consecutive games. He is the Cowboys' all-time leader in games played, catches, and receiving yards. He caught a pass in 130 consecutive games until the streak was stopped late in the 2016 season.

Parcells and Jerry Jones became father figures to Witten. His own father at first would come around to the Jason Witten Youth Football Camp that Jason runs free for kids in Elizabethton during the off-season. Most people in town knew about Eddie's history, and he was hard to miss on the sidelines. When someone offered to go over and ask him to leave, Witten said, "Hey, he's fine." Witten introduced his father to his kids, but he has no ongoing relationship with him. "I wanted him to know that I forgave him and he could move forward even though there were mistakes," he said. "I wouldn't be where I am today if it wouldn't have happened. As crazy as it may seem, there's a lot of good he taught me and I appreciate that."

* * *

ESPN's *E-60* did a piece on Witten in 2014 in which his father was interviewed. Witten said he was disappointed his father would not come clean about the abuse he put his family through, which forced them to leave him. "He had the opportunity to just say, 'You know what, I screwed up,' but he got real defensive," Witten said.

He called his father and told him he had his chance to set the record straight, "but you chose to run the other way." They rarely see each other now. Witten elected to take on domestic violence with the same determination he used in attacking line-backers and strong safeties. "The older you get, the more you can recognize how influential your upbringing is on what shapes you in life," Romo said.

It put Witten in an awkward position when teammate Ezekiel Elliott was accused of domestic violence. "I'm not privy to all the information that's gone on over the last year," Witten said after the NFL announced a six-game suspension for Elliott. "I'd say this: There's no place for a man to put his hands on a woman. Most of you know that's a situation that's affected my family as a younger kid, so I put in a lot of work and attention and have a platform to step out and speak on stopping domestic violence."

It took time for Witten to open up to Romo about his family life after they made the Cowboys as rookies. Once Witten realized what a special friend Romo was going to be, he filled him in on his childhood. "It doesn't mean you can't come out of it and do great things and be a great person," Romo said. "You do also understand how much impact the father has on his children. It's a testament to Jason and his family and his grandparents and his mother that he turned out this way. Jason changed the future of the Wittens by wanting to be different. His kids are now going to see how he loves his wife, loves his kids, and is a great father. That's going to be instrumental in how they treat their kids and their wives. I think that's a testament to him seeing that and deciding 'I'm going to be different.'"

* * *

Jason Witten had just won the Bob Lilly Award for the sixth time in 2016. It is voted on by the Cowboys fans and given to the Cowboy who "best represents the highest level of achievement, sportsmanship, dedication and leadership like that of the Dallas Cowboys Hall of Famer Bob Lilly."

Each of the first five times Witten won, the award was presented at halftime of a Cowboys home game. Witten was in the locker room and had his wife, Michelle, and his children on the field to accept the award from Lilly, the first player the Cowboys picked in their first draft in 1961, the first Cowboy inducted into the Ring of Honor, the first Cowboy selected to the Pro Football Hall of Fame.

The sixth time Witten won the award was different. It was late in the season, and the Cowboys decided to make the presentation before the game. Lilly, who was given the nickname Mr. Cowboy by Roger Staubach and other teammates, was on the field with Witten's family. Cowboys executive Charlotte Jones Anderson and then Witten himself joined them.

Lilly moved over to stand next to Witten. "Hey," Lilly said. "At some point they just have to change the name of the award to the Jason Witten Award."

Witten was flattered, but the best from Lilly was yet to come. "I'm telling you—you're Mr. Cowboy," he said.

Just to make sure Witten fully grasped what he was saying, Lilly said it again. "I'm telling you, you're Mr. Cowboy."

In Witten's mind, that was the highest compliment from a man he deeply admired. Lilly was a great player and so was Witten, and the reason he had been around long enough to win the award six times was because he had been a player good enough to stick around that long. But the reason he won it six times had nothing to do with his having more than 1,000 catches—and only Jerry Rice, Tony Gonzalez, and Larry Fitzgerald had more—or with his having played more games for the Cowboys than anybody else. He was an All-Pro off the field.

Witten had heard people call him the modern-day Mr. Cowboy, but now the original Mr. Cowboy was telling him the name belonged to him.

The honor was indescribable to Witten. It was like the "Yankee Clipper" name being handed down by Joe DiMaggio. Witten walked off the field with his wife and daughter, one of his four children. As they approached the locker room, Michelle looked at him and said, "Did he just say that?" All Witten could say was, "That was unbelievable."

He thought about how he came into the NFL as a kid still trying to make sense of what had transpired in the past eight years of his life: his father dumping the family off on a highway when he was eleven years old, moving to Tennessee with his mother and brothers, living with his grandparents, playing for his grandfather the high school coach, earning a scholarship to Tennessee, being a third-round pick, learning how to be a pro from Parcells, making a lifelong friend in Romo, and now the most respected Dallas Cowboy in team history tells him, no, young man, *you* are the new Mr. Cowboy.

Witten's head was spinning. That was how much it meant to him. The Cowboys went out and beat the Bucs. Dak Prescott targeted Witten ten times. He caught all ten passes.

Lilly had such high standards that he cost himself a lot of money in his post-NFL life. The *Dallas Morning News* ran a story in 1998 with details about the Coors beer distributorship that Lilly was awarded in Waco, Texas, following his retirement in 1974. The most he ever made in his fourteen-year career with Dallas was $80,000, and the story said he was now running a business bringing in ten times that amount.

One day, he saw the details of a traffic accident that was caused by drunken driving. "A whole bunch of Coors cans had fallen out on the highway, and he realized, 'Those young boys were drinking my product,'" Lilly's wife, Ann, told the *Morning News*.

Lilly could not live with the thought that he'd somehow contributed to the accident. He gave up the distributorship. "Had he kept the business, it would have been worth millions today," Ann Lilly said. "And I can tell you, we're not millionaires. But we're happy."

Witten won the award for the seventh time in 2017. He says there will always be just one Mr. Cowboy. That's Bob Lilly.

Witten helped establish the Jason Witten Collegiate Man of the Year award in 2017, with criteria similar to what the NFL uses for the Payton Award: great leadership on and off the field. The first winner was Central Florida linebacker Shaquem Griffin, who had his left hand amputated at an early age because of a rare bone defect. Oklahoma State quarterback Mason Rudolph and Alabama defensive back Minkah Fitzpatrick were the other finalists. The award was presented at The Star after the season.

Witten's SCORE Foundation makes a $10,000 contribution to the athletic scholarship fund of the winner's college. Charlotte assisted Witten in setting up the award.

"I've never been around somebody who represents so fully what the Dallas Cowboys should be," she said. "He has overcome such a challenging past and been able to internalize that and use it to do something stronger and powerful for the future. He can engage people at any level and get them not only to listen, but inspire them to be better. At some point in his life he realized he had an opportunity to be a part of the problem or a part of the solution. He chose to go with the solution and take everyone on his journey. I just don't think there are many men like that."

He received the ultimate honor just one day after he retired. A nine-day-old giraffe at the Dallas Zoo was given the name Witten.

* * *

Jason Witten and Tony Romo hit it off the first time they met on the Marriott bus. They had flown into Dallas for rookie mini-camp in 2003. Witten was a third-round pick, a tight end from Tennessee. Romo was a free agent quarterback from Eastern Illinois University. They picked up their belongings at baggage claim, and there was not even a Cowboys representative waiting for them.

They were just rookies after all.

Witten and Romo were the only two players on the Marriott shuttle bus when it picked them up at Dallas/Fort Worth International Airport. Neither had heard of the other. Witten was a sure thing to make the team. Romo was going to have to catch the eye of Parcells early and often to stick around.

"Hey, you here for the Cowboys camp?" Witten asked.

"Yeah," Romo said.

It wasn't quite Humphrey Bogart and Claude Rains in *Casablanca*, but it was the start of a beautiful friendship. "The joke is now, I didn't know who he was but he should have at least known what the hell my name was," Witten said. "I was the third-round draft pick."

How could Witten be expected to know Romo? He was a no-name free agent. Even though the Broncos and the Cardinals outbid the Cowboys with larger signing bonus offers, Romo wanted to give it a shot with Parcells and his offensive coordinator, Sean Payton, who had also played quarterback at Eastern Illinois.

The shuttle pulled up to the Dallas Airport Marriott North, the hotel the Cowboys used for rookies when they first got to town when their training facility was at Valley Ranch. It was also the team hotel the night before home games when they played at Texas Stadium.

Witten and Romo got off the bus. Now what to do?

"You want to go across the street and get pepperoni pizza?" Romo asked.

"No. This is the weekend I've been dreaming about my entire life. I'm not going across the street and having pepperoni pizza," Witten said.

Romo accepted Witten's excuse and took a rain check. They would have plenty of pizza together. "For fourteen years we got to play together and all the highs and lows that we experienced," Witten said. "Not only on the field, but personally to see us become men and get married and have children. To think that two guys came in at that young of an age and then to be the leaders of the football team. Ultimately, we never won a championship together and that's something we'll both have to live with. It's hard. Man, we emptied the bucket. We left everything out there trying to achieve it."

Championships form lifelong bonds, even for those in the locker room who otherwise have nothing else in common. Witten and Romo never even made it to an NFC Championship Game together, but from the day they met it was as if they had known each other forever. They didn't have the championships that brought Troy Aikman and Michael Irvin so close and did the same for Emmitt Smith and Daryl Johnston.

Aikman had a clean-cut image, was the face of the franchise, a three-time Super Bowl champion, so it was risky when he showed up in a Dallas courtroom for Irvin's drug trial in 1996. Irvin was busted by police in an Irving, Texas, hotel room.

Also present in the room: ten grams of cocaine, one ounce of marijuana, two topless dancers, and former teammate Alfredo Roberts.

"Hey, can I tell you who I am?" Irvin said to police.

They already knew.

So did Aikman. Irvin was an incredibly talented player who had issues. Aikman wasn't going to abandon him.

"It was in support of him as a friend, not in support of what he did," Aikman said.

Irvin pleaded no contest and was given four years probation and suspended five games by the NFL.

More than two decades later, Irvin detailed what it meant to him that Aikman, his quarterback, was there for him in his time of greatest need. It brought tears to his eyes and they were real. It was the lowest moment of his life, and Aikman came downtown even though Irvin told him to stay home and not risk tarnishing his reputation. Aikman appeared on the tenth day of the trial and took a seat with Irvin's family.

"I see Troy as a brother. Period," Irvin said. "I just love him for everything he stands for, everything he is. He's great at everything he does. If there is anything I need, I go to Troy. He'll be there for me even if I say don't do it."

Aikman grew up in Henryetta, Oklahoma, went to school at the University of Oklahoma, played for Barry Switzer, broke his leg, and transferred to UCLA. Irvin grew up in Fort Lauderdale as the fifteenth of seventeen children. He got himself in more trouble than seems possible off the field in his days with the Cowboys, but he subsequently found religion and straightened out his life. He has helped his family financially and been a mentor for his brothers and sisters, nephews and nieces.

Irvin is a loyal man. He will do anything for a friend. Aikman's loyalty hit home for him. "It meant the world," Irvin said. "He looked past my shortcomings and said, 'That's my brother and I'm going to be there and I'm going to show up and support him.' I said, 'Don't do that. Don't put yourself in that situation,' but he did and it means a lot. It means a great deal."

They won Super Bowls and helped each other get into the Hall of Fame. They were the two hardest workers on the Cowboys team. Aikman never let Irvin down even when Irvin kept screwing up. He became a big brother to him.

Even though he made the Hall of Fame in his third year on the ballot, Irvin knows he could have been better if he'd stayed away from drugs and clubs. If he had a chance to replay those years, he would handle it differently. "Oh God, yes," he said. "The only way you make sense out of the decisions you made as a young man and things that didn't go right, is if I could use it to help others."

The relationship between Emmitt Smith and Daryl Johnston was special, too. Johnston was one of the last great fullbacks in the NFL. He could run with the ball, he could catch it, but his strength was as a lead blocker creating holes for Smith to become the all-time leading rusher in NFL history. He would sacrifice his body to keep tacklers off Smith. How could you not love a guy for that?

Smith broke Walter Payton's rushing record in 2013, and Johnston, in his role with Fox television, was on the sidelines to witness it firsthand. Smith came over to hug Johnston immediately after setting the record.

"I'm glad I could be here. I wouldn't have missed this for anything," Johnston whispered in Smith's ear.

Smith took a step back, then embraced Johnston again. He put his right hand behind Johnston's head and brought him closer. Smith was crying.

"Thank you, man," Smith said.

"I enjoyed everything I did for you. You made it fun, buddy," Johnston said.

* * *

Witten and Romo became so inseparable that Terrell Owens's paranoia about their relationship led to his departure from Dallas after just three seasons and just one year after the Cowboys had extended his contract. Late in the 2008 season before a mid-December game against the Giants, Owens went to the coaches to complain that Romo had eyes only for Witten when he dropped back to pass. It was standard operating procedure for T.O., who had Hall of Fame ability as a wide receiver but felt the need to destroy his quarterbacks. He did it with Jeff Garcia in San Francisco and Donovan McNabb in Philadelphia.

Even though Jerry Jones went against the wishes of Parcells to sign Owens after the Eagles cut him following the 2005 season, he developed a good rapport with Romo on the field. They hit it off right away, with Owens catching 85 passes for 1,180 yards and 13 touchdowns in his first season in Dallas, far surpassing Witten's numbers. Parcells left after the season and was replaced by Wade Phillips. The Cowboys were the best team in the NFC in 2007 with a 13-3 record, and T.O. had another monster season with 81 catches for 1,355 yards and 15 touchdowns. Witten exploded with 96 catches for 1,145 yards and 7 touchdowns. By his third year with the Cowboys, T.O.'s numbers and the number of team victories dropped, which is a combustible combination in T.O.-ville. In 2008, Owens had 100 more receiving yards than Witten, but Witten had 12 more catches. The Cowboys won nine games and missed the playoffs.

As the season was crumbling, Owens went in to meet with offensive coordinator Jason Garrett and dragged along fellow wideouts Roy Williams and Patrick Crayton. There were reports that Owens believed Romo and Witten were meeting on the side and drawing up plays that eliminated T.O. as a potential target. Owens never took into consideration that he dropped an awful lot of passes and Witten held on to everything thrown in his direction.

"I'm not jealous of Witten," Owens told the *Dallas Morning News*. "I'm not jealous of nobody. I can take the approach that I got paid so screw everything, but that's not me. I just want to win. I'm not trying to create a war of words with anybody. I thought we had a productive meeting and I just talked to Jason [Garrett] about Tony reading the whole play because other people are open besides Witten."

Tension was building. Owens and Witten got into a shouting match at the Friday practice two days before the game against the Giants. "The things that happen in the past with the other quarterbacks that I've had made me go to [Garrett] instead," Owens said. "I didn't want to have any problems with Tony, so I went to Jason. I don't want people to say if I go to Tony and tell him he's not doing what he's supposed to be doing, then people will say we have a problem. I don't want to create that situation."

In January 2008, eleven months before Owens told the teacher on Romo, he put on one of the all-time great dramatic performances defending Romo after the Cowboys were upset by the Giants in a divisional-round playoff game at home. The Cowboys had a bye on wild card weekend and Romo and his then-girlfriend Jessica Simpson—along with Witten and his wife and linebacker Bobby Carpenter and his wife—took advantage of the downtime and went on a weekend junket to Cabo San Lucas in Mexico. It was a relatively quick two-and-a-half-hour flight.

Even before the Cowboys lost the game to the Giants, Romo was catching grief for not staying in Dallas with his head in the playbook, watching tape and scouting New York vs. Tampa on television. Instead, the perception was that he was frolicking on the beach with his superstar singer girlfriend, with the play-offs the furthest thing from his mind. Witten and Carpenter, his two closest friends on the team, dodged the ridicule, but Romo was made out to be the celebrity quarterback with his priorities out of order. Romo knew any blame would fall on him as the quarterback.

"You're young. You don't know any better at the time," Romo said. "At the time, you think you're just going to get away. Everyone else heads to Vegas. I thought going to sit at a pool and watching football at a house down there is something that seemed intelligent at the time."

Intelligent until pictures of Romo and Simpson started to circulate.

"When you look back, it wasn't very smart," Romo said. "But that was so little in the grand scheme of things. We went down there and literally did nothing. Obviously, the optics didn't look good."

T.O. was the star of a bizarre interview-room performance the following weekend at Texas Stadium just across the hall from the locker room. Romo threw an end zone interception from the Giants' 23-yard line with nine seconds left in the game, finishing off the Cowboys' shocking 21–17 loss. Owens came into the interview room wearing sunglasses and it wasn't long before a disingenuous waterworks show started.

"That's my teammate," Owens said while crying. "That's my quarterback."

Why was Owens so broken up? He was a competitive player, for sure, and the loss hurt. But if you truly want to be skeptical, or in this case realistic, Owens was already lobbying for Romo to throw him the ball even more the following season. But then when things didn't go his way, he turned on his quarterback. After the 2008 season Jones cut him.

When Jones released Romo in the spring of 2017, Owens took a playful jab at himself when he tweeted, "That's my quarterback! 1st, I wish him health and 2nd I wish him the best place for his success as he closes out his career."

Romo turned down an opportunity to continue playing with the Houston Texans and retired when he was offered the number one analyst job for CBS. He was an instant success in the booth. Witten, at least for one more season, continued his career. It was all about the work ethic. "The secret is in the dirt," he said. "No one was going to outwork me. I relied on grit."

* * *

Witten and Romo started their NFL careers together on the Marriott bus back in 2003. What they went on to accomplish together and apart was made even more impressive by how unexpected it was.

Romo ranks first in passing yards and touchdowns in Cowboys history, with Aikman second. Aikman played in nine more games, but Romo threw for about 1,200 more yards, and had 83 more touchdowns and 24 fewer interceptions. Romo's numbers completely blow away Roger Staubach's.

Here's the difference: Aikman won three Super Bowls. Staubach won two Super Bowls. Romo won two playoff games.

It pains Jerry Jones that he went through the Romo era without making it to the Super Bowl. Romo got to the playoffs just four times and never made it past the divisional round. He made the big mistakes at the worst times. Just about every year the Cowboys would be alive in the final game having a chance to advance it to the postseason, and each year it seemed Romo committed crucial errors. He was also unlucky: his fumbled snap on the winning field goal attempt against Seattle in the 2006 wild card round; the loss to the Giants as the number 1 seed in 2007 when he ran into a red-hot team that would go on to beat the undefeated Patriots in the Super Bowl; Dez Bryant's apparent catch in Green Bay late in the fourth quarter of the 2014 playoffs being overturned by replay, a catch that would stand today after a 2018 rule change; and his back injury in the third preseason game in 2016, allowing Dak Prescott to take his job and never give it back.

"I look back and 2007 might have been my best team," Romo said. "The team in 2014 was really good, but 2007 had a really good defense. When I say that, I think we were seventh or eighth. I never really had a top five or six defense. I was just young. As I got older, I was a much better player. When I look back, you wish you were a little older, a little better during that time."

Staubach and Aikman embraced Romo as the next in line of great Cowboys quarterbacks. Staubach was a national figure coming out of Navy. Aikman was the first pick in the draft. Romo's claim to whatever fame he had the first few years was doing an impressive impersonation of Brett Favre, his hero growing up in Wisconsin. He is among the best undrafted rookie free agent quarterbacks in NFL history.

"There is always going to be an empty cold feeling by not winning a Super Bowl," he said. "You wanted to do it for people who rooted for you, that you loved, who were meaningful in your life. I wanted it for Jerry and for Stephen and Charlotte and Jerry Jr. and Witten. All the special guys you played with over the years. I just feel it was my job to bring it to them."

Jones put together what looked to be a playoff-contending team in 2016 with rookie running back Ezekiel Elliott, the fourth overall pick in the draft, expected to take the pressure off Romo and pick up big yards behind the dominant offensive line. That part of the Cowboys' game was missing in 2015 when Jones allowed DeMarco Murray to sign with the Eagles, even though he had just set the Cowboys' single-season rushing record. But once again, Romo was injured. He suffered a compression fracture in his back in the preseason game against the Seahawks. In the 2015 season, Romo broke his collarbone early and broke his collarbone late, and the Cowboys were 3-1 with him and a dreadful 1-11 without him. Why would it be different this year? They liked what they had seen from Prescott, the fourth-round pick, in camp, and he was the best player in the NFL in the preseason games. But there are a lot of players who are All-August and then don't even make it out of September. There are plenty of teams that are undefeated in the preseason, then have trouble winning when the lights come on for the real games.

The Cowboys decided to stick with Prescott and not bring in a veteran to start or compete with him. They signed journeyman Mark Sanchez as insurance, but knew if they had to play him, the season was over. Prescott and the Cowboys lost the season opener to the Giants and then ripped off eleven straight victories. Dallas never put Romo on injured reserve, so he was eligible to return whenever he was healthy. In training camp, the old saying is, "You can't make the club in the tub," and once the season starts an injured player doesn't even feel like part of the team.

It was clear when Romo went down in Seattle that he wasn't getting back on the field soon. By no means would this be the first time Witten would have to play without his best friend.

* * *

A day or two after Romo's injury, his cell phone buzzed. The text message that popped up on his screen was long. He looked at the text and saw it was from Parcells, his first coach in the NFL.

The mental image of Parcells sitting at home in Saratoga, in upstate New York, typing on his iPhone, is precious. One of his daughters or maybe his granddaughter taught him how to operate it. Parcells is old-school in so many ways, but he took the plunge and learned how to keep up with the latest technology.

Romo had stayed in touch with him after Parcells left the Cowboys and always took his frequent advice to heart. Romo and Witten traveled to Canton in the summer of 2013 to join a bunch of other Parcells Guys from his days with the Giants, Patriots, and Jets for their coach's induction into the Hall of Fame. Witten and Romo were seated in the audience for Parcells's speech along with Phil Simms, George Martin, Vinny Testaverde, DeMarcus Ware, and former assistant coaches Bill Belichick and Sean Payton. Fellow Hall of Famers Lawrence Taylor, Harry Carson, and Curtis Martin were on the stage with Parcells.

Witten and Romo were at Parcells's post-induction party under a huge tent on the Hall of Fame grounds. Parcells had always warned Romo about becoming a "celebrity quarterback," and other than his high-profile romance with Simpson and his desire to play on the PGA Tour as a hobby, he tried to remain as low-key as possible playing one of the most high-profile positions in sports: quarterback for America's Team.

Parcells was asked at Canton that weekend to name the best quarterback who had ever played for him. Simms was a nearly perfect 22 of 25 in the Super Bowl. Jeff Hostetler won the Super Bowl with an amazing run in the 1990 playoffs after Simms was injured late in the season. Drew Bledsoe took him to a Super Bowl in New England. Testaverde nearly ended the Jets' Super Bowl drought playing for Parcells. There was just something about Romo that Parcells loved.

"What do you want him for?" Parcells said as he started to answer the question. "If you want them for fighting it out, just fight it out to the death, it's Phil Simms. If you want him to just pass the ball, make this 100 percent passing picturesque and classy, then I have to have Vinny Testaverde. If you want to play the modern game, elusive and gets away, then give me Tony Romo."

It bothered Parcells to see that Romo was going to miss significant time in 2016. He picked up his phone and typed his thoughts: "You're in a dark place…nobody believes in you but you…the seasons start dwindling…there's a new kid that everybody is going to say is ready to take over…you feel like an outsider…don't feel sorry for yourself…this is the time to show them what you've got."

Romo texted back to Parcells: "Don't count the kid out yet."

Parcells meant it as motivation, but his text had a dreary tone to it. Parcells is a wise football man. He always knew how to hit the right hot button for his team. When he thought one of his older players was fading down the stretch of a long season, he would put a one-gallon gas can in their locker asking if they had anything left in the tank. He would leave mousetraps in lockers when he sensed players were taking an opponent lightly for what's known as a trap game sandwiched in between two difficult games.

"I love Coach. I love Bill," Romo said. "He was instrumental in my career. He's smart. He's old-school. At the core, our connection is just competition. We both love it, crave it, almost need it. I like that's he tough and can be hard on you."

Romo was finally cleared to play in November. The Cowboys were 8-1 with an eight-game winning streak. The talk in Dallas had transitioned from "When will Romo be ready?" to "The Cowboys can't bench Prescott." The organization was uncomfortable turning its back on Romo but had no choice.

On November 15, two days after an exhilarating victory in Pittsburgh, and with no apparent path to the field, Romo made a concession speech for the good of the team. Many of the words and phrases he used that day, in a speech that was so well received, were taken from the text message sent to him by Parcells months earlier. He started off by saying that getting injured, when he thought this was his best Cowboys team, was "a soul-crushing moment for me."

He went on to say:

But then here you are sidelined without any real ability to help your teammates win on the field. That's when you're forced to come face-to-face with what's happened. Seasons are fleeting. Games become more precious. Chances for success diminish. Your potential successor has arrived, injured two years in a row and now in the midthirties, the press is whispering, everyone has doubts, you've spent your career working to get here. Now we have to start all over. You almost feel like an outsider. Coaches are sympathetic, but they still have to coach and you're not there. It's a dark place. Probably the darkest it's ever been. You're sad and down and out and you ask yourself, "Why did this have to happen?" It's in this moment you find out who you really are and what you're really about.

He spoke for a couple of minutes and walked off the podium and didn't take any questions. He thought about Parcells.

"No question, some of those words are his," Romo said later. "They were just exactly right. He just gets it. He can be right there with you. He can be tough, too, but he knows. It's relatable."

Romo's career was all but done. The Cowboys already had the number 1 seed locked up going into the regular-season finale in Philadelphia. Romo arrived at Lincoln Financial Field knowing he would get in his first game of the season and knowing this would in all probability be his last appearance in a Cowboys uniform. Even though Jones had said a few weeks earlier that he envisioned Romo making a contribution in the postseason, that was unlikely unless Prescott was injured. Romo played one series against Philadelphia, led an 81-yard drive, and ended it with a 3-yard touchdown pass to Terrance Williams. He completed 3 of 4 passes.

Romo was determined to be the best teammate possible to Prescott. He liked the kid and wanted him to succeed. He never publicly complained about Jason Garrett not giving him an opportunity to win his job back, but it did strain if not ruin their relationship. They used to attend Dallas Mavericks games together. They even traveled to Durham, North Carolina, to watch Duke play basketball. Garrett and Romo were friends, but when Garrett didn't put Romo back on the field when he was cleared to play, the relationship began to fracture. Romo's concession speech to Prescott was not cleared through Garrett. He did not have advance notice of what Romo was going to say. Garrett was a career backup quarterback and could not relate to the emptiness Romo was feeling. Shortly before the Cowboys cut Romo in the spring of 2017, a group of Cowboys went to American Airlines Arena to see the Mavericks play the Golden

State Warriors. Present: Garrett, Witten, and offensive linemen Zack Martin and Travis Frederick. Noticeably absent: Romo. They all posed for a picture with Steph Curry.

The head coach's job is to make decisions that are best for the team, and the way Prescott was playing, Garrett risked losing credibility in the locker room if he returned Romo to the starting lineup.

"Obviously, Tony wanted to play. He's a competitor," Garrett said. "That's one of the great things about him. He's as good a competitor as I've ever been around. We made the decision to play Dak Prescott through the season. He did a great job for us. That's not an easy situation for a guy like Tony after he's been a starter and such a great player for us for a long time. As it turned out, because of his injuries the last couple of years, he decided to move on. He and I have a great friendship. I have incredible respect for him."

The Cowboys fell in love with Prescott at the Senior Bowl in 2016. Garrett and his staff were selected to coach the North squad. The Jacksonville Jaguars staff had the South squad. Prescott, who played at Mississippi State, was on the South team. The Cowboys coaches heard from the Jaguars coaches that Prescott was the best quarterback at the Senior Bowl, better than Carson Wentz, who went second overall in the draft to the Eagles a few months later. Prescott was named the game's MVP and was selected by the Cowboys in the fourth round after they were outbid by Denver trying to trade up for Paxton Lynch in the first round and then the Raiders jumped one spot ahead of them at the top of the fourth round to take Connor Cook.

Prescott took a step backward in his second season after an outstanding rookie year. His touchdowns decreased from 23 to 22, which is negligible, but his interceptions jumped from 4 to 13 and the victories went from 13 to 9. The focus was on him during Elliott's six-game suspension and he did not take his game up a level. Dallas lost its first three without Elliott, with Prescott throwing no touchdowns and five interceptions. One reason he was 13-3 as a rookie and had a bright future despite regressing in 2017 was the support he received from Romo during his rookie year. "I never felt the presence of somebody over my shoulder," Prescott said. "The deal about football, the deal about teams, the deal about time, is it goes on, no matter how great someone is."

If Jerry Jones had just made the decision himself, Romo would have been back in 2017. Dallas could have fit Romo's $14 million base salary into its salary cap with Prescott making only $540,000 in the second year of his rookie deal. But it would have been counterproductive for Romo and for the team. It was the quarterback controversy that no team wants. Jones spent the first part of the off-season in 2017 looking to trade Romo, but teams knew he would eventually be cut, so nobody was willing to give up anything of significance. It was time for the Cowboys to move on to the next generation and time for Romo to retire. Romo had no desire to live away from his young family by moving by himself to Houston, which was ready to sign him, or even possibly Denver, and for the short-term it wouldn't have made much sense for them to come with him.

The idea of playing was intoxicating to Romo. The thought of playing in a new city and learning a new team and possibly getting hurt again was not. Romo's decision to retire was made much easier by, and perhaps prompted by, an offer from CBS to be the lead analyst on its NFL games. On the same day in April that CBS announced he would be replacing Phil Simms in the booth, the Cowboys released Romo at his request, which at the very least left him in control of his own football fate if he ever changed his mind.

* * *

Romo's departure hit the Jones family hard. Jerry thought of him as his third son. Stephen thought of him as his second brother. None of them wanted it to end this way. They wanted to win a Super Bowl delivered by Romo. But fairy-tale endings for quarterbacks rarely happen in the NFL. Not everybody gets to walk away like John Elway.

"It was hard for everybody," Stephen Jones said. "It was tough for the whole organization, starting at the top. It was difficult for me. Tony and I had long visits when he got hurt. The conversation started with Tony saying, 'I like this Dak kid. I think he can at least get us half the games.'"

Then as the victories piled up, Romo told Jones, "I guess if he wins them all, I'm going to be in trouble."

The Cowboys could not bench Prescott. Just like Bill Belichick could not bench Tom Brady when Drew Bledsoe was ready to reclaim his job in 2001. It paid off for the Patriots when Brady won the first of his five Super Bowls. But the Cowboys lost in the divisional round at home in a heartbreaking last-second defeat to Aaron Rodgers and the Packers on the final play of the game. That left the Joneses to at least wonder if Romo could have won the game. "Tony is a competitor," Stephen Jones said. "He obviously thinks, 'Hell, if I had been quarterbacking the team, we would have won the game.'"

Does he think that?

"That's just so unfair for everybody to speculate that one way or the other," he said. "Jerry would be more open to it and say I think we might have won the game. Jerry is also Dak's biggest supporter. He is our future. At the same time, you had thoughts of what Tony might could do."

Romo's retirement was hardest on Witten. Witten wrote a

long, touching good-bye letter to him in which he said Romo had the leadership of a five-star general, the charisma of Joe Namath, and the competitive fire of Michael Jordan.

"I am forever grateful to have had you as my QB. Your God-given talent and ability has positively impacted not just my life, but my entire family. I am proud to call you my dear friend and brother for life," Witten wrote.

Romo said the letter was something he "cherished and is really one of the most meaningful things anyone has done for me. Jason doesn't do anything like that halfway. There is one thing we have in common. We are not fake. We're not doing things unless we believe in it. I feel honored that he put those words down and then shared them with the world. Football brought us together, and it created a bond that will last a lifetime. I go to him with important things and he is the same way. We have a unique, special relationship, and I hope a lot of people have a chance to have that in their life."

Witten narrated a tribute to Romo that was shown on the AT&T Stadium video board before Romo's first game in Dallas with CBS. Romo was shown in the corner of the board watching the video. It contained highlights and mentioned Romo's twenty-four fourth-quarter comebacks.

Of course, when Witten retired, Romo returned the favor with a heartfelt letter about his buddy: "It's hard to describe how special Jason Witten is. Sometimes in life you are lucky to come across someone that will change your life. Most of the time you don't realize at the moment the profound impact and impression someone will have on you. The difference with Jason Witten is that I knew right away the impact he would have on me. Not only was Jason Witten the most talented, humble and hardest working individual on our football team, but he was one of the most genuine, good-hearted people you could ever meet."

Even though Witten thought he was coming back in 2018 until the ESPN offer, he cried after a loss to the Seahawks in the fifteenth game eliminated Dallas from the playoffs. At the final team meeting the day after the season ended, Garrett made special mention of Witten and his teammates gave him a standing ovation. Many of them showed up at his retirement press conference just over four months later.

Witten's iconic helmetless run against the Eagles on his favorite play, "Y Option," a hook route that he and Romo had perfect chemistry executing, was shown on all the highlight shows the day he retired. Witten caught Romo's pass and his helmet came flying off after a big hit from Philadelphia safety Malcolm Jenkins broke his chinstrap. Witten ran 30 yards, without his helmet. He had three concussions in his career, but not on that play. His only injury was a bloody nose, but it could have been worse. "It's the defining play of my career," Witten said. "I'm sure my family was saying, 'What in the world is he doing? Get down.' It was an amazing play."

Witten's journey will likely culminate in the Hall of Fame, where he will have a difficult decision to make: Who presents him? Will it be his grandfather, Bill Parcells, Jerry Jones, Tony Romo, or Witten the giraffe?

CHAPTER FOUR

One Ego Too Many

Jerry Jones was on a family vacation and in line renting skis for his kids at Snowmass in Aspen shortly after the Cowboys became the first team to win three Super Bowls in four years.

You never know who you will bump into coming down the slopes of the rich and famous.

Jones turned around, and right behind him was Bill Belichick.

It was early in the off-season in 1996, and Jones and Belichick were in the same place geographically but in much different places mentally. Jones had just won the Super Bowl without partner-turned-adversary Jimmy Johnson, the most satisfying moment of his life in football, and Belichick had just been fired by the Cleveland Browns, the low point of an otherwise stellar career in coaching, as owner Art Modell decided to move the team to Baltimore without him.

Belichick was so disliked in Cleveland that Modell actually said he didn't want Belichick, a noted sourpuss, bringing the negative vibe with him to Baltimore as the Browns/Ravens established an identity and fan base in their new city. Modell fired Belichick despite the Browns making the playoffs in 1994 and beating Bill Parcells and the Patriots in a playoff game. They were struggling at 4-4 in 1995 before Modell sabotaged Belichick and his team by announcing he was relocating the storied franchise after the season. The Browns won only one of their last eight games as the situation in Cleveland went from unbearable to toxic. Modell was hung in effigy, and Belichick was already hated because he had run off hometown hero Bernie Kosar two years earlier and explained it in his usual mumbled monotone.

In a different place and time, Jones and Belichick might have been a great combination in Dallas. Two years earlier, if he had been available, Belichick would have been a better choice than Barry Switzer to replace Johnson, even though Belichick was two decades away from being considered the greatest head coach in NFL history with the help of Tom Brady. But if there ever could have been a seamless transition from one control freak to the other, sharing the same philosophy, who are great friends and annually talk shop on Johnson's boat in the Florida Keys, it would have been Johnson handing off to Belichick.

Jones didn't have a job to offer, and Belichick was reuniting with Parcells as an assistant coach in New England. "We didn't do an interview," Jones said. "I wanted to encourage him. I didn't talk to him about our job at the time."

It was many years later when Johnson and Troy Aikman were having a beer after the Divorce of the Century, an unfortunate ego-driven chapter in Cowboys history when Jones paid Johnson $2 million to go away and do anything but coach the Cowboys after winning back-to-back Super Bowls. Aikman was now the lead analyst for the NFL games on Fox, and Johnson was part of the studio team for the Fox pregame show, but Johnson's departure still irritated Aikman.

He may never forgive Johnson for not finding a way to make it work with Jones. The Cowboys were so young and so talented they might have won another two or three Super Bowls in a row if Johnson had remained. At the very least, they could have become the first team to win three in a row.

The quarterback put down his beer and looked at his former coach, with his piercing blue eyes doubling as poisonous arrows.

"We could have been Brady and Belichick," Aikman said.

Aikman was filled with remorse, but Johnson didn't flinch. Even telling the story, Johnson has no regrets about what could have been. "Those things aren't important to me," he said.

They were to Aikman. "I don't know that we would've won more Super Bowls," Aikman told the *Dallas Morning News*. "I say that with the understanding and appreciation of how difficult it is to win a Super Bowl. But regardless of that, I strongly believe we would've remained competitive for a longer period of time with an opportunity to achieve greatness at the conclusion of each season had Jimmy remained our coach."

Johnson walked away from the best team in football when it was just hitting its peak with its best players—Aikman, Michael Irvin, Emmitt Smith, Darren Woodson, a bruising offensive line, a dominant and deep defensive line—because he could no longer deal with his boss.

If Aikman was distraught by Johnson's departure and the ensuing chaos with Barry Switzer's hands-off, no-discipline approach, then Irvin was beside himself with regret. He had played for Johnson at the University of Miami and arrived in Dallas one year before his coach. Irvin loved Tom Landry, but Johnson was his guy. Irvin also became close to Jones and still is, but Johnson was such an important part of his life, and he left Irvin when they were all in the prime of their careers. "I was very upset with that decision. It's their decision," Irvin said. "They are two smart guys. Alpha males. There is no doubt in my mind with Jimmy we win more Super Bowls. No doubt in my mind we win four in a row. Not just four in a row. We may come back and get a fifth or a sixth with Jimmy. People were always talking about Jimmy and were worried about him burning out. Belichick is doing great still and he's been there forever. I would have loved to have seen that kind of stay with Jimmy and Jerry. I will say that I really hoped and wished that Jimmy would have let Jerry play a little bit more like he wanted to. He just wanted to play with his team."

Their egos were just too big. Jimmy couldn't handle Jerry and Jerry couldn't handle Jimmy.

"Jimmy was maniacal about winning football games. Kraft and Belichick have that, but Kraft allows Belichick to run it," Irvin said. "Go ahead and run it and I'll make all of the business decisions. Run it. Jerry wants to bring all his guys in the locker room and I ain't got no problem with that. But if we just lost, you got to know Jimmy is not with any of it. Jimmy wouldn't let us eat on the plane back home if we lost. In the fourth quarter, I would be joking with guys but I wasn't joking, 'Come on man, dude, eight minutes left, are we going to eat today or what?'"

Really, no food?

"Jimmy got so hot. When he gets hot, he gets crazy," Irvin said.

When the flight attendants brought out the food on the flight after the Cowboys lost a road game, Irvin claims Johnson prevented them from serving. "Take that cart back," he barked.

He would starve his players?

"Yeah." Irvin laughed. "We ate five hours before the game. If we lost, we wouldn't eat until we got home."

Switzer let them eat. He was probably first in line. He just wasn't as good an NFL coach as Johnson. He didn't win nearly as much.

Not one bit of second-guessing has ever entered Johnson's mind about what he left behind.

"No," he said. "One hundred percent no."

He and Aikman could have set the bar so high that Brady and Belichick would still be jumping to reach it.

"Well, it's a priority for me to be happy," Johnson said. "It got to the point it was more work than it was happiness. I was handling all the personnel as well as coaching the team. It was seven days a week around the clock. Then obviously there was some tension there at the end."

Brady and Belichick won five Super Bowls and made it to eight in their first eighteen years together. Two of those seasons don't even count. Brady threw only 3 passes as a rookie in 2000. He tore his ACL in 2008 halfway through the first quarter of the first game and missed the rest of the season. That means in Brady's first sixteen seasons as the full-time starter, right up through the 2017 season, when he turned forty years old five weeks before the opener, the Belichick-Brady tandem made it to the Super Bowl in 50 percent of their seasons together. Aikman and Johnson made it to the Super Bowl—and won it—in two out of five seasons, 40 percent, but more were surely on the way.

Even without Johnson, the Cowboys advanced to the NFC Championship Game in 1994 and lost to the 49ers, and the following year beat the Steelers in Super Bowl XXX. They did it with Switzer, a young assistant coach with Arkansas under Frank Broyles when Jones and Johnson were teammates in the early '60s with the Razorbacks.

If the Cowboys won a Super Bowl with Switzer, who viewed

the Cowboys as an unexpected last football job, it's a given they would have done just as well with Johnson and probably better. Aikman and Johnson eventually had a great relationship, but it was strained in the first year. Aikman was just getting settled into Dallas after the April 23 draft when Johnson shocked him by taking his Miami quarterback Steve Walsh with the first overall pick in the supplemental draft on July 7. Aikman felt betrayed.

What message was Johnson sending? Was this any way to begin a relationship?

"It was really bizarre," Aikman said in an NFL Films documentary. "I didn't know what exactly that meant."

Johnson had recruited Aikman when he was coaching at Oklahoma State, but Aikman elected to play for Switzer at the University of Oklahoma. When he transferred from Oklahoma after breaking his leg and the offense was no longer designed to feature the passing game, Johnson was at Miami. Once again, he recruited Aikman. This time he went to UCLA.

The rookie coach and the rookie quarterback were supposed to form a partnership. But Walsh's presence made Aikman question Johnson's end game. "It impacted me being an ally for Jimmy very early on in my career," Aikman said in the documentary. "He already had a relationship with Steve because they went back to college. I had no relationship with Jimmy. I had turned him down twice already."

Walsh's arrival created friction between Johnson and Aikman. Johnson's intention was to immediately flip Walsh in a trade, figuring teams in a quarterback-needy league would line up to get him and bring back more than the Cowboys invested. He never intended for Walsh to even make it to training camp. But his plan did not work at first, and Walsh stuck around all season. All Johnson accomplished was alienating Aikman, who believed Johnson was scheming to play Walsh despite the tremendous disparity in their ability. Aikman could throw a football through a brick wall, but Walsh's fastball could barely break a balloon.

After a 1-15 season in '89 in which Aikman did not play in the only victory—he was injured and Walsh started—Johnson knew that for Aikman to develop he had to get rid of Walsh so Aikman could play with a clear mind and not look over his shoulder. Besides, he wanted to recoup the draft choice he'd spent. It was an awful rookie year for Aikman. He lost all eleven of his starts, had only 9 touchdowns and 18 interceptions, resented the quarterback controversy Johnson created, and was humiliated by a comment Jones made about him that was meant as a compliment during his first training camp but instead came out as a Jerry-ism.

"All I can say right now is he looks good in the shower," Jones said.

Johnson was able to find a buyer for Walsh in the off-season when the Saints gave him picks in the first, second, and third rounds. His gamble paid off, even if the pick he used on Walsh in the supplemental draft would have been first overall in 1990. It didn't really matter, because nearly halfway through the 1989 season Johnson set up the future with the Walker trade. He used one of the draft picks he acquired to move up and draft Emmitt Smith in 1990, adding him to Aikman and Irvin. They soon became known as the Triplets.

Aikman and Johnson found common ground in the strangest place. Jimmy loved aquariums, and it turned out Aikman thought that was a pretty cool hobby. Johnson invited Aikman over to his house to teach him the intricacies and nuances of maintaining a fish tank, and their relationship took off.

As the bond between Johnson and Aikman became stronger, the bond between Jones and Johnson was deteriorating. The first sign of trouble occurred in 1989 just a few weeks into their first season together. Dallas was 0-5 and had been blown out in four of the losses. Jerry and Jimmy had inherited a bad team from Schramm, Landry, and Brandt, and Johnson knew there was no quick fix. The only way out was to trade his one marketable commodity. Johnson leveraged interest on running back Herschel Walker from the Cleveland Browns and pulled off the best trade in NFL history by trading him to the Minnesota Vikings for a lifetime supply of premium draft picks. If nothing else, Johnson won the trade because he used one of the picks to move up in the draft to select Smith, who turned into a much better player than Walker.

Once the trade was fully digested by the public, it became clear that it was one-sided in the Cowboys' favor and Johnson was given all the credit. He deserved it. He was the one who came up with the unique concept of opting for draft-choice compensation instead of the Vikings players he received in the deal, and it turned around the Cowboys franchise. Johnson kept Jones on a need-to-know basis and didn't loop him in until Jones called Falcons owner Rankin Smith to create even more leverage with Vikings general manager Mike Lynn. Jones's major involvement was negotiating Walker out of his no-trade clause. He didn't want to leave Dallas. Jones convinced him it was a good career move by writing a check for $1.25 million and buying him two cars, including a Mercedes, and a house in Edina, Minnesota.

Dallas won just one game and Jones was taking most of the criticism. Johnson had won a national championship at Miami, but he had no players in Dallas, so he escaped much of the blame. Was Jerry in over his head? It looked that way early on. The real problems began when the Cowboys started to turn it around in 1990 with a 7-9 record, at the time the biggest one-season improvement in team history. If Jones was going to take the blame for the 1-15 season, then he wanted some of the credit as the Cowboys began to transition into a playoff team. Johnson was not willing to share the credit with the man who hired him and was paying him. Jones was not content to just work on the business side and fix all the financial problems he'd inherited.

It was Johnson's idea to trade for troubled 49ers defensive end Charles Haley in 1992, which flipped the balance of power in the NFC from San Francisco to Dallas. Jones's contribution was picking Haley up at the airport. Johnson would come up with personnel ideas on long jogs around Valley Ranch with his coaching staff or sitting at his favorite watering hole with his beloved Heineken and nachos. Johnson was hailed as a genius and Jones didn't appreciate the chill coming around the corner from the coach's office.

If Jones and Johnson ever were close friends, it's not possible for it to happen again, but Jones is no longer ice cold. "The fact that I've gotten to be involved in the whole picture of the NFL for all these years has diminished any real sensitivity that I have about somebody giving Jimmy credit as opposed to what credit I do or don't get," Jones said.

* * *

The mood in Dallas on Monday mornings from September through December is determined entirely by one thing: Did the Cowboys win on Sunday? The morning coffee tastes better, the talk shows are not as harsh, and the buzz around town is palpable. In year three of the post-Landry era, the Cowboys were in the playoffs for the first time in six years. As the 1991 playoffs began, journeyman Steve Beuerlein was at quarterback playing for Aikman, who suffered a partially torn ligament in his right knee on the Sunday before Thanksgiving and missed the last four games of the regular season. Even so, the Cowboys were 11-5, their best record since they were 12-4 in 1983.

There was controversy in Dallas as the playoffs began in Chicago. Beuerlein was 4-0 subbing for Aikman, but Troy felt he was ready to return for the playoffs. Johnson decided to go with the hot and healthy quarterback and stuck with Beuerlein. "Obviously, if Beuerlein had not played as well as he's playing, we'd be playing Troy at less than 100 percent because he'd give us the best chance to win," Johnson said at the time. "Steve Beuerlein playing well is what's kept Troy from playing right now. If Troy were 100 percent, it would be a different story, but he's not."

The Cowboys beat the Bears for their first playoff victory since 1982. Johnson decided to start Beuerlein again the next week in the divisional round in Detroit. When Dallas fell behind 17–6 in the final minute of the first half, Johnson picked that odd moment, rather than the start of the third quarter, to make the change back to Aikman. The Cowboys wound up losing 38–6. In the locker room after the game, Aikman told Randy Galloway of the *Dallas Morning News* that he was going to request a trade. He asked him to hold off on writing the story. The day after the game, Johnson called Aikman into his office and pledged his allegiance to him. Aikman did not ask for a trade.

Johnson was accumulating the best young talent in the NFL, and in another year or so, the Cowboys were going to be contenders for the Super Bowl—as long as they didn't implode from the struggle between Jones and Johnson over the credit for the quick turnaround. Jones had a favorite sign he kept on his desk in Arkansas for fifteen years in the days when he was trying to a hit a gusher, or "glory hole," as an oilman. It said: "If you are willing to give others credit, you can conquer the world." If only he still had the sign and ordered another for Johnson.

Jones and Johnson played up their friendship when Jones pulled off what was perceived to be a hostile takeover in Dallas and brought Johnson along for the ride. They were tied together although they were such different people. Jones was pure dollars and what made financial sense. Johnson was all football. The most misrepresented aspect of the Jones-Johnson relationship was that they were very close friends from their days playing together at Arkansas. Jones was a year older but was redshirted, so they were the same year in their eligibility. Johnson has always bristled when it was suggested that their longtime friendship should have carried them through the tough times in Dallas.

"We were roommates on the game trips, even when we stayed in a hotel before home games," Johnson said. "We were friends and because of the football trips, we were roommates."

They were roommates, Johnson emphasized, because the room assignments were done alphabetically. They both played offensive guard until Johnson switched over to the defensive line, where he made the all-conference teamand was better known as "Jimmy Jump-Up." They were starters on Arkansas's 1964 national championship team. Johnson didn't hesitate when asked who was the better player. "When they picked the all-time [Arkansas] team of the sixties, I'm on that," he said.

They graduated together and stayed in touch, but it wasn't like they made a point of seeing each other on a regular basis in the twenty-five years between Arkansas and the Cowboys. "Jerry went into business," Johnson said. "I saw him at the horse races at Hot Springs one time. He went into insurance and gas and oil. He was in Oklahoma City when I was at

Oklahoma State. We visited a few times. Then Stephen, his son, came to our football camp at Oklahoma State. We stayed in contact."

Johnson initially flirted with the Cowboys in 1988 before anybody in Dallas had ever heard of Jones. He received a call from Tex Schramm. The rumors were out there that the Eagles were interested in hiring Johnson. Schramm knew all about Johnson because Gil Brandt was the godfather to college coaches, a de facto employment agency helping coaches get to bigger and better jobs.

"Tex told me, 'Tom [Landry] is going to retire soon, and I just wanted to touch base and see what your interest might be,'" Johnson said.

Schramm's plan was to bring Johnson to Dallas as the defensive coordinator with an agreement that he would succeed Landry when either he retired or Schramm convinced him to retire. Schramm had tried the same thing when he hired Paul Hackett from Bill Walsh's staff in San Francisco to be the Cowboys' passing-game coordinator in 1986, with the implied understanding that he would succeed Landry. That didn't go over well. Landry was not even thinking about retirement and resented Hackett from the day he walked into Valley Ranch. Hackett was around for Landry's final three seasons, and Landry reduced his responsibility each year. Johnson did not need to take an intermediate job. Either he was going to get the NFL head-coaching job he wanted or there was no reason to leave the University of Miami.

When Johnson accepted the invitation to sit with Landry, Schramm, and Brandt in the Cowboys suite for Super Bowl XXIII in Miami, he claims, "I didn't have any thoughts of being the coach at that time."

Not long after the Super Bowl, Johnson said Jones called

to ask a favor. He knew Johnson had a relationship with Schramm.

"Could you call Tex Schramm and tell him that I am a legitimate buyer?" Jones said.

Johnson had a lot going on at Miami with recruiting, but he placed the call to Schramm.

"Hey, Jerry is a legitimate buyer. He's a good guy and he has the money to do it," he told Schramm.

Johnson moved on. He didn't think much about his old college friend buying the Cowboys. Jimmy was in the Dallas area weeks later for the Doak Walker banquet in Fort Worth. Schramm was also there. When Johnson was at the dinner, Jones left him a message at the hotel to call him back. Johnson checked out of his hotel the next morning and was on his way to the airport when he looked at his messages. One of them was from Jones. Said it was important. He waited until he arrived at the airport and returned Jones's call just before he was to board his flight back to Miami.

"I really might be buying the Cowboys, but I have to make a decision about the complex. There is a $5 million note on that complex and it's going to be due. If I do buy the Cowboys, I might have to make a decision on that note," Jones said.

"Okay," Johnson said.

"Can you go over to the complex and take a look at it and tell me what you think?" Jones said.

Jones wanted Johnson to give him a scouting report on the Cowboys training facility at Valley Ranch. If he didn't want it to be part of the deal, his option was moving the operation full-time to Texas Stadium. Johnson grabbed his suitcase, hailed a cab, and went to Valley Ranch, which is only fifteen minutes from Dallas/Fort Worth International Airport.

There was an understanding by now that if Jones bought the team, Johnson was going to be coaching it. "I don't know if we ever talked about it," Johnson said. "It's just a given that was going to happen."

Johnson pulled up unannounced in front of Valley Ranch. He was a high-profile college coach, he was in town for a dinner, and he was stopping by to say hello. Why would Tex, Tom, or Gil question that, especially after Johnson sat with them for the Super Bowl?

Johnson knew what he was doing was disingenuous. "It was kind of an awkward situation," he said. "Of course, Tom and Tex and Gil, they had no clue what was going on."

Cowboys owner Bum Bright intentionally kept Schramm out of the loop. Initially, all buyers were screened by Schramm, who would decide whether they were worthy of an audience with Bright and his financial people. Any time an owner suggested he was going to be hands-on or even implied Schramm's power would be reduced, his application was tossed in the trash. Schramm owned 3 percent of the Cowboys, but he was looking to protect his day-to-day job.

Johnson was given a tour through the complex. The coaching offices were nice. Jones's office would be close but not too close. The locker room was huge. There was plenty of space for team meetings and position meetings. The weight room was covered but not enclosed. There was no indoor practice field. The Cowboys had been in there just four seasons and it still had that new-car smell.

"It feels like a country club around here. I can work through that," Johnson said in a joking way to Jones.

"Great," Jones said. "I'm sending my plane down to pick you up."

Johnson got in a car to head back to the airport. Jones had his private plane waiting to take him to Little Rock. They went over the game plan and flew back to Dallas, where Jones had

Johnson sit in on the final meetings with Bright. That night, they were discovered by Ivan Maisel, the college football writer for the *Dallas Morning News*, who had been staking out the Mansion on Turtle Creek all day looking for Jones and even possibly Johnson. Word had broken that the deal was imminent. When Maisel came up empty at the hotel, sports editor Dave Smith told him he could call it a night. He took his fiancée, Meg, to a Mexican restaurant named Mia's.

Maisel walked in and his eyes grew wide. Sitting right there in the restaurant having a couple of cold ones were Jones and Johnson. They had been all over the news for twenty-four hours already but felt no need to be discreet. This was before the days of cell phones, so Maisel did not have a phone he could whip out of his pocket to take his own pictures. He walked over to the pay phone, calmly called the office, and told them to get a photographer over to Mia's ASAP. The result was perhaps the most famous picture of the Jones-Johnson era with them sitting at their table yukking it up. The backlash when the *Morning News* hit the newsstands the next morning was intense. Not only were Jones and Johnson out celebrating in public, but they were toasting each other at—unbeknownst to them—Landry's favorite restaurant.

Jones and Bright reached an agreement in principle the morning after Mia's, and soon Jones and Schramm were headed on Air Jerry down to Austin so Jones could fire Landry in person. Jones had already sent Johnson back to Miami so he could avoid the hysteria in Dallas.

* * *

By the time the Cowboys made the playoffs in 1991, Jones and Johnson had grown further apart. "You heard the old deal, that success and failure, both those are frauds and falsely influence situations," Jones said.

It took Jones three years to straighten out the Cowboys' finances. It took Johnson three years to get the Cowboys into the playoffs. Jones left the football decisions to Johnson, but as the president and general manager, he had final say. He gave Johnson a ten-year contract—Johnson's only request when Jones negotiated with his attorney, Nick Christian, was to pay him the same as he was making at Miami—and wasn't about to second-guess his greatest strength, which was his evaluation of personnel and the ability to make favorable trades.

The ten-year contract was Jones's way of emphasizing to Johnson they were partners for the long term. Johnson had no intention of staying that long, but if it made Jones feel better, so be it. The length of the deal was not unprecedented in Dallas. After Landry had won only thirteen games in his first four seasons with the expansion Cowboys and folks in Big D were calling for him to be fired, owner Clint Murchison did just the opposite. He gave Landry a ten-year contract extension. "We knew each other well. Jimmy was Jimmy," Jones said. "Jimmy told me two years, two and one half years into it, 'The idea of thinking about coaches staying in a situation as long as Coach Landry did, is just not realistic, it's just not the way it works.'"

Jones had no emotional attachment to Landry when he fired him. He didn't know him. He had never met him. Even when he attended a game against the Giants in the 1988 season and sat in a suite with his wife, Gene, and daughter, Charlotte, and Cowboys icon Roger Staubach and his wife, he didn't meet the Cowboys coach before or after the game. He had his eye on buying the team, convinced himself if the empty seats he saw that day continued for a year or two he could live with it, but he couldn't have imagined that just months later he would fire the only coach the Cowboys ever had.

As the Cowboys blew past the Bills to win the Super Bowl following the 1992 season, the distance between Jones and Johnson began to widen. Instead of enjoying that they had brought the Cowboys back to life together, Jones made it clear that Johnson worked for him and Johnson made it clear that the football decisions were his. Jones considered himself a football man and wanted everybody to know he had his fingerprints on every move that Johnson made to improve the team. Johnson knew the truth: Jones handled the money; Johnson handled the players. They were both great at what they did. That wasn't enough for either one of them.

During his negotiations with Bright to buy the team, Jones made it clear that if he was to become the Cowboys' owner, he wanted to replace Landry with Johnson, his friend from Arkansas. If that was a deal breaker, Jones told Bright, then the deal was off. Bright had no problem with Jones's plan at all. In fact, it elevated Jones's standing in Bright's mind. Bright despised Landry, who snubbed him at a cocktail party in Dallas after he bought the team, which Bright never forgot or forgave. Bright was embarrassed, and once the Cowboys started to slip, he became publicly critical of Landry and wanted Schramm to fire him. Time after time, Schramm resisted. Bright never interceded on football matters, so if Schramm wasn't going to dismiss Landry, he was not going to do it.

Now this was different. Bright was selling the team and Jones wanted Landry out. Bright raised his hand and volunteered to do the dirty work so Jones did not look like the bad guy. Jones, to his credit, said he would take the responsibility and do it himself. Besides unloading his team for much-needed cash to help bail out his other businesses, Bright was most pleased that Landry was finally gone.

It was months before the sale was approved by NFL owners, but Jones had already changed coaches and moved into his new office at Valley Ranch. He set up shop in temporary quarters until he forced out Schramm and then took over his office. Johnson was working around the clock in Landry's old office. They were making decisions as if Jones officially owned the team, which he did not. Not only had it not yet been brought up for a vote, but Jones and Bright still had financial issues to work out. The NFL subsequently changed its rule and prohibited any new owner from making changes until he officially was voted in by the other owners.

As they were putting the final touches on the deal months after it had been announced at the Saturday Night Massacre, Jones and Bright came to a crossroads: They could not agree on a handful of contract clauses that involved several million dollars. The deal would not be official until everything was signed off on, even though Landry was gone, Johnson was in, and there was no putting the toothpaste back in the tube.

"What would you do if I just picked up and went back home to Little Rock, Arkansas?" Jones asked Bright.

Bright didn't even hesitate. He flashed a big smile.

"Well, I got me a new coach," he said.

* * *

One of the signature moments in Cowboys history took place in the cramped visitor's locker room at Candlestick Park in San Francisco. Dallas defeated the 49ers in the 1992 NFC Championship Game and was headed to the Super Bowl for the first time since 1978.

"How 'bout them Cowboys!" Johnson shouted.

The Cowboys then finished the deal with a 52–17 victory over the Bills in Super Bowl XXVII.

Jerry and Jimmy.

Jimmy and Jerry.

They were the toast of the NFL. All the losing in the first year brought them closer together. It was Jimmy and Jerry against the world. An oilman from Arkansas and a college coach from Texas, via Miami. They put together one of the greatest turnarounds in NFL history and did it before having the benefit of free agency. But winning split them apart. As Jones and Johnson went at it behind the scenes like Ali and Frazier, Jones was making amends with Landry and bringing him back into the Cowboys family. After Jones's visit to Landry's country club in Austin to fire him in late February 1989, the only contact they had was at the Giants-Bills Super Bowl in Tampa in early 1991. They happened to be dining at the same restaurant and were cordial to each other as they passed on the way to their tables. Jones had invited Landry to be inducted into the Cowboys Ring of Honor at Texas Stadium in 1990 but was rebuffed. Jones had taken over from Schramm as the one-man nominating committee, and he felt extending the olive branch to Landry by putting his name up inside the stadium would be the first step to saying he was sorry about how things were handled. Jones really did have a lot of admiration for Landry and often said one of the reasons he bought the team was a result of the success Landry had achieved.

Landry could be a stubborn man on and off the field. His players were frustrated by his love affair with the outdated Flex defense, but he stuck with it. The offensive linemen didn't like rising up before getting into their stance prior to the snap, but it was Landry's way of causing confusion for the defense by hiding the running backs behind the big linemen. He was stuck in his ways, even as the rest of the league had long ago caught up with his innovations. He was a proud man and Jones had taken his team away from him. He was going to make this man squirm before taking his rightful place in the Ring of Honor. Jones cringed when he saw signs on the highway calling Landry out as a baby for not accepting his invitation to join the team's elite.

But what could he do? Landry snubbed him.

"I had a great friend that was the head of a very prominent grocery chain in the Dallas area that had become real good friends with Coach Landry," Jones said. "He set up a meeting with Coach Landry and me at his house."

Bill Parker was the president in the Dallas market for Kroger's. He was close to Landry. He was close to Jones. "He's one of the best friends that I ever met," Jones said.

Jones spoke with Parker about the problems he was having with getting Landry to agree to be inducted. Landry had gone into the Pro Football Hall of Fame in 1990, one year after he was fired. After the three of them sat around for a little bit in the living room, Parker had lunch set up in the dining room and left Jones and Landry alone. They spoke for two hours.

"Coach Landry was great," Jones said. "We at that time agreed to bury the hatchet, so to speak. We just talked about the circumstances and how he looked at it. Tom was very open and he just said, 'I want to do this. We should do this.' I don't think one person ever heard that story except my immediate group."

They each got what they wanted. Landry made Jones pursue him and went into the Ring of Honor on his own timetable. Jones knew he could not put anybody else in the Ring of Honor until he was able to get Landry to agree. "The thing that hurts me the most is when people say I am unforgiving

131

for Jerry and everything," Landry said. He was inducted during the 1993 season at halftime of a game against the Giants, the team for which Landry had played and later been an assistant coach. Jones thought it was appropriate that Landry went into the Ring of Honor in a season when the Cowboys were the defending Super Bowl champions. During the ceremony, Landry thanked Jerry. "I have no animosity," he said. "Considering what Jerry paid for the team, he had the right to do anything he wanted to. I'm happy with the way the Cowboys are going now. The hard feelings are over."

Now Jones had the clearance to add to the Ring of Honor, with Tony Dorsett and Randy White going in the next year. Jones waited until 2003 to induct Schramm, who was the man who came up with the concept in the first place, which is now copied by just about every team in the NFL. Schramm was teary-eyed at the press conference that April to announce he was going to be inducted, but he died in July and was inducted posthumously in October. There was no reason for Jones to make Schramm wait that long. He was eighty-three when he passed away. Jones and Schramm never developed a relationship after Jones pushed him out, although for a few years Schramm kept his suite at Texas Stadium right next to the press box. The NFL owners stalled approving the sale to Jones until he came up with an acceptable package to make Schramm comfortable for the rest of his life. A silver-and-blue parachute.

Jones and Landry saw each other now and then before Landry died from leukemia in 2000. Landry attended the dinner and celebration Jones had the night before the inductions of Dorsett and White. "It's not quite the Hall of Fame in Canton, but it's pretty nice," Jones said. "Coach Landry was a big part of that. From that time on, we were very cordial."

Jones was proud that his grandson John Stephen, who is

Stephen's son, won the Tom Landry Award in 2017 as the out-standing high school football player in the Dallas area after back-to-back state titles playing quarterback for Highland Park High School. Tom Landry Jr. presented the award. "The award was particularly appreciated by us and me because of my back-ground with Coach Landry," Jones said.

One year after Landry died, Jones had a bronze statue of Landry erected outside Texas Stadium. When the Cowboys were in the process of moving to their new stadium in 2009, Jones had the statue put in storage for safekeeping. One week before the first regular-season game against the Giants, the statue was unveiled in front of Gate A. Johnson won as many Super Bowls in five years as Landry did in twenty-nine years, and with two decades having passed, Jones appears to be soft-ening and will eventually induct Johnson into the Ring of Honor. That would be confirmation of his contributions even if it creates the perception that it marginalizes what Jones meant to the team's success. Jerry has the only vote, so Jimmy has been waiting. A statue? Forget about it.

Jones was able to take a deep breath once he made amends with Landry. Following an 0-2 start to the 1993 season due mainly to Smith's holding out, the Cowboys were back on track as the season came down the home stretch. Jones should have been feeling pretty good about his team and his business.

In reality, things were only getting worse. His cold war with Johnson was about to escalate.

* * *

What was Jimmy thinking?

Just a few days before the Cowboys played the Giants in a winner-take-all for the NFC East title and the NFC's top seed in the playoffs, big trouble emerged in Dallas. In an interview with ESPN, Johnson said he was intrigued by the possibility of being the coach and general manager of the expansion Jacksonville Jaguars, who would begin play in 1995. The Cowboys were about to play one of the biggest regular-season games in their history and the coach, who always demanded his players be all-in or find another place to work, was openly talking about another job.

He later explained, "I was asked about Jacksonville, and what I said, instead of the standard line, was that any time you have a job, you're willing to listen to other opportunities."

Jones was incredulous. He went ballistic. His team was trying to put themselves in the best position possible to repeat for the first time as Super Bowl champions, and his coach, under contract at $1 million per year through the 1998 season, had lost his focus. "It's up to me," Jones said. "I have no intention of making a coaching change. To have this as an issue is a joke."

Right then it was clear that Johnson was beyond unhappy. Jones values loyalty, and Johnson was being disloyal. "I do know that I was very much aware that he was illegally talking to Jacksonville," Jones said, thinking back to that time. "I was very aware of that. I was told by people that overheard and saw it. He was under a long-term contract and he was sitting there feeling out Jacksonville.

"I don't want to sound in any way, and I am, I guess, a little bitter," Jones said. "But I don't have to go back too far and remember what caused me to have the rationale and the thinking that we need to make a change."

Dallas beat the Giants on the road, won two playoff games, and made it back to the Super Bowl, and once again they faced the Bills. It was much tougher this time. Aikman was coming off a concussion in the NFC Championship victory against the

49ers and was out of sorts. There was also not the customary off week between the conference championship game and the Super Bowl, giving him less time to recover. The Cowboys shifted their focus to the running game, and Smith brought Dallas back from a 13–6 halftime deficit with two second-half touchdowns to win 30–13, and for the first time in their history the 'Boys defended their championship. Smith ran for 132 yards and was named the Most Valuable Player.

Johnson now says he had his mind made up before the Super Bowl that he was done in Dallas. He had his Corvette driven from Dallas to Atlanta so it would be closer to his home in the Florida Keys. The winning Super Bowl coach and the MVP get little or no sleep Sunday night after the game before they are required to be at the final news conference at 8:30 a.m. Monday. On the limo ride over to the media headquarters with Smith, the rumors were circulating that Johnson wanted out.

"You know," one person in the car said to Johnson, "if you win three in a row you're automatic in the Hall of Fame."

"I can't tell you 100 percent that I am going to stay," he said.

The flirting with Jacksonville still bothered Jones. "I should have been more tolerant," he said. "When we won those back-to-back Super Bowls, it was more than either one of us could have realistically ever really thought could happen to us that soon. It's like two people who know each other well, like brothers, you could get intolerant with somebody you know well much quicker than you can with somebody who is more arm's length."

By the time of the league meetings in Orlando in late March, Jones was looking for a reason to sever his relationship with Johnson. Things had not improved after the Super Bowl, but if Johnson was so set on leaving, he would have been gone by now.

Jones needed one more reason to fire Johnson. He got it in Orlando. The NFL throws an annual cocktail party at the meetings. Owners, head coaches, general managers, and media are invited. The league headquarters were at the Hyatt. The party was at Disney's Pleasure Island and was hosted by ABC. Johnson was sitting at a table with former assistants Dave Wannstedt, who had left to coach the Bears after the first Super Bowl, and Norv Turner, who had just been hired by the Redskins.

The table included some people who had been fired by Jones, including vice president of player personnel director Bob Ackles. It wasn't long after Jones bought the Cowboys that he went through a staff reduction to cut costs. "I had over twenty employees sue for every type of discrimination when I made the change with them—race, sex, health, age," he said. "I went to a jury trial and won it. They wouldn't settle. Anybody could tell you that to take a case like that and go to a jury with it is dangerous territory."

Jones emerged unscathed in court. But on this night in Orlando, he felt disrespected after he walked over to Johnson's table and raised his glass and proposed a toast to the Cowboys' success. It didn't go over well when some people at the table naturally were still bitter over Jones firing them. If a toast can fail, then Jones's toast failed. Johnson did not have his back and drink to Jerry, and Jones was furious.

The party moved back to the bar in the lobby of the Hyatt. It was past midnight when Jones came through and spotted a few reporters sitting at a table. "I'll be back," he said.

When he returned a half hour later, Rick Gosselin and Ed Werder of the *Dallas Morning News* were waiting for him. Jones sat down. He might have been drinking a bit. On the twenty-year anniversary of Gosselin and Werder sitting with Jones until 4 a.m., with the bar closed, the lobby empty, and the rest of the NFL world sleeping, Gosselin published this play-by-play in the *Morning News*:

> Jones asked us how important was it to have a franchise quarterback such as Troy Aikman in the championship equation. He asked us how important it was to have a franchise running back such as Emmitt Smith in the equation. He asked us how important it was to have a franchise wide receiver such as Michael Irvin in winning titles.
>
> We discussed the merits of all three of those positions. Then Jones asked us what turned out to be his $2 million question: How important was the head coach in a championship equation.

The next line from Jones to the two reporters detonated the explosion that blew up the Cowboys:

"There are 500 coaches who could have won the Super Bowl with our team."

There was no Twitter, no social media, but after only a few hours Johnson was made aware of what Jones said. He not only checked out of the hotel, he checked out mentally. He was done with Jones. He jumped in his car and drove back to the Keys.

One week later, after having some preliminary talks about trying to make it work, Johnson demanded Jones settle his contract. Jones gave him $2 million to disappear. "There is nothing you can trade me for those five years we had together and what we went through together and how it worked out," Jones said. "There is nothing you can give me to have one more day of it."

Jones went home late that night. Gene was already in bed. She knew Jerry better than anybody and never could understand why he couldn't leave well enough alone. It wasn't like Jerry and Gene socialized with Jimmy and his girlfriend, Rhonda, a former hairstylist who later became his second wife. Gene wasn't losing a close friend because her husband fired Jimmy. But she knew how nervous Jerry was putting together the sale and how much Jimmy was instrumental in making it work.

"I come home, and of course Gene has been watching the news and finds out about it. I lay down. It's as silent as anything you can imagine," Jones said in his Hall of Fame speech. "After I laid there a minute, she just looks over and said, 'You can't stand it, can you? You just absolutely, when it gets going, you just got to get in it and mess it up.'"

Jerry was not in the mood to explain himself.

"I just shut up and went to sleep," he said.

He earlier had thought back to a conversation he had with his father after he first bought the team.

"My daddy called me," Jones said. "I had consulted with him, but I hadn't really shared with him the significant amount of money involved or the significance of what the Cowboys could be. My motivational fear was to lay an egg."

This is how he recalled the conversation with his father:

"You better be successful or you will be known to the whole country as a failure the rest of your life," Pat Jones said.

"Dad, you really made my day," Jerry said.

"I didn't mean it that way. You cannot drop the ball here. There is too many people looking at you," Pat said.

That made a lifetime impact on Jerry. Was he doomed to ultimately fail because he couldn't handle success and dumped the best coach in the NFL?

Four months later, Johnson was sitting on his boat parked in the backyard dock at his house in Tavernier in the Florida Keys. He was relaxed and not expressing any regret about leaving

Dallas, but clearly was upset at feeling disrespected by Jones. After a night of nachos and Heinekens, the next day he managed to serve up some well-measured digs at his former college roommate and former Cowboys boss.

"I really feel like I had accomplished a tremendous amount in five years. I was very proud of it," he said. "To be sloughed off like I was, it hurt. Just tossing out that he could hire anybody to coach this team to win the Super Bowl bothered me. It bothered my ego. I put together a team that won Super Bowls. Evidently, he doesn't appreciate that. What else could I do for the guy? I was hurt when Jerry said five hundred coaches could've taken that team to the Super Bowl. Are there five hundred coaches out there who could have made the personnel decisions and put together a team that won two Super Bowls starting from scratch?"

A few years later, Switzer, who won three national championships at Oklahoma, also won the Super Bowl in his first and only NFL job after having not coached for five seasons, and Jones had his answer.

"There may not have been five hundred," Jones said. "But we know there's at least one other."

Jones said Johnson's enthusiasm for the job had slipped, and as soon as they saw they were not working together as a team, he wanted to make a change. "I didn't want to invest any more time with him," he said.

Johnson had it written into his contract that all football decisions belonged to him. Now that he was gone, Jones would no longer be the GM in title only. All the decisions belonged to him. His first was to hire Switzer, who was there for the money and the NFL pension. In his second season, he proved Jones right. If Switzer could win the Super Bowl with Johnson's players, maybe there were 499 other coaches who could do it as well. But Johnson had also picked the players, something

Switzer could never do. Switzer's presence in his old office frosted Johnson.

Then Switzer embarrassed the organization on his way to training camp in Austin in 1997, when he was arrested at DFW Airport with a loaded .38-caliber revolver in his carry-on bag. Switzer explained he'd tossed it into his bag to hide it from children visiting when he had people over at his house and forgot to remove it before heading to the airport. But if the coach is supposed to be the leader and set an example, Switzer struck out.

Time has not taken care of all the wounds. Jones bragged when he hired Johnson that he was worth five first-round draft picks and five Heisman Trophy winners, and five years later he paid him to leave. "I did nothing but build Jimmy Johnson up, and I was doing it at a time when I was really getting beat up real good about Tom Landry," Jones said. "Inordinate success must be dealt with like inordinate failure. I agree that it looks like you didn't deal with success that well. I'm known for doing better when times are hard than when they are good. I really am known for that as far as what grade I make."

Even though it was a given at the time that Johnson was making the personnel decisions, Jones was crying out for his share of the credit and could not stay in his lane. "There was always that argument about who picked the players and who didn't because I was the general manager and he was the coach," Jones said. "All of those arguments are null and void if the owner decided we will do it or not do it."

The Cowboys came as close to winning three and then four championships in a row as any team will likely ever come. In the 1994 NFC Championship Game in San Francisco, they fell behind 21–0 in the first quarter, moved to within 38–28 in the fourth quarter, and were driving to make it a one-score game when cornerback Deion Sanders got away with pass interference on Irvin deep in 49ers territory to put an end to the comeback. San Francisco overwhelmed San Diego in the Super Bowl. Dallas would have done the same. The next year, the Cowboys beat the Steelers in the Super Bowl.

Jones had supplemented the roster by signing Sanders in 1995 and he was instrumental in Switzer's winning the Super Bowl. In his first draft without Johnson by his side one year earlier, Jones picked guard Larry Allen from Sonoma State. Allen made it into the Hall of Fame before Jones.

Jones doesn't believe the Cowboys would have won any more championships had Johnson remained. That is just him rationalizing. "The odds of doing any better than we did are huge," he said. "I don't wistfully look back and think we could have done better than what we did with Barry and won another Super Bowl."

* * *

Johnson worked for HBO and Fox for two years before getting what was his NFL dream job: coaching the Miami Dolphins. He had moved back to the Florida Keys during his time away from the game and didn't want to leave South Florida again. He campaigned to be the next Dolphins coach almost as soon as he packed up his car and left Dallas in the spring of 1994, even though the legendary Don Shula, the NFL's all-time winningest coach, had no intention of retiring. He was offered the Bucs job in 1996 and turned it down. He was offered the Dolphins job and accepted.

But the Jimmy Johnson who showed up in Dallas in 1989 was not the Jimmy Johnson who was given total control by Dolphins owner Wayne Huizenga. He didn't have the energy for another rebuild. He didn't have his coaching staff, his "crew," around him. Wannstedt was in Chicago. Turner was in Washington. Many of the others were locked into contracts in Dallas.

Johnson spent four disappointing years in Miami. He made the playoffs three times but never won more than ten games in a season. He won two playoff games but never got past the divisional round. He feuded with quarterback Dan Marino, the most popular player in South Florida's history. Johnson quit after his third season following the death of his mother late in the season, but Huizenga talked him into staying. Wannstedt, who had been fired in Chicago, joined his staff in Miami for the fourth year, so at least Johnson had his buddy with him.

The last game of his coaching career was a humiliating 62–7 loss in the 1999 playoffs to the Jaguars, the expansion team he had eyed five years earlier.

"No one thought more of Jimmy than me as a coach," Jones said.

Jones won a Super Bowl without Johnson. Johnson didn't win anything without Jones.

"You see what he did when he was in Miami," Jones said.

Two decades later, Jones is not over Johnson.

The truth is they were a great one-two punch in Dallas. They needed each other more than either one of them will ever admit.

"That was an interesting time for all of us," Jones's daughter, Charlotte, said. "I think everyone probably was caught off guard with, 'How in the world did we wind up in this situation?' But my father values trust. Jimmy had a different vision than what Jerry had. Unfortunately, that started together and it ended in two different places. When you don't share the same destination, then things don't work. In that moment that it happened, I'm not so sure it was clear to the rest of us. It has become very clear since then, and looking at it, Jimmy had other pursuits. He wanted to go in a different direction. If you do, then so be it and off you go. I think when you get in the moment and everything that surrounds what we do is so intense, you got to know that the guy in the foxhole with you has got your back."

Even though Jones made that crack about Johnson's lack of achievements in Miami seven months after his Hall of Fame induction, it was evident in his speech that he knows how important Johnson was to him and the Cowboys. They had seen more of each other that weekend than they had since Johnson had left Dallas twenty-three years earlier. Johnson was the presenter for Miami defensive end Jason Taylor, whom he'd drafted for the Dolphins. The inductees and the presenters were scheduled at the same events for three consecutive days in Canton. At the induction ceremony, they were sitting just a few feet apart: Jerry with Gene and Johnson with Taylor.

Jones did the right thing by giving Johnson credit for their success in Dallas in their five years together. One of the most compelling parts of Jones's speech:

I wouldn't be here today if it weren't for Tom Landry, Tex Schramm, and Gil Brandt, who is sitting in the audience. I couldn't have built the Cowboys today if it weren't for what they did, the shoulders I stood on. I'm deeply indebted to those three.

But the changes were really inevitable. There was no real easy way to do it. I wanted someone I knew. I wanted someone I knew well. I wanted someone that could get it done to be our coach. I wanted Jimmy Johnson. I said he'd be worth five first-round draft choices or five Heisman Trophy draft winners. Of course, I sure did get laughed out of town when I said it. It was my first experience as an owner and a general manager in making a difficult and very unpopular decision.

Jones then looked over a few feet to his left where Johnson was listening to him with great interest.

"Jimmy, it was a great decision. You were a great teammate. You were a great partner. To the contrary of popular belief, we worked so well together for five years and restored the Cowboys' credibility with our fans," he said. "We were back-to-back, we were driven, we had thick skin, we took all the criticism they could dish out. I thank you."

If only they had been able to put their egos on hold for a few more years and been willing to acknowledge how important they were to each other, Johnson and Aikman could indeed have been Belichick and Brady.

CHAPTER FIVE

Crossing Enemy Lines

Jerry Jones was on his private plane, the one with the Cowboys metallic blue star on the tail, waiting for a special guest to join him in a holding area on the tarmac at Teterboro Airport in Bergen County in northern New Jersey.

There was one week to go in the 2002 NFL regular season when Jones set up the chips and dips and drinks aboard his jet.

His guest for snacks and some football talk was Bill Parcells.

Parcells used to work a few miles down the road off Route 17 at Giants Stadium, when he coached the Giants to a pair of Super Bowl victories and later took the Jets to their first AFC Championship Game in sixteen years. In between, he helped the Patriots get to the Super Bowl.

Now he was out of coaching. He was out of football. He was going out of his mind.

Parcells stepped down as coach of the Jets after a disappointing 1999 season, a year that began with Super Bowl aspirations but ended in the first half of the opener when quarterback Vinny Testaverde tore the Achilles tendon in his left leg diving after a fumble by future Hall of Famer Curtis Martin.

Testaverde's backup was Rick Mirer, whom Parcells had

passed over with the first overall pick in the 1993 draft, with the Patriots taking Drew Bledsoe instead. He made the right decision then. He made the wrong decision this time. Mirer, from Notre Dame, was supposed to carry many of the same traits as former Irish quarterback Joe Montana, but in his seventh season he was nothing more than a journeyman hanging on in the hopes of getting one last shot.

As soon as Testaverde went down, Parcells lost interest in the season. Eight months earlier, the Jets had a 10–0 lead on John Elway and the Broncos three minutes into the third quarter of the AFC Championship Game in Denver. If they could just hold on, the Jets would be heading to their first Super Bowl in thirty years, and Parcells would be heading into New York sports immortality, taking both New York football teams to the Super Bowl. But the Jets being the Jets—a team that won Super Bowl III in the greatest upset in pro football history but has never been back in the big game—they were outscored 23–0 the rest of the way. Afterward Parcells was so drained it looked like he had carried the ball twenty-five times into a wall of 350-pound defensive linemen.

It was a minor miracle that in Parcells's second season, after taking over a team that Rich Kotite had driven into a ditch with records of 1-15 in 1996 and 3-13 in 1995, he had won twelve games and a playoff game. He had squeezed a career year out of the journeyman Testaverde and then loaded up in the off-season to make a Super Bowl run in 1999. Elway had retired after winning back-to-back championships, and the Jets were a favorite to get to the Super Bowl.

Once again, Same Old Jets.

Parcells knew his plans had gone to hell the moment Vinny went down. The Jets lost their first three games and were 2-6 at the halfway point when he made the switch from Mirer to Ray

Lucas, a jack-of-all-trades-type player. Lucas energized the Jets and they won six of their final eight games, and Parcells second-guessed himself for not making the change to Lucas earlier. Parcells stepped down as coach after the season.

Jones could not have been more thrilled after winning Super Bowl XXX against the Steelers in his second season without Jimmy Johnson. But the Cowboys continued to get picked apart in free agency. They beat the Vikings in a wild card game in '96 but then lost to the second-year expansion team Carolina Panthers in the divisional round. The next season they didn't make the playoffs, and Jones gave Switzer a one-way ticket back to his couch in Oklahoma. Jones hired Steelers offensive coordinator Chan Gailey and the Cowboys immediately were back in the playoffs as NFC East champs with a 10-6 record. But they lost in the wild card round at Texas Stadium to the Cardinals, whose one previous playoff victory came in 1947. The next year, Gailey went 8-8, the Cowboys made the playoffs again, this time as a wild card, and lost in the first round to the Vikings on the road. That was it for Gailey. Jones fired him and promoted defensive coordinator Dave Campo, but he was painfully over-matched. There was one game left in Campo's third straight 5-11 season when Jones waited for Parcells to come on board.

The Cowboys had become irrelevant. Jones was trying to get voters to pass a measure in Arlington in 2004 to provide $325 million in public funding for a new stadium by way of a tax increase. One more season of 5-11 in 2003 could sabotage the vote.

Parcells, the ultimate fix-it man in football, was being asked to help build a stadium. "We were wanting to turn the corner with our team and hadn't gotten it done," Stephen Jones said. "We also understood we needed to do it sooner than later, because we did have a stadium referendum coming up. Bill was aware of that when we talked to him. At the end of the day, our polling showed—surprise, surprise—people think more positively about you when you are winning versus when you are not doing so well. We heard a lot of good things about Bill and felt he would be a good fit for us and we could turn the corner quickly."

Parcells might not stick around very long, which Jones had to know if he studied the scouting report, but he always left with the team in much better shape than when he arrived. Parcells won two Super Bowls in his last seven seasons with the Giants after he was 3-12-1 his first year. He quit four months after the second title due to a heart condition that eventually required surgery, although when he stepped down he would not concede it was health related. No team was more dysfunctional than the Patriots, but he took them to the Super Bowl in his fourth year. He quit a couple of days later. He teased Jets fans in 1998 and then left one season later.

The issue for Parcells: He ran out of New England because he convinced himself that Patriots owner Robert Kraft meddled too much after he took away Parcells's power in the draft room. That prompted one of the best of the many great Parcells-isms: "It's just like a friend of mine told me. If they want you to cook the dinner, at least they ought to let you shop for some of the groceries."

Kraft did not own the Patriots when Parcells was hired in 1993. He bought the team in 1994 for a then-record $172 million when it was on the verge of being moved to St. Louis. Parcells and Drew Bledsoe were the two most valuable assets he inherited. Parcells and Kraft worked well together for a year or so until Kraft became more comfortable in the football business and Parcells decided to freeze him out. If Kraft made Parcells claustrophobic, then welcome to life in a telephone booth with Jones, the socks-and-jocks guy.

The issue for Jones: After running off Johnson, he hired three straight puppets in Switzer, Gailey, and Campo.

Yes, Mr. Jones.

Of course, Mr. Jones.

Whatever you say, Mr. Jones.

Thank you for the job, Mr. Jones.

Can I get your slippers and a pipe, Mr. Jones? How about a nightcap?

That might have stroked Mr. Jones's ego, but it hadn't won him enough football games in the last seven years. If Jones thought Johnson was secretive and dismissive and rebelled against being a team player, all Jones had to do was call Kraft to find out what it was like for an owner to feel like he worked for the coach.

Parcells and Jones have different recollections of who played matchmaker, although they agree it was not Yente from *Fiddler on the Roof*. Parcells said he received a call from Raiders owner Al Davis, with whom he had a close relationship. Davis also became a mentor to Jones when he bought into the NFL.

"You need to be honest with me now," Davis said to Parcells.

"I'm always honest with you, Al," Parcells said.

"You think you might consider the Cowboys?" Davis asked.

"I haven't thought about it," Parcells said.

"You think about it and let me know. Make it pretty quick," Davis said.

Davis was acting as an intermediary, and Parcells believes Jones asked Davis to detect if Parcells would be willing to rescue his sagging franchise. Parcells did as Davis asked and got back to him quickly; he told him he would be happy to talk about the Cowboys job with Jones.

Jerry Jones never played a down in the NFL, but he was the featured attraction at the 2017 Hall of Fame ceremonies. Once he's started talking and built up momentum, he's harder to stop than a 240-pound running back. Jones went for 36 minutes and 50 seconds in an entertaining and often poignant speech. *(Courtesy of James D. Smith/Dallas Cowboys)*

It was appropriate that Jimmy Johnson was on the stage with Jerry Jones on his big night at the Hall of Fame. The presenter for Dolphins defensive end Jason Taylor, Johnson was more responsible than anybody for Jones's three Super Bowl rings. Jones was generous in recognizing Johnson's contributions, although it was Jones's business smarts that got him elected. *(Getty Images [Joe Robbins / Stringer])*

Tony Romo and Jason Witten met on a bus from the airport to the hotel for rookie minicamp in 2003 and became such close friends that Terrell Owens once accused Romo of freezing him out of the offense and throwing only to Witten. They played 13 years together, and Romo completed 649 passes for 7,287 yards and 37 TDs to Witten. Romo holds most of the Cowboys' passing records, and Witten is their all-time leading receiver. *(Courtesy of Sam Smith/Dallas Cowboys)*

Mr. Cowboy, meet Mr. Cowboy. All-time great Bob Lilly presents the Bob Lilly Award (what else?) to Jason Witten before a late-season game in 2016. The award is voted on by Cowboys' fans and goes to the player who best exemplifies Lilly's achievements, sportsmanship, dedication, and leadership. On their way off the field, Lilly told Witten he was the new Mr. Cowboy. Witten responded by catching all 10 passes thrown his way by Dak Prescott against the Bucs. *(Courtesy of James D. Smith/Dallas Cowboys)*

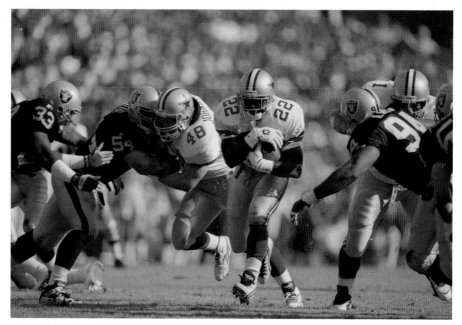

The affectionate "Moose!" calls for fullback Daryl Johnston followed the Cowboys from Texas Stadium to Giants Stadium and around the league. No one was more appreciative of Johnston's blocking skills than Emmitt Smith, who cashed in by rushing for more yards than any player in NFL history. Johnston was on the sidelines working for Fox Sports when Smith broke Walter Payton's record, and Emmitt came right over to share a long embrace with Moose. *(Courtesy of the Dallas Cowboys)*

Quarterback Dak Prescott and running back Ezekiel Elliott are the Cowboys' future. Both had fabulous rookie years in 2016. Prescott played so well when Tony Romo was injured that Romo, rather than moving on and playing for the Houston Texans, opted for retirement and a job with CBS. Prescott's play slipped when Elliott was suspended six games in 2017 for domestic violence. *(Courtesy of James D. Smith/Dallas Cowboys)*

Gene Jones is the matriarch of the Jones family, and their three children are the heirs to the Cowboys kingdom. Gene is a former Miss Arkansas USA. She and Jerry met at the University at Arkansas and were married while still in college. When Jerry couldn't win Gene a teddy bear at the state fair on their first date, he snuck off when she wasn't looking and bought her the biggest one he could find. Jerry selected Gene to present him at his Hall of Fame induction. *(Courtesy of the Dallas Cowboys)*

The Cowboys are a $5 billion family business. Jerry Jones has made sure to surround himself with his family, with oldest son Stephen (left), daughter Charlotte, and son Jerry Jr. holding the three highest management positions in the organization under Jones. *(Courtesy of James D. Smith/Dallas Cowboys)*

Jerry Jones will likely run the Cowboys until the day he dies. But plans are in place for the Cowboys to remain in the family for at least the next two generations. After Jerry has passed, Stephen (left), Jerry Jr., and Charlotte will each control 33 percent of the team. Stephen, as the oldest and the one who has been with his father from the day he bought the team, will inherit the Cowboys' vote at the league meetings. *(Courtesy of James D. Smith/Dallas Cowboys)*

Those were the days! Jerry Jones and Jimmy Johnson were the toast of the NFL after the Cowboys won the Super Bowl just three seasons after Jimmy and Jerry were 1-15 in their first year in 1989. They won another trophy the next year before the Jimmy-Jerry relationship imploded and Jones paid him $2 million to leave the Cowboys. *(Courtesy of the Dallas Cowboys)*

Bill Parcells was accustomed to getting his way, but when he took the coaching job in Dallas in 2003, he knew the final say belonged to Jerry Jones. Before the 2006 draft, Parcells was so upset when he was told the Cowboys planned to take DeMarcus Ware over Marcus Spears that he threatened to boycott the draft. He showed up, of course, and the Cowboys were able to draft both Ware and Spears in the first round. *(Courtesy of James D. Smith/Dallas Cowboys)*

Jerry Jones needed a coach to restore credibility and help a stadium tax bill pass in Arlington. Bill Parcells wanted back into coaching after being out for three years. Parcells and Jones were a potentially volatile combination, but they got along just fine, although Parcells made the playoffs just twice in four years and left Dallas without winning a playoff game. *(Courtesy of James D. Smith/ Dallas Cowboys)*

Jason Garrett is the second-longest tenured coach in Cowboys history behind Tom Landry. The difference: Landry had five Super Bowl appearances and two Super Bowl victories in twenty-nine years compared to Garrett having two playoff appearances and one playoff victory in his first seven full seasons as head coach. But Jerry Jones has the only vote that counts, and he is Garrett's biggest supporter. *(Courtesy of James D. Smith/Dallas Cowboys)*

Tom Landry's two worst seasons as Cowboys coach were his first, when he was 0-11-1; and his twenty-ninth and last, when he was 3-13. After Landry was fired by Jerry Jones, he played hard to get when Jones wanted to induct him into the Ring of Honor, but he made his first appearance at Texas Stadium since getting fired when he held a press conference with Jones in July 1993 to announce he would be honored that November. *(Courtesy of the Dallas Cowboys)*

Nothing about the Cowboys stays a secret, but somehow Jerry Jones's lunch with Tom Landry in 1993 at the home of a mutual friend remained hush-hush until right now. Jones had tried for years to convince Landry to be inducted into the Cowboys' Ring of Honor. It was not until their clandestine luncheon when they sat down face-to-face for the first time since Jones fired him when he bought the team in 1989 that Landry finally said yes. *(Courtesy of the Dallas Cowboys)*

The Saturday Night Massacre. On February 25, 1989, Cowboys president Tex Schramm introduced forty-six-year-old Jerry Jones as the new owner of the team. Schramm and Jones had just returned from Austin, Texas, aboard the latter's private plane after Jones had fired Tom Landry in the restaurant of Landry's country club. Schramm would soon be fired as well. *(Courtesy of the Dallas Cowboys)*

The Cowboys' five Lombardi Trophies are an impressive sight at The Star. Only the Steelers, with six, have won more. Tied with the 49ers and Patriots, Dallas has been stuck at five since the 1995 season. In the more than two decades since their last championship, the Cowboys have won only three playoff games, never more than one in any season. Tom Landry and Tex Schramm were responsible for the first two trophies. *(Andrew Myers)*

Everson Walls was the ultimate teammate to Ron Springs in 2007 when he donated a kidney to help him regain quality of life. They were named honorary captains for the Cowboys' season opener at Texas Stadium. Springs lapsed into a coma months later when he went in for what was supposed to be minor cosmetic surgery and never recovered. The deaths of Springs in 2011 and Robert Newhouse in 2014 were devastating to their close friends on the teams from the 1970s and the 1980s. *(Getty Images [Scott Cunningham / Contributor])*

When Ezekiel Elliott and the running backs have their position group meetings, there is history and inspiration on the walls, with the two leading rushers in team history staring right at them. Emmitt Smith is the NFL's all-time rushing leader with 18,355 yards; and Tony Dorsett is ninth with 12,739 yards. Elliott's career got off to a great start in 2016 when he rushed for 1,631 yards, the second-highest total for a rookie behind Eric Dickerson's 1,808 yards in 1984. *(Courtesy of James D. Smith/Dallas Cowboys)*

Troy Aikman and Michael Irvin won three Super Bowls together and helped put each other in the Pro Football Hall of Fame. But their bond runs much deeper than their football accomplishments. Aikman showed up in a Dallas courtroom to support Irvin during his 1996 drug trial. More than two decades later, Irvin is still appreciative that Aikman had his back when it would have been easy for him to walk away. Aikman said he supported Irvin as a friend, though he did not support what he'd done. *(Courtesy of the Dallas Cowboys)*

Jerry Jones had his greatest success with the Triplets: (*from left to right*) Michael Irvin, Troy Aikman, and Emmitt Smith. The Cowboys were the first team to win three Super Bowls in four seasons and perhaps would have won even more if Jimmy Johnson remained as coach. Jones and the three players are all in the Hall of Fame. (*Courtesy of the Dallas Cowboys*)

Jerry World cost $1.3 billion. A large American flag to hang in a stadium costs $1,500. Yet when the Cowboys' new stadium opened in 2009, there was not one permanent American flag in the building. The Cowboys didn't feel there was a logical spot to permanently display the flag. That was odd, considering Jones's strong stance during the NFL's Anthem controversy in 2017. They found a spot later in the season. (*Courtesy of James D. Smith/Dallas Cowboys*)

It was supposed to cost $650 million, with Jerry Jones and the city of Arlington splitting it down the middle. Jones was responsible for over-runs. By the time he finished with all the bells and whistles and video boards, the final price tag on the retractable-roof palace was $1.3 billion. The stadium has become the standard for opulence in the NFL. *(Courtesy of James D. Smith/Dallas Cowboys)*

The NFL draft is the league's second-biggest event each year, right behind the Super Bowl. Despite the screw-up at AT&T Stadium for Super Bowl XLVIII, when there were missing seats for tickets that were sold, the league gave Jerry World another chance by allowing it to host the 2018 draft. All went well for the NFL, except for Roger Goodell getting booed again. *(Courtesy of James D. Smith/Dallas Cowboys)*

It's a toss-up: Watch the game live at AT&T Stadium or watch it on the video board. The picture is so big and so clear that it's mesmerizing. Jerry Jones came up with the idea of putting in a board that stretches about fifty yards after seeing a smaller version at a Celine Dion concert in Las Vegas. (*Courtesy of James D. Smith/Dallas Cowboys*)

Frisco, a Dallas suburb, wanted a $90 million indoor high school stadium. They also wanted the Cowboys to set up shop in their growing little town. The Cowboys took their money and built the stadium for $170 million and in return were given ninety-one acres to develop, which became The Star, the home to their new headquarters as part of a $1.5 million complex with restaurants, shops, and a sports medicine facility. (*Andrew Myers*)

Cowboys players can't complain about the workplace. The team went all out in providing a state-of-the-art locker room at The Star. Until the Cowboys moved into Valley Ranch in 1985, which was followed by their move to The Star in 2016, the locker room at their old practice facility in North Dallas was in a blue aluminum shack. The players had plenty of company, as the place was roach infested. (*Andrew Myers*)

The lobby at The Star looks more like a five-star hotel than the headquarters for a football team. There is a sculptured light fixture hanging from the ceiling, with the practice field in the background. The locker room is downstairs, the coaches are on the lobby level, and the executive offices are on the second floor. Office space is also leased to various companies and organizations. *(Andrew Myers)*

The team that eats together—well, maybe one day they will win a Super Bowl together. The Training Table on the bottom level of The Star is not only for the players but the rest of the Cowboys staff as well. The idea for the staff to mingle with the players and coaches came from Jerry Jones Jr. after he visited the cafeteria at the NFL headquarters in New York. The players get tired of seeing each other all day and have embraced spending time with people from other departments. *(Courtesy of James D. Smith/Dallas Cowboys)*

best interest. Then you get out there and you're not doing something that allows you to be satisfied mentally. You know, I wasn't soliciting offers. It's just that things once in a while come your way. But Dallas was a long way from pretty much everybody that I care about. Other than that, I'm glad I went there. It was a good experience for me. I learned a lot, and hopefully I left them with something. I don't know that I did. But I think I did."

Parcells called Johnson just once for the scoop on working for Jones. "I always got along with Jimmy pretty well," Parcells said. "I didn't know him real well. Everything was positive from Jimmy's side."

Johnson gave his blessing. He said he thought it could be a winning formula for a couple of years, but then "they might get under each other's skin."

They had one more meeting before shaking hands on the deal. It lasted five hours in Garden City, Long Island, where Parcells lived during his four years with the Jets. Jones and Parcells didn't have much history with each other. They would meet up on the field before Giants-Cowboys games. Jones would come over and sit with Parcells and Davis at the scouting combine workouts in Indianapolis. They would speak on the phone when Parcells had final say with the Patriots and Jets, and Jones would call him to talk about a trade.

One of Parcells's mentors when he was promoted to head coach by the Giants in 1983 was Landry. Even though they were competing in the same division, Landry went out of his way to assist Parcells in any way he could. Parcells would wander over during pregame warmups and strike up a conversation. If Landry liked you, and he enjoyed Parcells, he didn't feel the need to hide secrets even in an ultra-paranoid business. Landry was a former Giants cornerback and assistant coach—in fact, he was a player-coach in his final two years as an active player—and he still had a close friendship with Giants owner Wellington Mara. Mara was also fond of Parcells, so it was no surprise that Landry treated him kindly. It didn't take Parcells more than his first season as the Giants' head coach to realize he was knee-deep in a volatile business. He won three games, his mother and his father each passed away during the season, and General Manager George Young would have fired him if University of Miami coach Howard Schnellenberger had wanted the job. Parcells was granted a reprieve by Young and changed his coaching style. He had a hard time with the transition from defensive coordinator to head coach, because many of his players were the same but the relationships had to be different.

By 1984, he was back to being true to his personality. He was a loathsome hard-ass. The players loved him, but only on the days they didn't hate him. It worked. The Giants won the Super Bowl in 1986 and again in 1990, which was Landry's second year in retirement. Parcells did not hold it against Jones that he had fired his friend.

"I talked to Coach Landry after he left the Cowboys and told him how grateful I was to him and how fortunate I was to be able to consult with him from time to time," Parcells said. "But it's just the passing of the torch. That's the way the business is. Hey, you get a new owner, and God knows I had three or four new owners myself. I know what happens. It's going to be different."

It was a gamble for Jones and Parcells the moment they signed the contract. Jones did not want to get into daily battles like he did in the final years with Johnson. Parcells felt Kraft emasculated him by taking away his personnel powers, and he could not go through that again. Jones liked to shop for the groceries and Parcells liked to do more than cook the dinner. Jones admired Parcells's ability to win and Parcells admired Jones's ability to make money. "Bill had a much different background than Jimmy," Jones said. "Bill grew up in a family in a pretty sophisticated business. They're very different people. Bill has a real deep loyalty strength, as witnessed by who he brings on his staff. Both of them are, of course, great coaches, and both have great qualities. But they are not alike."

The Cowboys had fallen hard and Jones was so desperate to get back into playoff contention that he might have hired any accomplished coach but Johnson. He also needed the new stadium approved. It held the key to the Cowboys' financial future. If Parcells had not taken the job, who knows, maybe Jones would have just decided to coach the team himself. His routine was to descend from his suite to the sidelines in the fourth quarter and stand within shouting distance of his coach, so maybe he would eliminate the middle man, put on the headset, and coach the team and have nobody to blame but himself.

Fortunately, it didn't come to that. Jones had fourteen years and three Super Bowls of equity built up, and Parcells was ready to buy in and go after another ring. "I knew he was very active and I think the general reaction overall to him in the league was, 'Who is this guy?'" Parcells said. "There was a group of the more conservative and more established owners, just like when CEOs change in business, not everybody is readily accepted. Some people weren't open to his ideas and his visions. But when they won and they got Jimmy there and they won the Super Bowl, that got everybody paying attention."

Parcells promised there would be no confrontations with Jones. He needed to make one last run at the Super Bowl for peace of mind and his legacy, and the Cowboys had all the ingredients he wanted: They were a bad team and Parcells excelled in reclamation projects. They had a big-money owner. They were the Dallas Cowboys. He arrived in Dallas and found an apartment in a seventeen-story building off McArthur Road and Texas State Highway 114 in Las Colinas, not far from Valley Ranch and very close to a good pizza place, a rarity in the Dallas area but a necessity for a Jersey guy. Nobody in Big D asked him any questions about why he stopped coaching the Jets. They weren't interested in his Giants history, either. They just wanted to know if he would win in Dallas.

* * *

Jones embraced Parcells's arrival, but at the same time he was setting off warning signs. He made sure everybody knew he was still in charge, and even a future Hall of Fame coach was not going to marginalize him like Johnson did. "I am what I am," Jones said.

He was a ruthless businessman, but he could also turn on the charm. Parcells was a ruthless coach, but there could just as easily be a twinkle in his blue eyes. "I'm a salesman and there's nobody who can get to me quicker than another good salesman," Jones said. "But the facts are I'm the ultimate decision maker as long as I own the team."

The presence of Parcells immediately gave the Cowboys credibility. Troy Aikman, who had retired after twelve seasons following multiple concussions and a debilitating back injury, had been out of football two seasons when Parcells was hired. He had flirted with the Chiefs, Chargers, and Dolphins, but ultimately stayed away. He had the obligatory press conference with tears. Aikman had been frustrated with Switzer, Gailey, and Campo, but the opportunity to play for Parcells got his attention. "If Bill Parcells were to come to my home and tell me how much he wanted me to play and how much I could help him and the team win, I think it would be worth considering," he said. "Don't know then that I would do it, but how could you not at least hear him out?"

Parcells didn't stop by Aikman's house. Aikman stayed retired.

* * *

There are only three places Parcells could have made his next stop after the Jets that would have pissed off Giants fans: Philadelphia, Washington, or Dallas. If you loved the Giants, you hated the Eagles and Redskins but absolutely despised the Cowboys. Now that Parcells was in Dallas, he was a traitor. How could he switch sides in one of the most vicious NFL rivalries? He was asked that question when he showed up wearing a golf shirt with the Cowboys star at a media breakfast at the NFL meetings in the spring of 2003. "I've coached against the Giants before," he said. "It's really not new for me. It's over a decade since I was the coach of the Giants. A lot has happened."

When he was elected to the Pro Football Hall of Fame in 2013, in his mind he went in as a member of the Giants, although unlike the baseball Hall of Fame in Cooperstown, players, coaches, owners, and executives do not designate a team they are representing.

When a writer from New York who previously worked in Dallas covering the Cowboys asked Parcells about the mind-set of jumping to the enemy, he said, "Well, you used to work in Dallas and now you work in New York."

The writer's response: "I'm not sure that is quite the same."

He was much more philosophical about his job-hopping after two decades had passed and he talked about how transient the profession had become over the years. Nick Saban, the best college coach of his era, went from Michigan State to Louisiana State University to the Miami Dolphins to Alabama in the span of just twelve years. The Giants needed Commissioner Pete Rozelle to step in and prevent Parcells from leaving after the Giants learned on their charter flight home from their Super Bowl XXI victory over the Broncos in Pasadena that he was trying to broker a deal with the Falcons as coach and general manager. Rozelle cut off negotiations. Parcells wound up staying four more seasons with the Giants and winning another Super Bowl.

"You recognize the profession that I was in has changed appreciably over the years," Parcells said. "Where back in the day prior to me coming of the age where I could have potentially been a head coach, there was quite a bit of stability in the coaching profession and a lot of places there were coaches, particularly in college football, which is what I was aspiring to do, who were there for years and years: Bear Bryant, Woody Hayes, Bud Wilkinson, Frank Howard at Clemson, Joe Paterno, Bo Schembechler. There was a lot of stability in a lot of places."

Teams began playing more of a national schedule. They were developing their brand. There was enormous pressure to get into the big-money bowl games. Notre Dame secured its own national television contract with NBC. "That affected stability in the coaching profession," Parcells said. "When you look at professional football, there were coaches in the league, when I was there in more formative years, that were there for a long time. Coach Landry and Chuck Noll were stable for a long time. George Allen moved a couple of places. Chuck Knox moved to a couple of different places. By the time it got to me, I'll just put it this way in one sentence: The coaching profession became appreciably more transient. Both in college and the pros. There are several pro coaches who have had multiple jobs."

The Cowboys were not the only team romancing Parcells toward the end of the 2002 season. He wanted to get back into coaching so badly that he was willing to go back to college and was in serious talks with the University of Kentucky. He had not worked as a college head coach since the 1978 season at the Air Force Academy. Parcells's hobby of owning Thoroughbred racehorses had turned into a passion. Kentucky's campus in Lexington was only eighty-one miles from Churchill Downs in Louisville, and even if none of his horses made it to the Kentucky Derby, he would be able to visit the track any time he wanted.

He spoke to Lee about joining his staff if he took the job at Kentucky, but the Cowboys job sure was more appealing, even if it meant twice a year playing the Giants, the team he rooted for as a kid in New Jersey and wound up coaching. He had faced the Giants with the Patriots and the Jets, but standing on the Cowboys sideline would be perceived much differently. "I didn't really look at it like, 'Oh, I'm being disloyal to the Giants.' I never felt that way," he said. "It was an opportunity, a chance to coach a team. I still wanted to coach. I was probably going to the University of Kentucky if I didn't go to Dallas. I was thinking about Kentucky pretty strongly. Obviously, the horses and everything, it was the location I was enamored with."

Parcells had not lived in Texas since he was the linebackers coach at Texas Tech in Lubbock from 1975 to 1977. He had coached in either New Jersey, New England, or Long Island since 1981. He was also going to have to adjust to his boss, the owner of the team, being the general manager. If there was a draft-room argument and he wanted to curse out the general manager, he was going to have to think twice about it. He took over a 5-11 team from Campo, and for the first time in his four head-coaching stops, he made the playoffs in his first season. It took two years with the Giants, two years with the Patriots, and two years with the Jets. The Parcells magic worked right away in Dallas as the Cowboys finished 10-6, with Quincy Carter starting all sixteen games.

Carter was picked by Dallas in the second round of the 2001 draft. He was the third quarterback taken after Michael Vick, who was the first overall pick by the Atlanta Falcons, and Drew Brees, who was the first pick in the second round by the San Diego Chargers. Vick was on his way to the Hall of Fame until his career was put on hold when he served eighteen months in prison for running a dog-fighting operation in Virginia. Brees is a lock to make it to the Hall of Fame. Carter came to symbolize the Cowboys' inability to replace Aikman. He started eight games as a rookie, was nearly cut his second year after getting into a sideline argument with Jones, and then emerged as Parcells's starter in 2003 by beating out Chad Hutchinson. The Cowboys attempted 510 passes during the regular season and Carter was responsible for 505. He had 17 touchdowns and 21 interceptions.

The Cowboys lost at Carolina in the wild card round, but the season was a success. Jones's team was relevant again, just in time for the stadium vote.

The following summer was filled with optimism. Parcells was just getting warmed up. Big things were expected. He actually thought the mobile Carter might give him someone to build with until the Cowboys could find a real franchise quarterback. But Carter turned out to be someone Parcells could not trust. If you play quarterback for Parcells, the one thing he won't tolerate is not being accountable and reliable and being there for your teammates.

Parcells was able to put up with Lawrence Taylor's cocaine

problem because he was the best defensive player in NFL history, and he truly loved LT and worked behind the scenes to save his career and save him from himself as LT tried to snort his way out of the league. The perception was that Parcells enabled Taylor, but the truth is he did all a coach could possibly do to assist a friend in trouble. When a player says playing eighteen holes of golf is the best way for him to go through drug rehab, there is an issue.

Carter was different. He was a young player. He was not a star. He was a mediocre talent fortunate to be a starting quarterback in the NFL. He was already in the NFL's drug program when he flunked his second test in the summer of 2004. In the off-season, the Cowboys signed Testaverde, now forty years old but a physical freak who could still sling it, and traded for Drew Henson, the former Michigan quarterback once considered better than Tom Brady in Ann Arbor. Henson had not played football since 2000, after deciding baseball was his first love. He had been projected to be the first pick in the 2002 draft by the expansion Houston Texans if he had not given up football.

As soon as the Cowboys got word that Carter had flunked another test, they cut him. Carter would have been fined four game checks by the NFL, but he wouldn't have been suspended unless he flunked a third test. Parcells and Jones didn't have the desire to find out if bad things indeed happened in threes.

Carter was gone.

"I just know that I am saddened by this turn of events," Parcells said. "I just couldn't keep him in my plans."

"This was not a difficult decision at all," Jones said.

Parcells announced that Testaverde would be the opening-day starter against the Vikings. Henson was expected to be the backup, but he was beaten out by Tony Romo. Romo dressed for six games during the 6-10 season but did not throw a pass. Parcells gave Henson an opportunity to show he could still be the player he was at Michigan.

Dallas got off to a miserable 3-7 start and Henson received his first opportunity to play in loss number seven to the Ravens. He came off the bench in a 30–10 defeat and completed all 6 of his passes for 47 yards with a touchdown. Did the Cowboys have something here? Parcells wanted to find out more. He needed to find out more. He gave Henson the start four days later in the Thanksgiving Day game against the Chicago Bears. Even though the Cowboys were out of the playoff race, the late-afternoon slot always attracted a huge national television audience. This was going to be Henson's chance.

The Bears were 4-6, not much better than the Cowboys. Henson was 4 for 12 for 31 yards in the first half, and the teams went into the locker rooms tied at 7. When the Cowboys offense ran on the field for the first possession of the third quarter, Testaverde was back at quarterback. Henson did not take another snap for the Cowboys. He was third on the depth chart in 2005 behind Bledsoe, the latest of Parcells's former quarterbacks to join him in Dallas—he had played his first four seasons in New England for Parcells—and now Romo was solidly entrenched as the number two. The Cowboys assigned Henson to play in NFL Europe after the 2005 season, and Parcells cut him toward the end of training camp in 2006.

The good news for Jerry was that the stadium bill passed in November with 55 percent of the vote. Arlington raised its sales tax by 0.5 percent and also raised the tax on car rentals and hotels. It would be five years before Jerry World would open, and while it was likely Parcells would be out of Dallas by then, his presence at the time of the vote certainly helped.

There was something about Romo that energized Parcells going into the 2006 season even though he had yet to step on the field during his first three seasons. He had the "it" factor, a magnetic personality that made him a natural leader. He also had some on-field wild-child Favre in him that needed to be kept under control. He was fearless but a little too careless with the ball. Parcells was taking it slow with him. Sean Payton, who was Parcells's offensive coordinator for his first three seasons in Dallas before he was hired as the head coach of the Saints, was on the phone with Romo during the last two rounds of the 2003 draft. Payton and Romo had Eastern Illinois in common.

At the time, the Cowboys' depth chart was not intimidating: Carter, Clint Stoerner, and Chad Hutchinson. Payton developed a quick rapport with Romo and offered him a signing bonus of $10,000, when the going rate was $2,500 to $5,000. But the Cowboys were not the only team after Romo, and four others were also offering $10,000. The Cowboys raised their offer to $15,000. Parcells and Jones each got on the phone to give Romo a sales pitch. Payton got word that Arizona offered $25,000.

"Tell him, shit, we'll match it," Jones said.

Payton convinced Jones that Romo knew the Cowboys opportunity was the best fit for him and not to raise his offer. Not that Jones needed the money, but he was grateful Payton saved him ten grand. When Payton was hired by the Saints in 2006, his first phone call after he settled in went to Parcells. He wanted to trade for Romo. Parcells refused, and the Saints instead signed free agent Drew Brees, but only after the Dolphins doctors told Saban that he was too much of a medical risk coming off serious surgery on his throwing shoulder.

Parcells didn't bring back Testaverde in 2005 and signed Bledsoe to a three-year contract. It worked well for the first ten games of the season, with Dallas winning seven. But they slumped down the stretch and finished 9-7 and out of the play-offs for the second straight season. Parcells had now coached the Cowboys for three years and had made the playoffs just once; he was still without a playoff victory.

In a strange twist, it was Romo who both brought the Cowboys back to life in 2006 and weeks later ended Parcells's coaching career.

This time for good.

Bledsoe was 3-2 going into a Monday night game at Texas Stadium against the Giants. Romo had continued to collect dust on the bench. In his first three years plus five games he had not yet thrown one pass in the regular season. The Cowboys invested a lot of time in a no-name, undrafted free agent who so far could not get on the field when Carter, Hutchinson, Testaverde, Henson, and Bledsoe all had been given opportunities to varying degrees by Parcells.

Romo stood on the sidelines, was a good teammate to Bledsoe, and kept his mouth shut. Then Parcells had seen enough...of Bledsoe. The Cowboys were trailing the Giants 12–7 and had a second and goal at the 4-yard line when Bledsoe threw a bad pass and was intercepted by Sam Madison at the 1 with 1:33 left in the first half. Parcells was disgusted. The one thing a quarterback must never do in striking distance is turn the ball over and take points off the board. This was Bledsoe's fourteenth season in the NFL, and if he hadn't figured it out by then, it just wasn't going to happen. At half-time, Parcells told Romo he was up. His first pass against the Giants, the first pass of his career, was intercepted by middle linebacker Antonio Pierce. Romo finished his night with 2 touchdowns and 3 interceptions and 227 yards passing. Dallas lost 36-22, but Romo brought enough life to the offense that Parcells named him the starter.

Bledsoe would not take one more snap the rest of the season. He would not take one more snap the rest of his career. At the end of the season, he retired. Bledsoe became the answer to a pretty easy trivia question: Who lost his job to Tom Brady in New England and Tony Romo in Dallas?

* * *

Parcells is like a sponge absorbing knowledge. His four years with Jones taught him more about the business world than any of his eleven previous stops as a coach in college or the NFL, or even the one year he worked in real estate in 1979 when his wife got tired of moving around and he turned down a job he had already accepted to be on the Giants defensive staff. He was miserable out of football, and his absence lasted only one year before he took a job as linebackers coach in New England.

When he moved back to Texas, he faced the usual coach's dilemma: buy or rent? He wasn't quite sure, because as usual he wasn't sure how long he would be staying. Jones suggested the Starwood, a development in Frisco with a twenty-two-mile drive to Valley Ranch. It was still more than a decade before the Cowboys would move their corporate headquarters and training facility into a $1.5 billion extravaganza in Frisco.

Parcells went to look at the houses. He liked what he saw.

"Who developed this?" Parcells asked his real estate agent.

"Jerry Jones and his partners," the agent said.

"If I was to buy one of these houses, who would handle the insurance?" Parcells asked.

"Blue Star would handle," the agent said.

"Is that Jerry's insurance company?" Parcells said.

"Why, yes it is," the agent said.

Parcells left without buying. He needed to think it over. He drove back to Valley Ranch and was laughing to himself in the car at a story he planned to tell Jones. He parked in his spot outside the facility and went to find Jerry. He told him that in Pennsylvania the workers for coal mining companies bought just about everything they needed for their personal use in the company store. Groceries, household items, toiletries, and the like. The money was deducted from their paychecks.

Jones giggled. He knew where this was going. He knew Parcells had just come back from visiting one of his houses insured by one of his companies.

"By the time I'm finished with you, you are going to be getting about 10 percent of what you are making," he told Parcells.

They had a good laugh.

Parcells said to pump the brakes on that one. He decided to rent a few minutes from Valley Ranch to cut down on his commute. Jones did not own the building.

Jones and Parcells truly had fun with each other. They were the same generation with very different backgrounds but both extremely competitive. Jones would send Parcells footballs and apparel to sign. One day, Parcells sent him a bill. "Several thousands of dollars," Jones said.

Parcells decided to charge Jones for his autograph. Jones in turn sent Parcells a bill for all the time and phone calls he made in his office at Valley Ranch for the nonfootball business he conducted on Cowboys property. "He was working on his stocks and bonds all the time," Jones said.

They called it even.

Jones had moved training camp to the Alamodome in San Antonio the summer before Parcells's first year with the team. It was the fifth different camp setup for the Cowboys since Jones bought the team; the Cowboys had trained in Thousand Oaks from 1963 to 1989.

Parcells hated training camp in the Alamodome.

The coaches and players stayed in a downtown hotel and were bused over to the stadium in the morning for two-a-day practices. After the first practice, the players were served lunch in the dome, and if they hustled there was time to go back to the hotel, grab a nap, and be back in time for the afternoon practice. The Cowboys set up cots in the luxury boxes at the dome for players who wanted to eliminate the travel time and get more naptime. It was an unusual sight to behold. Large men in their twenties and thirties sleeping on undersized beds in the middle of the day in a stadium suite. It was convenient, but there was no turndown service or chocolates on their pillows. The field was artificial turf, which players hate. The dome was climate controlled, which they liked, but not ideal for coaches to get players into game shape for the season.

"That's a bad place to have training camp," Parcells said. "No disrespect to the city, but we were practicing in the Alamodome. You're like a mole. You're in the dark all day."

The coaches' offices were in the dome. They would arrive early in the morning, several hours before sunrise, and by the time they left it was so late at night that it already had been dark for hours. "You feel like you're living in the Lincoln Tunnel," Parcells said. "And when you tried to take your team outside to practice, which I tried to do a couple of times, it's a hundred degrees. It's pretty humid down there. It's a tough place to practice football for very long. You got a lot of cramps, pulled muscles; you got a lot of things that aren't conducive to developing your team."

Jones had good news for Parcells. The next year the Cowboys would hold camp in Oxnard, California. It was the site the Raiders used when they were playing in Los Angeles. Jones had taken the team there in 2001. It was a great setup in Oxnard.

Players and coaches were housed in the Residence Inn adjacent to the practice fields. It was a two-minute walk from their rooms to the locker room and field. It was self-contained. There's a huge grassy area used as a parking lot for the fans, and the Cowboys draw huge crowds. The Rams were in St. Louis. The Raiders had moved back to Oakland. The Cowboys were adopted as Southern California's team. Best news for Jones: No bitching from Parcells. He loved Oxnard.

"It got up into the low eighties in the afternoon," Parcells said. "At seven at night, it was back in the low sixties. It was a perfect place. We could run a lot. Our players were not dehydrating a lot. You could practice pretty hard. I liked it out there."

There's nothing Parcells likes more than running his players through rugged two-a-day practices. If he was coaching today, he would have a hard time with the limited practice rules that were part of the 2011 collective bargaining agreement, in which camp practices were cut down to one per day.

That is quite different from the camp Parcells ran when he was named Giants head coach in 1983 and the team spent the summer getting ready for the season at Pace University in suburban Pleasantville, New York. The players called one of Parcells's drills the "Pace Party." This was an invitation-only event and nobody wanted to be on the guest list. Parcells matched the guards against the inside linebackers. Tackles on defensive ends. Tight ends on outside linebackers.

"Man-on-man, head-on-head," defensive end Leonard Marshall said. "You knocked the living shit out of each other for twenty minutes. It wasn't fun. Trust me. I walked around with a bottle of Tylenol the first two weeks of training camp."

Jones actually gave Parcells a headache when he told him he was being pressured by his sponsors to move training camp back to San Antonio. "Ford sells more trucks in Texas, and they didn't like seeing their signs up in California. Dr Pepper is big in Texas. In the Latin community it's big," Jones said.

"Now let me get this straight, Jerry. We got a $2 billion corporation and we're worried about selling fucking soda?" Parcells said.

Jones laughed.

"You don't know how right you are," he said. "If you can sell soda, you can sell potato chips. If you can sell potato chips, you can sell hamburgers. If you can sell hamburgers, you can sell French fries."

Parcells listened in amazement. "He had a whole litany of things that were derived from selling Dr Pepper," Parcells said. "That's part of my learning curve. You know what is ironic? They went back to San Antonio for a while, but now they go to California every year."

* * *

During Parcells's four years in Dallas, Jones looked out for him financially. One day he came to him and offered to make him part of a business transaction he was excited about.

"I want to put you in a deal," Jones said.

"I don't want to go into any deal," Parcells said.

Jones insisted, but Parcells refused to sign. Jones was buying a bunch of Papa John's pizza stores in Texas and gave Parcells a share at no cost to him. "I don't want to do this," Parcells said. "I don't deserve this."

He was gone from the Cowboys for a few years when a check arrived in the mail. He opened it. There was a check for $100,000 from Papa John's. Parcells felt guilty but cashed the check. Not much later, same thing. Another check for $100,000. The pizza business was booming. This went on for a couple of years.

"It was pretty good," Parcells said.

* * *

Parcells has only good things to say about Jones now, but they did clash over "the player," which is what Parcells called mercurial and controversial wide receiver Terrell Owens.

Never *Terrell* or *Owens*, and certainly not *T.O.*

The player. Lowercase.

Parcells didn't call Lawrence Taylor "LT," but at least he called him "Lawrence" or "Taylor." Despite LT's drug problems, Parcells never gave up on him. He also had a genuine affection for him, which he never developed for T.O.

Owens was a Hall of Fame receiver, but in Parcells's mind, he dropped too many passes and was just a bit too much in love with himself. "I love me some me," was Owens's calling card, but it was not what Parcells preferred to hear from his players. Owens didn't have off-the-field issues, he did not have a drug problem, he wasn't out late at night; he just wasn't Parcells's kind of guy.

Parcells wanted no part of Owens. He didn't want him on the team. Jones did. After Philadelphia coach Andy Reid twice suspended Owens in 2005, the Eagles cut him after the season. That didn't make much of an impact on Parcells until Jones told him he wanted to sign him. When Parcells took the job with the Cowboys, he knew that Jones owned final say. It was part of the deal. The owner was the general manager. That was different from what had transpired in New England. When James Orthwein hired Parcells in 1993, he became the savior. Season ticket sales soared. Orthwein needed Parcells and was thrilled to give him total control.

Jones came to Parcells and told him he wanted to sign Owens. Jones asked Parcells if he was close to anybody around Owens. Parcells always had a good relationship with Drew Rosenhaus, who was now representing Owens. He offered to hook them up even though he was against signing him. "I'm the one who got Rosenhaus to meet with Jerry," Parcells said. "I knew they were going to talk. I didn't know what was going to happen. I was a little surprised when they signed him."

Parcells was not part of the conversation when Jones spoke to Rosenhaus at the combine in Indianapolis. One month later, Jones signed Owens to a three-year, $25 million contract, which was startling if only because Owens disrespected the Cowboys' storied history when he was with the 49ers by running out to midfield after each of his two touchdown catches in a game in 2000 and posing with his arms up in the air on the blue star at Texas Stadium. The first incident happened without any repercussions. When Emmitt Smith scored for Dallas, he ran out to the star to defend the Cowboys' turf and slammed the ball down, as if driving a stake into the ground. When Owens then scored again, he once again sprinted from the end zone to the star and started to pose when Cowboys safety George Teague came over and leveled him.

Now Jones was bringing this knucklehead to Dallas?

Parcells was in Florida and didn't show up at Owens's introductory press conference. It was Jones sitting by his side. The owner tried to sell all's-well-with-Parcells, but it was impossible to buy. "Bill is very much on the page here, very much," Jones said. "We're not just in the business here of walking problems through the door to create challenges. We've got enough on our own."

One month into the season, Owens was taken from his home by ambulance to the hospital. He was recovering from a broken hand and taking Vicodin for the pain. He claims he had an allergic reaction to the medication but reports soon surfaced that he attempted to commit suicide, which he vehemently denied.

"It's very unfortunate for the reports to go from an allergic reaction to a definite suicide attempt," Owens said.

Before Owens was able to speak for himself, Parcells held his usual midday daily press briefing. He was overwhelmed with questions about Owens's condition. He appeared dispassionate and uncaring as he brushed off the inquiries, once again never referring to Owens by name, just as "the player."

Parcells had no patience for the constant drama surrounding the ultimate drama queen.

"When I find out what the hell is going on, you will know," Parcells said. "Until then, I'm not getting interrogated for no reason."

It was obvious he refused to mention Owens's name, although he denies it. "That's another bunch of bullshit," he said. "Here's what happened. The day he had this incident where they had to take him to the hospital, a suicide or something, I don't know where the guy is. I don't know where he is. All I know is what I am being told without any corroboration. I'm finally in this conference and I'm being badgered about what is going on. I said, 'Look I don't know where the player is.' And then they went and said I called him 'the player.' Did I? I guess so. But I wasn't doing it in that context. I don't know where the guy is and I don't know what has happened. What do you want from me? I don't have anything. That's the truth. It's just the same bullshit."

Parcells was gone from Dallas after the 2006 season. One year with Owens was one year too many.

"You try to make things work," Parcells said. "You know, he wasn't a bad kid. He didn't use bad language. It's a complicated story. He has a narcissistic disorder. He can't help it. You see traits and you know."

As far as Parcells was concerned, Owens was not dependable. If he was told to run a route at twelve yards, he might run it at eight. If his assignment was to block, he might just run by the defender. He wasn't consistent catching the ball.

"Whatever you put in there, it's not enough," Parcells said. "I've had a couple of guys like that. He has a hole in his bucket."

Parcells did not leave the Cowboys because of Owens. He retired from coaching, and this time it was final, after a heartbreaking loss to the Seattle Seahawks in the wild card round of the playoffs. Dallas made the playoffs by finishing second to the Eagles in the NFC East with a 9-7 record. Parcells felt if they could get by the Seahawks, he could get his team into the NFC Championship Game and then potentially the Super Bowl. If they beat the Seahawks, they would next play in Chicago and face quarterback Rex Grossman. Parcells had defeated Joe Montana three times in the playoffs. He would have come up with a defense to eat up Grossman, an inferior quarterback.

He had switched to Romo earlier in the season, and the kid was now on a roll. Parcells had kept him in mothballs for three years, and he was gaining confidence and swagger each week. He won five of his first six starts, reminiscent of the success Brady had in New England immediately after he, too, took over for Bledsoe. But the Cowboys stumbled down the stretch, unusual for a Parcells team, and lost three of their last four. Even so, Parcells was optimistic going into the playoffs.

He felt even better when Romo drove the Cowboys from their 28 to a fourth down at the Seahawks 2 with just 1:19 left in the game. The scoreboard: Seahawks 21, Cowboys 20. Parcells sent in veteran kicker Martin Gramatica to attempt a chip-shot 20-yard field goal, the same distance as an extra point. The Cowboys were poised to go ahead by two and then keep Matt Hasselbeck out of field goal range and move on to the divisional round at Soldier Field. Seattle had already used all three of its time-outs.

The great coaching career of Bill Parcells ended on an aborted field goal attempt. It ended because Romo, the holder, dropped a perfect snap, then had no choice but to rise up and run with the ball. He sprinted to his left and was stopped short of the goal line. Parcells had been victimized by sudden finishes in his coaching career. Flipper Anderson of the Rams ended the Giants' season in 1989 when he scored on a 30-yard pass from Jim Everett barely one minute into overtime and kept running right up the tunnel and nearly out of the door into the Giants Stadium parking lot.

This was worse. Parcells had poured every bit of his being into getting the Cowboys this far. He was sixty-five years old. The thought of starting the cycle all over again just to get the Cowboys back into position where a chip-shot field goal could win a playoff game was exhausting. The roster evaluation, the combine, free agency, draft preparation, organized team activities, minicamp, training camp, the marathon season of sixteen games—he could not deal with it. He didn't know from what source the energy would be provided.

"I love Coach. I love Bill," Romo said.

Two weeks and two days after Romo dropped the snap, Parcells retired from coaching again.

He told Jones, "Just the realization of all the things that you got to do to get back to that chance, there is so much involved. It's really hard. It's time to go."

"I was afraid this could happen," Jones said.

Jones is so persuasive he can sell ice cream on an ice-cold day at the ballpark, but he had no luck convincing Parcells to change his mind.

"I couldn't talk him out of it," Jones said. "I wanted him to stay so bad."

The Cowboys were on the verge of being Super Bowl contenders. Jones pleaded with Parcells for one more year. No go.

"I don't have anybody that I've ever enjoyed working with any more than Bill," Jones said. "He was that much of a joy to work with."

Parcells departed Dallas and would split his time between his home in Saratoga, New York, close to the racetrack, and his apartment in Jupiter, Florida, where he and Belichick for years lived two floors apart. Parcells would become executive vice president of football operations for the Dolphins late in the 2007 season, but when Wayne Huizenga sold the team to Stephen Ross just thirteen months after Parcells arrived, he was faced with the prospect of a new owner for the fourth time. Parcells had signed a four-year, $16 million contract with the Dolphins that contained a clause allowing him to opt out if Huizenga sold the team and still collect his contract in full. Early in the 2010 season, Parcells departed Miami with his money.

This time, he surely was done with football for good...until another high-profile opportunity came his way. Sean Payton, the protégé he treated like a son, was suspended by Roger Goodell for the entire 2012 season after his involvement in the Bountygate scandal with the Saints. Payton asked Parcells if he would run his team in his absence. Parcells gave it serious consideration. He didn't want to coach again but didn't want to turn his back on Payton. He ultimately decided he just could not do it. He was likely to make the Hall of Fame in 2013, and a return to coaching would restart the clock on the five-year waiting period.

Parcells lived to regret leaving the Cowboys one year too soon, just as he'd left the Patriots one year too soon. He had accumulated great young talent with the Patriots but let his distaste for Kraft overwhelm him and force him out. By the 2007 season, with Parcells concentrating on his horses and Jones hiring Wade Phillips to replace him, Romo was forced to grow up as a quarterback, and he led Dallas to a 13-3 season and the number 1 seed in the NFC.

Phillips ran a loose ship. There is little chance Parcells would have allowed Romo out of the country to vacation in Cabo with his girlfriend one week before a playoff game. There is also no chance Parcells would have allowed Jones to distribute tickets to the NFC Championship Game to his players in the days before the Giants game in the divisional round. The Cowboys first needed to beat New York, of course, to get to the Championship Game. Jones got ahead of himself by giving each of his players two tickets and it cost the Cowboys. New York coach Tom Coughlin found out about it and informed his players right before the game. Big Blue already hated the Cowboys. This gave them another reason to get fired up and Coughlin made sure to use it as motivation.

After R. W. McQuarters intercepted Romo in the end zone with nine seconds left to clinch the victory, Coughlin gathered his players around him in the locker room and extended his right arm as if he were holding something valuable.

"Jerry just sent the tickets over," Coughlin said as his players roared. "So, we're all set."

* * *

That 2007 team was the one Parcells would have taken to the Super Bowl. He made an emotional decision too quickly after the loss to the Seahawks.

"I regret it, too," Jones said. "We might have gotten that done with Bill. I don't want to take anything away from Wade, but I know this team we had the next year with Romo playing at the level he was playing, it is really one of my biggest disappointments not to have gone on to the Super Bowl. We had the home field. We had it all."

Parcells was close to Jerry, and he really enjoyed working with Stephen Jones. He truly wanted to win a Super Bowl for them and become the first coach to win a Super Bowl with two teams. "They are good people," Parcells said. "I'll tell you what separated them from people in this business that I've run into that weren't good. When they tell you something, they're doing it. They will stick by their word. Jerry did so many nice things for people. I don't want to say he is so misunderstood, but he's really a benevolent guy. That's a nice trait to have when you help people."

Parcells made the Hall of Fame in 2013. Jones joined him in 2017. Parcells learned about marketing from Jones and how selling soda is still important to a billion-dollar football operation. But what did Jones learn from Parcells? He discovered it was okay to disagree with his coach as long as it was not based on ego and a competition to get the credit. Parcells believed in "I go by what I see" in making personnel decisions and didn't let emotion interfere with his judgment. That allowed Jones to cut Dez Bryant, one of his favorites, when he trusted his eyes and saw that Bryant no longer was able to gain separation from cornerbacks and that he dropped too many passes.

Parcells has stayed involved in football in a mentoring role with many of his former assistants who went on to become head coaches, including Payton and Minnesota's Mike Zimmer. Payton and Zimmer were on Parcells's staff with the Cowboys. He also had an impact on Stephen Jones, who is in charge of the team's football operation. "I just learned so much from him," Stephen Jones said. "We just had a great relationship. It was important for Jerry to make that work. We came up with a great structure. I had such a tremendous amount of respect for Bill."

There were times when Stephen took Parcells's side when he disagreed with Jerry.

"What! Goddamn it!" Jerry screamed at Stephen.

Then Stephen and Jerry would get into it.

Parcells left the Cowboys wanting more from him. This time, he had nothing left to give.

CHAPTER SIX

Teammates to the End

Robert Newhouse, the old man in the dorm room, warned Tony Dorsett, Ron Springs, and Dennis Thurman that the road trip was a really bad idea. It was too late and too far and practice the next morning was too early.

They were sitting around in their first-floor suite at training camp at Cal Lutheran University in Thousand Oaks, California, a beautiful town set in the middle of the Santa Monica Mountains just twelve miles from the Pacific Ocean and fifty miles northwest of Los Angeles. The daily seventy-five degrees with a light breeze was perfect to help get through the grind of camp. Back home in Dallas, the temperature would flirt with an unbearable one hundred degrees every day in July and August, so the players were thrilled to get out of the Texas heat during the hottest time of the year, and many of them were also thrilled to leave their wives and girlfriends behind for an extended time with the boys and some new girls.

The Thousand Oaks nightlife didn't quite measure up to the bars and strip clubs in Dallas. It was lacking for excitement for young men in their twenties overloaded with testosterone and looking to blow off a little steam after another round of Tom Landry's two-a-days and evening meetings.

The El Torito restaurant on Moorpark Road in the early 1980s was a good pit stop for a quick meal and a margarita, but the bar scene left something to be desired. One of the Cowboys' most high-profile players had a little honey tucked away in the hills, and he checked into the Best Western when he felt the need to break curfew to seek female companionship. One time he was spotted racing to his car in the hotel parking lot at 8 a.m., scrambling to get back to campus, sign in for breakfast (the Cowboys took attendance), and get dressed and ready for morning practice without Landry or his chief lieutenant and offensive line coach Jim Myers realizing he was even gone. Other than the moral issue of players cheating on their wives and girlfriends, it was hard to blame grown men for wanting to escape and sleep on a mattress with a little more firmness than thin cardboard. Each summer the Cowboys would return, and it was big news in an otherwise sleepy town. The local women anticipated their arrival and the players didn't disappoint.

Dorsett, Thurman, and Springs didn't have anything in mind other than escaping dorm life for a few hours. Newhouse looked at his watch as his teammates finished planning their itinerary. It was 11 p.m., and Myers had already checked to make sure all four of the players in Newhouse's suite were safe and sound if not tucked in. Except for Newhouse, they had been waiting Myers out before busting loose.

"We called it going over the wall," Dorsett said.

Dorsett, Springs, and Thurman needed action and were headed to Los Angeles. Maybe it would be a bar that Thurman knew from his college days at the University of Southern California. Maybe one of them would use their connections to stop by and visit Hugh Hefner and his bunnies at the Playboy Mansion. Newhouse tried to convince his younger teammates they should stay put. That had about as much chance of working as Landry's plan when he actually rotated Roger Staubach and Craig Morton on every play in a 1971 loss in Chicago.

One by one, they considered Newhouse's wisdom and thanked him for his concern, and they were off. "House" was in his early thirties, four years older than Dorsett and six years older than Thurman and Springs.

"Y'all go ahead," he said.

Thurman was from Los Angeles, so this was a home game for him. He was their GPS. They snuck out the exit by their corner first-floor room and pretty soon were racing along 101 South to 405 South toward Los Angeles to hit up a few spots on Thurman's to-do list. "When you think about it, most of the time when we were going over the wall, if you were going to LA, you got a pretty damn good drive," Dorsett said. "Then try to get back before everybody starts waking up. It was quite a challenge. But we had a lot of fun."

His favorite place to stop by?

"Hugh Hefner's house," he said.

No doubt.

Soon after his roommates left, Newhouse put his head on the pillow.

There was a knock on the door.

"Jim Myers doubled back around and House was the only one there, and we got busted," Thurman said.

When they returned to campus at 3 a.m., they each found a note on the door from Myers.

"See Coach Landry when you get back."

Uh-oh.

According to Cowboys legend, Ed "Too Tall" Jones, at six foot nine the tallest player in team history, once felt the need for nocturnal entertainment. When he returned and pulled into his parking spot by the dorm, there was some stirring and he feared he was going to get caught. So he did the only logical thing. He stood by a tree with his arms stretched out like branches. Even if he got caught—and he didn't—Myers would have had to let him slide based solely on creativity.

Landry didn't burden his players with a long list of rules, but if you broke one of them, he was going to make you pay. A player could reduce the ensuing fine for breaking curfew as long as he satisfied one condition: He had to walk the fifty yards from his dorm to Landry's dorm by crossing a small campus street, knock on Landry's door, and inform him he had just returned to campus and been caught by Myers.

"You had to wake him up, dude," Thurman said.

The image of a half-asleep and pissed-off Landry standing in the doorway of his dorm room in his pajamas with a droopy sleeping cap with a pom-pom is precious. At least they found out he didn't sleep in his fedora.

Sheepishly, they had to knock on the door.

"Dennis, is that you?" Landry said.

How did he know?

"Yes, Coach," he said.

"I'm disappointed in you," Landry said. "Now go to sleep, okay."

The next morning at practice, Myers grabbed Newhouse outside the huddle and pointed at Dorsett, Thurman, and Springs. They could not stop laughing.

"They thought they were going to outfox the silver fox," Myers said.

* * *

One of the enduring qualities of football, as it desperately attempts to avoid being taken down by the concussion crisis, is the teamwork and leadership it develops, as well as lifelong bonds. It's a brotherhood that is strengthened even further if a team wins a championship. "A blood kinship" is how Bill Parcells describes the closeness of his players who have won a ring together.

Dorsett and Newhouse were on the Cowboys when they beat the Broncos in Super Bowl XII and lost to the Steelers the following year in Super Bowl XIII. Thurman was a rookie for the loss to the Steelers, and Springs arrived the next year in 1979. They never did all win a championship together, but they were as tight as brothers. Their dorm room, all the way down the hall and in the corner, was the heartbeat of the training camp.

"It was one of the funniest rooms," Dorsett said. "We talked a lot of smack. A lot of jive. It was the place everybody wanted to go. If there was a room that could make you feel better about being in Thousand Oaks, then that was the place to come."

"Everybody wanted to hang out in our room," Thurman said.

They began rooming together in 1980, and the living arrangement remained intact over the course of four training camps back when training camp was six weeks. Put the four years together, and they spent nearly half a year living together in separate accommodations. Enter the Newhouse Suite at your own risk of being teased. The living room was in the middle with a nice-sized couch, a few chairs, and a television. There were two bedrooms, and each had its own bathroom. Newhouse and Thurman were on one side, and Dorsett and Springs were on the other. There was a small refrigerator and a telephone on each side. (Cell phones were somebody's imagination.) That did it for modern conveniences.

"It was training camp," Thurman said. "You were supposed to be miserable."

By the time Staubach retired after the 1979 season, Dorsett was the biggest star on the Cowboys. He was the Heisman Trophy winner from Aliquippa, Pennsylvania, the home of Mike Ditka before him and Darrelle Revis after him. They all went to Pitt. The Cowboys traded up to take Dorsett with the second overall pick in 1977 and he became the only Hall of Famer in that draft. He was magic. His big eyes earned him the nickname "Hawk." He also had a big personality and a big smile.

Thurman was a cornerback who would move to safety later in his career. He was a huge Lakers fans, and to get under his skin, the players called him "Nate," for Nate Thurmond, the center for the San Francisco Warriors. Newhouse lost his starting fullback job to the more versatile Springs, but Landry kept him around for his special teams skills and leadership. Springs was a tailback but knew he would never take carries away from Dorsett, so he was resigned to playing as an undersized fullback, getting a half-dozen touches a game and maybe even being allowed to throw a left-handed option pass every now and then. His nickname was "Idi," because he looked like the Ugandan dictator Idi Amin. The nickname stuck after Springs showed up for a road trip dressed in a kanzu robe.

"We would play cards, play dominoes, and talk shit," Thurman said.

They were back in college but had only one book to study: Landry's thick offensive playbook for Dorsett, Newhouse, and Springs and his complicated defensive schemes put together in a binder for Thurman.

Newhouse, Thurman, Dorsett, and Springs were supposed to grow old together, attend team reunions, hang out drinking beer on the porch and tell jokes about Landry and how they spent their nights breaking curfew. Even if Landry appeared ice-cold in public, all the players eventually warmed up to him. He was a Christian man who never thought badly of anybody except Eagles coach Buddy Ryan. He was pure of mind and his players loved him. It pained him to cut a player, which was why he never allowed himself to become emotionally attached, as it deeply hurt him to end a dream. When Drew Pearson was behind the wheel in a horrific car accident in 1984 that killed his younger brother and ended his own career with the Cowboys, every time he awakened and opened his eyes in his room at Presbyterian Hospital in Dallas, Landry was by his bedside. Even as his family never gave Pearson the reassurance that they didn't blame him for Carey Pearson's death, Landry was the one to comfort him. The funeral took place back in Pearson's native New Jersey, but he was still in the hospital and unable to attend. Landry was with him to ease his pain.

"I loved Coach Landry," Pearson said.

Landry was the absentminded professor. He butchered players' names and was oblivious to the drug culture that swept through the NFL in the '70s and '80s. There were wild and unsubstantiated stories of abundant cocaine use by the Cowboys in the mideighties, prompting some to call them "South America's Team."

When free agent safety Bill Bates from Tennessee made the team as a rookie in 1983, he quickly earned the respect and admiration of the veterans for his big hits and disregard for his own body on special teams.

"The players like him so much they call him 'The Master,'" Landry raved.

The media, already aware of the nickname and its origin, tried to hold in their giggles, knowing that "Master" combined with Bates's last name was what his teammates had in mind.

But Landry's thought process did not take him there, and it never crossed his mind that the nickname meant anything other than that the veterans were fond of Bates's attitude and skills.

Bates stood out in a classic photo in 1985. Thurman was the leader of the defensive backs, and the group nicknamed themselves "Thurman's Thieves," to bring attention to their skills intercepting passes. The *Dallas Morning News* commissioned the group to pose dressed as gangsters sitting around a table. The defensive backs comprised seven African-Americans and Bates. When many of them showed up in the locker room for a Monday night game in St. Louis wearing the gangster hats they had purchased that afternoon in a mall attached to the team hotel, it caused friction with some of the conservative white players who questioned their commitment to the team. Thurman's Thieves wanted to win, but they also wanted to have some fun. Landry was oblivious to the turmoil around him.

* * *

It was not hard to imagine at the time a scene thirty years later with Dorsett flipping burgers on the grill, a drink in the hands of Walls, Springs, and Newhouse, as they hit their roaring sixties and made their way to their seventies, as they argued about who looked better.

They planned to be friends for life.

The plan didn't work.

Two of them didn't make it, and a third was struggling.

Football is a cruel sport. It can take away a man's mind. Life is cruel, too, and can take away middle-aged men way before their time.

Newhouse was the first to retire after the 1983 season. He

played his entire career with Dallas. Springs was waived by Landry right before the 1985 season after he was arrested for an altercation at a strip club—Landry, for sure, had never seen the inside of the Million Dollar Saloon—then played two years with the Bucs and retired. Thurman was cut by the Cowboys before the 1988 season and played one year with the Cardinals, who were coached by Gene Stallings, his former defensive backs coach with the Cowboys. He later coached for Stallings in Phoenix, the first stop on a long coaching career. Dorsett was gradually phased out by Landry after Herschel Walker arrived from the USFL in 1986 and was traded to the Broncos in 1988 for just a fifth-round draft choice. He played one season in Denver and then suffered a career-ending knee injury in training camp in 1989.

Newhouse went to work in the front office in player programs for the Cowboys. After finishing their careers elsewhere, Dorsett moved back into his house in Dallas, and Springs returned and bought a house with his family in Dallas. Thurman entered the coaching profession and worked for the Cardinals, USC, the Ravens, the Jets, and the Bills, but maintained a residence in Dallas. As happens with longtime friends, once their jobs separated them, the daily contact was over. They weren't sharing a dorm room, a locker room, training camp meals, a sideline, or daily jokes.

They never stopped caring about one another. Springs was the first to die in 2011 at the age of just fifty-four. Three years later, Newhouse passed away at sixty-four. Dorsett has been battling severe memory loss, which he attributes to absorbing too many hits to the head in his twelve-year career as one of the most electrifying runners in NFL history. That leaves Thurman to be thankful for his health but wonder what happened to his three best friends.

too. I will forget my keys, or a book, you walk right out of your house. For Tony, he may have gone to a restaurant a thousand times, and he starts driving there and he will forget his way. That doesn't happen to me. He's dealing with something a little bit different than I am dealing with. I just think I'm getting old. You have so much on your mind, you walk out of the room and forget to get your drink."

Springs died a complicated and heartbreaking death. He was diagnosed with diabetes in 1990 when he was thirty-four years old. More than fifteen years later, his condition had severely deteriorated. He had his right foot amputated. He was on the kidney transplant list for years. He was undergoing dialysis four hours a day, three days a week, and doctors said he couldn't wait more than another couple of years. He had no quality of life with failed kidneys. His son Shawn, a former first-round pick by the Seahawks who was now playing for the Washington Redskins, was a match and volunteered to give his father a kidney. It would have ended his playing career, and Ron would not let him do it.

* * *

In their days in Thousand Oaks, cornerback Everson Walls's room was two doors down the hall from the Dorsett-Springs-Newhouse-Thurman Suite. When he wasn't hanging out in his room with safety Michael Downs, Walls was with Dorsett and his crew. Walls is from Dallas and went undrafted after a stellar career at Grambling State University. He signed with the Cowboys as a rookie free agent in 1981 and emerged from a training camp that started off with nearly seventy rookies when there was no limit on how many players a team could take to camp. Gil Brandt, the personnel director, believed in bringing in quantity to find quality. The more players he brought in, the better the chance to uncover a diamond.

Walls was a gem on and off the field. He would often show his new teammates around Dallas to help them get comfortable. His mother was the team mom. He led the NFL as a rookie with 11 interceptions. He was the closest of the Cowboys in the back of the end zone to Dwight Clark when he made "The Catch," which sent the 49ers to their first Super Bowl in 1981. He accepted his responsibility with dignity but also pointed out that he had 2 interceptions of Joe Montana and a fumble recovery in the game. He is the only cornerback in NFL history to lead the league in interceptions three times. When Jimmy Johnson cut him after the 1989 season, Parcells signed him with the Giants and Walls saved their Super Bowl XXV victory over the Bills with a brilliant open-field tackle of the elusive Thurman Thomas on Buffalo's final drive of the game.

He was a finalist for the 2018 Pro Football Hall of Fame in his twentieth and final year on the ballot, but he appreciated the honor of making it that far in the process, even if in his heart he felt qualified to have been selected years earlier. Just like giving up the Clark touchdown, he forgot about the Hall of Fame disappointment within days. When the 49ers honored Clark—who had been diagnosed with ALS, better known as Lou Gehrig's disease—at halftime of a 2017 game against Dallas, Walls was the only Cowboy player from that era who made the trip to Santa Clara to support Clark along with thirty member of the 49ers from their 1981 championship team. They had become friendly in the years since The Catch, the equivalent of the Bobby Thomson–Ralph Branca friendship after the "Shot Heard 'Round the World," when Thomson's home run off Branca in the bottom of the ninth inning of a one-game playoff won the National League pennant for the New York Giants over the Brooklyn Dodgers.

Walls and Clark bonded when Clark told him that he was getting paid by Kodak for the use of a picture of The Catch, which led to Walls filing a lawsuit and being compensated as well. They made appearances together over the years and Walls texted with him when Clark revealed the ALS diagnosis. Walls felt compelled to make the trip to California on "Dwight Clark Day."

"I was afraid to talk to him at first, not knowing how he'd be," Walls told the *Dallas Morning News*. "The last time I had talked to him he was still healthy, walking his dogs. But we talked briefly and I gave him my love. I can't be mad about that play anymore. Whatever our journey, that dude is right there with me."

Clark passed away on June 4, 2018.

* * *

All of Walls's accomplishments as a Cowboys player were overshadowed by his kindness and love for Springs when he showed what it meant to be a teammate. Springs had no life at the age of fifty and no kidney donor. Walls was forty-seven with a long life to live. He wanted his friend by his side. He was tested to see if he would be an acceptable donor. He was a perfect match. He waited to break the good news to Springs to avoid being pressured into having the surgery immediately. He knew how much Springs looked forward to regaining the simple things in life such as being able to pee on his own. Walls donated one of his kidneys to Springs in 2007. That left him with one kidney for himself for the rest of his life. If anything went wrong with it, he wouldn't have a backup. It was a risk he was willing to take to give his friend back his life. Once Walls found out his O-positive blood type matched Springs's and he fit the other criteria needed for a transplant, he gave Springs the greatest gift imaginable.

"If you saw your friend wasting away, what would you do?" Walls said.

Dorsett was a nervous wreck. Two teammates. Two surgeries. Too risky. "Tony is so scared," Walls said. "He just wants to close his eyes and when they open up, everybody be okay."

Walls's mother tried to talk him out of giving up his kidney, but he would not listen. "You want me to save it for you?" he joked, trying to ease her concern. The families of Walls and Springs were close. Their wives were inseparable. Their kids were best friends. Walls's son introduced Springs's younger daughter to the man she wound up marrying.

In his thirteen-year career, Walls never once had surgery. This was the first surgery of his life. It was a big one.

The surgery took place on February 28, 2007. The kidney transplant went perfectly.

"Walls, I appreciate the kidney," Springs said afterward. "This kidney is a motherfucker. I'm pissing all over the place."

Walls and Springs became the faces of the true meaning of friendship and teammates—it's the first time one teammate had ever donated an organ to another. They formed the Gift for Life Foundation to educate people about ways to prevent chronic kidney disease and to dispel concerns about the living donor process. The Cowboys honored them as co-captains for the opening game of the 2007 season at Texas Stadium against the New York Giants.

The diabetes had deprived Springs of mobility in his hands. They were curled up in balls. On October 12, 2007, he went back to Medical City Dallas Hospital, the same hospital where

and friends, lost his father when he was eight years old, and ever since then he'd had a difficult time dealing with death. He had a twenty-nine-year-old nephew who died and Thurman could not walk by the open casket after experiencing that with his father. Thurman couldn't bring himself to visit Springs in the hospital after he went into the coma. The Ron Springs he wanted to remember was the instigator in training camp, the comedian in the locker room who once stood up on a bench at the decrepit team facility on Forest Lane on the day popular safety Benny Barnes was cut, and led a revival meeting.

"How long are we going to take this?" Springs shouted.

"Not long, brother Ron!" his teammates chanted.

This went on for a few minutes until Landry walked by, shot a dagger in Springs's direction. Springs then jumped off the bench and announced, "The meeting is over."

In the years when Springs was suffering from diabetes, Thurman made sure to stop by his old friend's house to check up on him. Thurman was an assistant coach with the Ravens, and Springs would tell him to pack some "Ravens gear" for him before he came back to Dallas. It was difficult for Thurman to go a long period without seeing Springs and then show up at his house to find him in a wheelchair.

"Here was a guy, when he first got to Dallas, Ron could do about anything he wanted athletically," Thurman said. "We would go play basketball, and he was a heckuva basketball player. We would go to the batting cages to hit baseballs, and he was a helluva baseball player. He could swing a bat. Then to go see him physically deteriorating was very difficult for all of us."

Thurman couldn't bear to visit him in the hospital just to see Springs lying in his bed. Every part of Springs's body was working except his mind. He started off bald when he went in for the procedure, and even his hair grew back.

"There was a couple of times I wanted to go by and see him," Thurman said. "I just couldn't pull myself to do it. I didn't want to remember Ron like that. I don't want to see people that I am close to, people that I love...I have an image of them standing, walking, laughing, joking. I would rather that be my last memory rather than seeing them lay motionless in a casket."

It was just past the twenty-year anniversary of Walls's Super Bowl–saving tackle of Thurman Thomas that a teammate from that New York Giants team killed himself. Walls and safety Dave Duerson had become good friends when Walls played for the Cowboys and Duerson played for the Chicago Bears and it was a bonus when Parcells signed them both in 1990. It was shocking news on February 17, 2011, when Duerson shot himself in the chest and died. It was later revealed, after his family followed through on his request and donated his brain, that Duerson suffered from CTE.

There was more bad news three months later.

Springs died of a heart attack on May 12, 2011, more than three and a half years after he went into the coma. Thurman traveled to Dallas for the funeral but couldn't walk in front of the casket. "I don't go to look at people in the casket anymore. It's a lasting image. I don't want that to be the last memory I have," he said.

Dorsett knows that Springs did his best to keep the big guys off him as his lead blocker. It's usually a thankless job. Daryl Johnston will never make the Hall of Fame, but Emmitt Smith might not have made it, might not have passed Walter Payton to be the NFL all-time leading rusher, if Moose hadn't cleared the way for him.

"Ron, that was my guy," Dorsett said.

Newhouse had a huge heart and was not only the wisest man on the team but also one of the most popular. He had massive forty-four-inch thighs—they required special tailoring for his uniform and clothes to fit—and that made him tough to bring down. When he got rolling, he was like a bowling ball, although he was best known for throwing a 29-yard option pass for a touchdown to Golden Richards to clinch Super Bowl XII.

"Newhouse was always the guy that knew little subtle things about you," Walls said. "He would tease the heck out of you. He was the guy who brings up all the inconvenient truths. No matter how good you were, he always remembered that moment that you messed up because he was around longer than anybody. You could be talking about a player that you revered as a kid and Newhouse would say, 'Yeah, I played with him.'"

Although Roger Goodell points to statistics that indicate the average football player has a longer life expectancy than the average male, it's not an easy sell. "I guess as football players we have become a little bit adapted to the fact that the guys don't hang around long like your uncles and grandfathers and all of those guys," Walls said. "There are always some kind of issues with former players and former teammates. It always seems to affect the ones that were the better players because they got all the playing time. They gave so much. They were utilized so much. It's a Catch-22. We depend on them the most, therefore we utilize them the most, and therefore they are the ones most affected by it and the ones you lose the earliest."

Newhouse suffered a stroke in 2010 and never bounced back. He was in the Mayo Clinic in Rochester, Minnesota, in need of a heart transplant, but he was physically not strong enough to receive one. He died on July 22, 2014.

"From a personal standpoint, it makes you think about your own mortality," said Doug Cosbie, who was in Springs's draft class and played tight end for ten seasons for the Cowboys.

"These are teammates. It makes you reflect life is short and you're not twenty-eight anymore. You are getting old. For me, it's difficult. You went through so much with them. It's like losing a family member."

Thurman was starting his sixth season as an assistant coach with the Jets when he got word right before training camp that Newhouse had passed. He texted with the Newhouse family.

"It was hard," he said. "You remember Newhouse's laughter. He had a big hearty laugh."

It took him back to the dorm room in Thousand Oaks, where all they had to worry about was making Landry's cut and sticking around another year. "It was a fun time but also a learning time," Thurman said. "There were times we had deep discussions about football and life after football and things we wanted to do. Newhouse didn't really know what he wanted to do when football was over. Dorsett didn't, either. I talked about wanting to get into broadcasting because that's what I wanted to do. I didn't know I was going to end up in coaching. Ron thought he would work with kids. We didn't really end up doing the things we talked about at that time. It's interesting how life takes you in different directions."

Newhouse retired after the '83 season just as Dorsett, Springs, and Thurman were in the prime years of their careers. The following season, in 1984, it was clear to Landry that Danny White had lost his grip on the team, and he opened the year with Gary Hogeboom as the Cowboys' starting quarterback. Landry eventually switched, but their record streak of twenty consecutive winning seasons that started in 1965 came to an end.

The physical problems of former players are much worse now than any single loss of a game, as their bodies break down from years of playing a brutal collision sport.

As Dorsett said: "It is what it is. If you play as long as I did, you are going to have something wrong with you." He stayed in touch with Adriane for many years, but that changed. "As time moves on, people move on," Dorsett said. "I have my own issues."

It was not supposed to be this way.

CHAPTER SEVEN

Jerry Jones, General Manager

In 1985, Jerry Jones invested $250,000 for a stake in a series of fledgling cell phone companies in six cities before the indispensable gadgets became just as much a part of daily life as socks and jocks.

Keys, wallet, cell phone.

Check.

Okay, ready to go.

For those with lots of disposable income to invest, there had been a lottery complete with Ping-Pong balls, and Jones ended up with 5 percent interest in six markets including San Juan, Winston-Salem, and Jacksonville. Jones was a risk taker in the business world, and he saw the incredible growth and potential once the technology developed that would make cell phones an extension of the hand.

Three years later, he was on a fishing trip with his son Stephen in Mexico. "For some reason, the next morning I got up and I was feeling pretty rough. I don't know why," Jones said as part of his trip-down-memory-lane speech at the Hall of Fame in the summer of 2017. "But I was drinking a lot of coffee, and I was reading the paper when I learned the Dallas

Cowboys were for sale. I found a phone in the lobby, and I got someone on the other end of the connection, and I said, 'You don't know me from Adam. And if I live to make it back to the United States, I'm going to buy the Dallas Cowboys. Hang-over be damned.'"

That led to the best business deal of Jones's forty-six-year-long life.

And also the worst.

The worst came first.

The deal for the Cowboys was a $154 million equity purchase. The only money Jones borrowed was against his assets. He didn't take out any straight loans. He sold his interest in the NBC affiliate in Little Rock. He decided to sell his stake in the cell phone companies.

"Sold them for $1 million," Jones said.

In just four years, he made a tidy $750,000 profit on his investment. That will pay for a lot of cell phone calls. The whole business was in its infancy stage and had not yet exploded. Cell phone towers were still being constructed. The telephone companies owned 75 percent of the six markets Jones invested in. He was among the investors in the other 25 percent. Jones needed to cash out to help buy the Cowboys. As smart as he is, if he had known what was about to happen, he would have found another way to raise the $1 million. He might have even gone to his favorite bank and just taken out a loan.

He cringes when he reveals what his $250,000 investment was valued at seven years later.

"My interest would have been worth $700 million," Jones said, give or take the cost of a few cell phone towers that would have required capital to construct.

That, he said, was the worst business decision he ever made.

He could have leveraged the $154 million it took to buy the

Cowboys and instead taken over a $2 billion company that might have eventually doubled its value. But he loved football, and he used his money to buy the Cowboys, who by 2017 were valued at $4.8 billion. That sounds great, but it's not like that $4.8 billion is in the bank or tucked away under his mattress at his home in ritzy Highland Park.

"I'm not interested in selling," Jones said.

Now, if he could have kept his cell phone shares and still bought the Cowboys...well, you can't have everything, even if you are Jerry Jones and accustomed to drawing an ace and a picture card on every blackjack hand.

When Jones showed up at Valley Ranch in February 1989, he immediately installed himself as the team's general manager. He considers himself a football man, and he could think of no good reason why he should establish a layer between himself and Jimmy Johnson by hiring someone else, especially when Jones had every intention of being involved in every football decision. While he was working hard the first few years to establish the Cowboys on solid financial ground, Johnson was the point man on the draft and trades and Plan B free agency, which impacted only the bottom of the roster. Unrestricted free agency did not come until 1993.

Jones studied the structure in Dallas that preceded him. Tex Schramm was the Cowboys' president and general manager. His first job in the NFL was as the public relations director of the Los Angeles Rams in 1947. He was later promoted to general manager and hired Pete Rozelle as the PR director. Schramm left the Rams in 1956 and worked as an executive at CBS Sports until Clint Murchison hired him to run the Cowboys when they were an expansion team in 1960. Schramm was instrumental in Rozelle's election as NFL commissioner in 1960, and no executive in the NFL was as savvy as Schramm in marrying football with network television. Jones did Schramm one better with the title of owner to go along with president and general manager. Schramm and Rozelle broke into the football business as public relations directors, which likely didn't prepare them any better for a career running a team or running the NFL than a former college football player running a multimillion-dollar oil-and-gas business.

Once Johnson left the Cowboys and his players soon left through retirement or free agency, it was up to Jones to replenish the roster. The NFL is a cutthroat business. Jones no doubt had more knowledge about the game than most owners, but he put the Cowboys at a disadvantage competing against football lifers like George Young with the Giants and Ron Wolf with the Packers. If Jones were to evaluate himself as the general manager in the post-Johnson era utilizing the same rubric he uses for his coaches, then no doubt he would have fired himself long ago simply based on the results. His drafts have been bad. His teams have been out of the playoffs more than they've been in. He emptied his pockets to buy the Cowboys and had no intention or desire to sit in his office and just work on the financials. He wanted in on the action, and he believed his presence as the general manager gave the Cowboys the stability other organizations lacked.

"If you look at it throughout the years, since I've come into the NFL, the average turnover for the general manger has been every bit as much as the head coach," Jones said. "So all you've done is enter into an equation when you yourself are going to make the ultimate decision anyway on the key issues."

If the owner was going to hire a GM who was going to pick the players and get fired, then Jones decided he might as well just pick the players himself. Hiring a GM, he reasoned, just adds "another moving part. All you got to do is look at the history. I think that my decision has been substantiated time and time again by the mere turnover that you have in GMs."

If the ultimate decision maker is the owner and he is involved in the day-to-day business, there is no need for a general manager. That's Jones's business model and he's sticking to it. "I couldn't have made this commitment to buy the Dallas Cowboys had I not been there to make the calls," he said. "The biggest money is spent on the players. Plus the fact that Tex Schramm had actually built the franchise to that point and done a magnificent job, and he had a media background and he's the general manager. He made the call to draft Roger Staubach. So my whole point was the Cowboys were the perfect template."

Even so, in the first twenty-four seasons without Johnson, the Cowboys made the playoffs just eleven times. They went through the Tony Romo era with just two playoff victories. As far back as 2012, before the Cowboys' streak of missing the Super Bowl had reached two decades, Bob Costas asked Jones in an interview on NBC's *Football Night in America* if Jones the owner should have fired Jones the general manager.

"Well, I think so, because he was there to dismiss," Jones said. "I have always worked for myself, and you can't do that. You basically have to straighten that guy out in the mirror when you work for yourself. But certainly, if I'd had the discretion. I've done it with coaches, and certainly I would have changed a general manager."

* * *

Jones is a brilliant businessman, but he is obsessed and determined to be known as a football man, a clever personnel man. George Halas was the player-coach-GM and owner of the

Chicago Bears. He won one championship as a player-coach and five more as an executive.

After Art Modell ran Paul Brown out of Cleveland, Brown became the owner-GM-coach of the Bengals when the NFL awarded an expansion franchise to Cincinnati in 1968. Brown coached the Bengals for eight seasons and made the playoffs three times, although he did not win a postseason game. His biggest mistake came after he stepped down as coach and promoted offensive line coach Bill "Tiger" Johnson to replace him rather than offensive coordinator Bill Walsh, who later won three Super Bowls with the 49ers.

"In the perfect world, the owner should be the general manager, just as it would be perfect for the head coach to be the owner," one former NFL general manager said. "But that is idealistic thinking. Jones has the right idea, but his flaw is he's trying to coach the team as the general manager by controlling whoever he hires. That doesn't work."

Jones has always had final say with the Cowboys even if it was just a formality when Johnson was setting up the deals. He's the owner. He signs everybody's checks. But if those checks don't have balances, then Jones could run wild and only the salary cap would limit his desire to collect stars once free agency began. As he found out, his son Stephen and his personnel department were not afraid to challenge him.

* * *

Jerry Jones made sure it was Prime Time in Dallas.

Even if Jones truly believes the Cowboys were not shorted any championships because he fired Johnson, not many shared his opinion. In the first year without Johnson, the Cowboys lost to the 49ers in the NFC Championship Game. Deion Sanders had signed a one-year deal with the 49ers after spending the first five years of his career with the Falcons. The 49ers won the Super Bowl with Sanders by finally getting past the Cowboys after losing to them in the two previous conference title games.

The pressure was on Jones. All he heard after the loss to San Francisco was that he could not win without Jimmy and how Barry Switzer was obviously not one of those five hundred coaches who could have won the Super Bowl with the Cowboys' talent. Basically, the same team that had beaten the 49ers the previous two years under Johnson lost to them under Switzer. In the '94 championship, the Cowboys had sixteen out of twenty-two starters remaining from the championship game one year earlier, including future Hall of Famers Troy Aikman, Emmitt Smith, Michael Irvin, and Charles Haley.

Just as Haley's trade from the 49ers to the Cowboys right before the 1992 season helped Dallas surge past San Francisco, the addition of Sanders to the 49ers secondary in 1994 helped swing the balance of power to the Bay Area. They had a legitimate cover corner to stick with Irvin.

Everybody knew that Sanders was nothing more than a one-and-done hired gun with the 49ers. He signed a one-year deal with San Francisco for a below-market $1.2 million. He wanted to raise his profile by playing on a championship team and hit the market again the next year. Sanders had picked the 49ers over the Chiefs, Dolphins, Saints, and Eagles, and a return to Atlanta. He was also playing baseball for the Cincinnati Reds. Despite their limited salary cap space, the 49ers were the best and most accommodating fit for Sanders.

Once the 1994 season was over, Jones set his sights on bringing Sanders to Dallas. He had to have him. He needed to hurt the 'Niners. He needed to help the Cowboys.

He was working with Stephen on the deal with Sanders's

agent, Eugene Parker. The Cowboys were very familiar with Parker. He also represented Emmitt Smith, and they had a contentious negotiation in 1993 that led to Smith holding out the first two games. Jones did have a tremendous amount of respect for Parker, and he was confident they could get the deal done for Sanders.

The deal was close enough that Parker came to Dallas to finish it off. The venue was Parker's room at the ritzy Mansion on Turtle Creek, the same hotel Jones stayed in when he was closing the deal with Bum Bright to buy the team. Stephen was in the next room preparing to consult with his father on the parameters of the contract before they agreed to terms. Stephen is his father's conscience and consigliere. He doesn't buy into star power.

It was 2 a.m. when Jerry entered the room where Stephen was waiting. Jerry was jacked up. Stephen was concerned that his father was about to destroy the Cowboys' salary cap. The NFL set it at $37.1 million for 1995, and Stephen was there to make sure his father didn't spend all they had remaining on Deion.

Jones had the numbers worked out with Parker: seven years, $35 million that included a signing bonus of $12.999 million. Deion was superstitious about the number thirteen. Jerry liked it. He was born on the thirteenth of October. Anyway, $12.999 million also sounded like a lot less than $13 million.

"You're really going to do this, aren't you?" Stephen said.

"Well, Stephen, it's done," Jerry said.

"It's what? My God, had I known you were really going to do this thing. . ." Stephen said.

"This thing is cooked now," Jerry said.

Stephen was a linebacker at Arkansas. He's considerably bigger than his father. He was also thirty years old at the time. His father was fifty-two. Stephen was livid. "Man, he shoves me right up against the wall, put that forearm around my neck and chest, and shoves me up," Jerry said.

This was a story that now makes him laugh. At the time, he grinned at his son, perhaps out of fear. "You are not going to hit me, are you?" Jerry said.

Jerry believed in buying and figuring out how to pay for it later. "I'll make it work," he told Stephen.

He did that when he bought the Cowboys. "I priced it based on what I thought it would take to buy it," he said. "Not how to make it work."

He did that in the oil-and-gas business, too. Football was a business with a hard salary cap. Stephen could have tinkered with the Sanders deal to make it more cap-friendly, but his father did not give him the chance. "At the time, we had Troy, Michael, and Emmitt, and we had them put to bed," Stephen said. "My thought was to get Deion to take a little less to keep the crew together."

Sanders's deal brought him even with Irvin and Smith and below Aikman. Stephen worried how they were going to tell the Triplets that they were now the Barbershop Quartet as far as money. "Leave it up to me," Jerry said.

Sanders's big signing bonus was accompanied by minimum salaries for the first three years before the salary jumped, keeping the cap number in the early years under control. The NFL soon outlawed structuring a contract in this manner. It became known as the "Deion Rule."

Stephen believes negotiating a deal of this magnitude requires a process. "Jerry thought the process was, 'Let's get this done,'" he said.

If the Cowboys had a traditional general manager who did not lead with his wallet, Sanders might never have made it to

Dallas. It was an awful lot of money for a cornerback, even one destined for the Hall of Fame. Sanders's presence forced offenses to cut off half the field. They were afraid to throw at him. It paid off in the Super Bowl for the Cowboys in Sanders's first season in Dallas, when the Steelers stayed away from him and kept testing Larry Brown on the other side. Brown picked off two of Neil O'Donnell's passes that had been thrown right to him. Brown, an unknown twelfth-round draft pick from Texas Christian University in 1991, was named the game's most valuable player and then signed a five-year, $12.5 million free agent contract to play for the Raiders. It was a big deal for any cornerback not named Sanders.

Jerry Jones 1

Stephen Jones 0*

*He was right. It was way too much money for a cornerback. But every owner would write a check for $35 million if they knew it would pay off in even one Super Bowl.

* * *

The Cowboys were among the first four teams to allow ESPN's cameras in their draft room when the inside look became a television staple in 1994. It was not the first time the Cowboys were out in front of the pack on innovative changes.

Gil Brandt was a baby photographer from Wisconsin obsessed with football when Schramm first hired him as a part-time scout with the Los Angeles Rams. Brandt later went to work in scouting full-time for the 49ers. When the Cowboys were granted an expansion team to begin play in 1960 and owner Clint Murchison hired Schramm to run it, among Schramm's first hires were Landry to coach the team and Brandt to find the players.

Landry left the Giants as an assistant coach after the 1959 season and was planning to get out of football and return to his native Texas in private business. Bud Adams of the brand-new American Football League pursued him to be the head coach of the Houston Oilers. Landry was considering the offer until Giants owner Wellington Mara, Landry's closest friend in football, called Schramm and told him if Landry was going to remain in coaching, then the Cowboys should hire him and keep him out of the AFL. Based on Mara's recommendation, Schramm hired Landry.

In their first season, the Cowboys were 0-11-1. The only game that prevented a winless season was a 31–31 tie at Yankee Stadium against the Giants in the next-to-last game.

Murchison, a businessman who inherited his money from his father's oil business and paid $600,000 to bring the Cowboys into the NFL, Cowboys, was the epitome of a hands-off owner. He was a bit of a recluse and was rarely seen around the team. He put all his faith in Schramm. He sold the Cowboys and the lease to Texas Stadium to Bum Bright in 1984 for $85 million. The biggest news Murchison created in his twenty-five years as owner was on the social pages. In 1973, Brandt divorced his wife Anne. They had been married in 1969. Murchison also divorced his wife Jane in 1973. Murchison married Brandt's ex-wife in 1975. It was her fourth marriage. Brandt never had any reason to believe Murchison was carrying on with Anne when he was married to her, although Murchison and Anne knew each other before Brandt married her.

Brandt continued to work for Murchison for another nine years until he sold the team. That would be front-page fodder these days for tabloids and blow up Twitter if the owner of a team wound up marrying one of his employees' exes. Murchison had major financial and health issues in his later years, spending the last part of his life in a wheelchair until his death in 1987.

The Cowboys were not included in the draft in their first year in 1960, but with their first-ever pick in 1961, they selected TCU defensive tackle Bob Lilly, who had a Hall of Fame career. Brandt picked Hall of Famers Mel Renfro, Bob Hayes, and Roger Staubach in his fourth draft. Landry had final say, but it was Brandt who did the work and put the draft board in order. Brandt was an innovator, and Schramm encouraged him to think outside the box.

"We went to the draft in 1961 and had a trunk full of black binders full of information," Brandt said. "Teams came in with rolls of quarters, Street and Smith's [football yearbooks], and copies of the *Billings Gazette*."

The rolls of quarters were for teams to use in pay phones during the draft. "It was $3.25 for three minutes," Brandt said. "A team would call Pappy Lewis at West Virginia and say, 'We need a tackle. You have any?' The Cowboys did not need quarters. They had all the information they needed in Brandt's black binders.

The Cowboys were the first to conduct pro days for draft prospects to work out for their coaches and scouts. The initial workout was at the University of New Mexico when Rudy Feldman was the coach. "We were the first to do that in 1970," Brandt said. "The draft was eleven days after the Super Bowl. We had time in the spring and we would call."

Brandt would request that Feldman have the entire team present for the Cowboys to run through workouts and to time. Feldman would ask why he wanted to time underclassmen. "It's good for the morale of your whole team. Everybody thinks they are a prospect," Brandt said.

This gave the Cowboys a head start on rising sophomores,

juniors, and seniors. "Our trade-out is we would take the whole coaching staff to dinner," Brandt said. "It would cost $500 to $600."

The Cowboys were the first to incorporate the use of computers for scouting into the draft in 1962. They invented the "black box," which is used to measure a player's agility and explosiveness. When Brandt's scouts would leave Dallas for bigger jobs, they would invariably use the black box with their new teams.

The Cowboys were always one step ahead during their glory days in the Landry era. Hayes was the 1964 Olympic 100-meter dash champion. Cornell Green was a basketball player. They traded up for Tony Dorsett. They invested a tenth-round pick on Staubach, who still had one season left and then had to serve his four-year commitment after graduating from the Naval Academy, and they invested a pick on Herschel Walker, who was in the USFL, and waited for the league to fold. Brandt found free agents like Drew Pearson, a receiver from Tulsa who played high school football in New Jersey with Joe Theismann; and Everson Walls, a cornerback from Grambling who grew up in Dallas.

Brandt and Schramm were never reluctant to brag about how far ahead of the rest of the competition they were. The NFL is a copycat league; it wasn't long before the Street and Smith's yearbooks were replaced by detailed scouting reports, and soon the Cowboys didn't have an exclusive on the use of computers. Still, the Cowboys were outperforming the other teams on draft day, which is the lifeline of every team. As the rest of the NFL began to catch up to the Cowboys' scouting methods, Brandt tried to outsmart them by using premium choices on high-risk, high-reward players. It didn't work. In the first round in 1982, he drafted Kentucky State cornerback Rod Hill. Hill was an amazing athlete who immediately alienated his teammates with his immaturity. The spotlight was just too big for him. He was supposed to be a prolific punt-return man, but he had such an inclination to run east–west, from sideline to sideline rather than straight up the field, that teammates began calling him "Shrine," as in the East-West Shrine Game, the popular college all-star game. In the second round that year Brandt selected Yale linebacker Jeff Rohrer. He had hit a gusher when he drafted Yale running back Calvin Hill in the first round in 1969. The Ivy League turns out an elite NFL player once every twenty years, and Brandt overplayed his hand. Rohrer, who was shocked that he was drafted so high, turned out to be a better locker room quote than he was a player. It was no surprise he was the smartest guy in the locker room.

When drug rumors persisted about Pitt quarterback Dan Marino right up until the 1983 draft, he began to fall through the first round. Brandt always prided himself on not only knowing everything about every player, but that he could name their parents, their siblings, and their high school coaches. He passed on Marino, even though Danny White had just lost three straight NFC Championship Games, and selected Arizona State defensive end Jim Jeffcoat. In the days leading up to the draft, he tried to entice the Colts into trading the overall number 1 pick so Dallas could take John Elway. Brandt offered Danny White in a package. The Colts wanted to substitute Randy White. Elway was traded to the Broncos. Brandt tried and failed in 1981 to move up to the Giants' number 2 spot to draft Lawrence Taylor. New York wanted LT and certainly was never going to trade him to a division rival. It was bad enough that Brandt traded backup quarterback Craig Morton to the Giants for a first-round pick that became Randy White. Brandt struck gold with the trades that brought Randy White and Dorsett to Dallas, but those days of unloading unwanted players for premium picks were over.

The Landry-Schramm-Brandt era ended with a whimper. Their last playoff victory was in 1982. They made the playoffs in 1983 and 1985 and missed in 1984, 1986, and 1987 before bottoming out at 3-13 in 1988, their worst record since they hadn't won a game in their very first season. Then they were all fired by Jones.

* * *

They deserved a better exit. Once Jones cut the check to Schramm, he was hired by the NFL to run their developmental league, the World League of American Football, consisting of teams in the United States and Europe. It was to be operated on a tight budget, but Schramm had no idea what that meant. He was one of the reasons the Cowboys were losing $1 million per month when Jones took over. Schramm enjoyed spending other people's money in excess, and now he had an entire league of owners paying his way. He knew only one way: first class. NFL owners considered the WLAF a minor league. The board of directors and Schramm clashed, and Schramm was fired in the fall of 1990, a few months before the league's first game. That was his final job in football before he passed away in 2003. Included in his legacy is his role as the godfather of instant replay in the NFL.

Brandt reinvented himself after his Cowboys career ended. He was not hired by another team, but he started to write for the NFL's website and co-hosted a show on SiriusXM radio. He eased into a role as draft guru and historian and became a valued treasure of the NFL. He even became close friends with Jones. When Stephen Jones's son John Stephen was leading Highland Park High School to a dramatic 53–49 comeback victory in 2017 to defend its 5A Division I state championship at

AT&T Stadium by throwing for a record 564 yards to bring his team back from a 49–39 deficit with three minutes to play, Brandt was sitting right next to Jerry in the owner's 50-yard-line suite.

Jones did not have to worry about the draft in his first five years of ownership. He had Johnson down the hall and around the corner at Valley Ranch taking care of things. Johnson devised the draft value chart, which assigned points to each draft pick depending on the slot. He used that to determine whether he was getting equal value or better as he traded up and down. He went for players who had productive college careers rather than any potential they might have shown in the "Underwear Olympics," at the Indianapolis combine. When Johnson departed, the pressure was on Jones. He did not face any challenges in the draft room from Switzer, Gailey, or Dave Campo.

Bill Parcells was going to be a different story. He did not have a history of a great spirit of cooperation in draft rooms. He battled with Giants general manager George Young for the eight seasons he was the head coach. Their contentious relationship may have had more to do with Young's coming close to firing him after Parcells was 3-12-1 in his first season in 1983 than an actual difference in philosophy. They won two Super Bowls together, with Young owning final say in the draft, but their relationship was never repaired. When Parcells was inducted into the Hall of Fame in 2013, his failure to mention Young in his remarks was glaring and unforgivable, especially because he mentioned Brandt, one of the Giants' main competitors.

Parcells had things his own way in New England for his first year in 1993, when James Orthwein owned the Patriots, and then for the first two years after Robert Kraft bought the team. Kraft took away Parcells's final say in 1996, and the Patriots drafted wide receiver Terry Glenn in the first round over

Parcells's objection. That battle for power led to Parcells leaving New England after he took them to the Super Bowl, even with Glenn a big contributor as a rookie. Parcells was his own boss with the Jets in his three years as coach and general manager, and in the final year with Gang Green when he was general manager only.

He accepted Jones's offer to coach the Cowboys knowing the owner was the general manager and the general manager had final say. Just coach the team. That was one of Parcells's favorite things to drill into his protégés. Now he had to listen to himself, but it was not going to be easy. He knew he wanted to play a 3-4 defense, so he had a profile for what kind of players he wanted at defensive end, defensive tackle, and outside and middle linebackers. In New York, he had Taylor to rush the quarterback from his right outside linebacker spot, lining up behind pass-rushing defensive end Leonard Marshall. Carl Banks was the linebacker on the strong side taking on tight ends and the running game, with Harry Carson and later Pepper Johnson and Gary Reasons calling signals from the inside linebacker position.

It was just a matter of time before Parcells was on one side of the aisle and Jones was on the other. In his first draft with the Cowboys, it came down to Oklahoma State defensive tackle Kevin Williams and Kansas State cornerback Terence Newman with the fifth pick in the first round. Parcells wanted Williams. Jones sided with the Newman camp. Williams went to the Vikings four spots later. Parcells was right on that one.

The big blowup finally happened in 2005, a year the Cowboys owned two picks in the first round, the eleventh and twentieth selections overall.

It was a year Stephen Jones had to assert himself with Parcells, a future Hall of Fame coach, and tell him, "That wasn't our deal. We're not going to go down that road," when Parcells kicked and screamed about the Cowboys' plan for their two number 1 picks rather than defer to Jones as he agreed.

Parcells wanted to take LSU defensive tackle Marcus Spears at number 11 after initially being all-in on University of Maryland linebacker Shawne Merriman. Spears would make the easy move outside to defensive end. Jerry and Stephen Jones and the Cowboys scouts wanted Troy defensive end DeMarcus Ware at number 11 and then see who was available at number 20.

"That really pissed Bill off," Stephen Jones said.

He found himself lecturing a man who was teaching him so many things about football and the NFL.

"Bill, you're the only one that wants to do this. All the scouts have worked their asses off," Stephen said.

Parcells can be charming. He treated the Cowboys scouts with respect and they loved him. "He was wonderful in the draft room," Stephen said.

This time, however, there was doubt Parcells was going to work the draft. He was arguing against Ware for just one reason: He was a hand-in-the-dirt defensive end in college, and in Parcells's defense he was projected as an outside linebacker. Parcells did not believe in using such a high pick and then gambling that the player could make a difficult position switch. He said that when he was with the Patriots, personnel guru Bucko Kilroy taught him never to take a projection in the first round, and the point was driven home in Parcells's talks with Brandt over the years.

"I was trained not to gamble on position transition," Parcells said. "I don't care what anybody tells you, you never know for sure if that is going to work until you get to doing it."

Parcells went to the Senior Bowl in Mobile, Alabama. The

Bucs staff was coaching the South team. Ware and Spears were teammates. Parcells asked Tampa Bay defensive coordinator Monte Kiffin to stand Ware up in a two-point stance so he could take a look at him at linebacker. "I thought he was a good player," Parcells said. "But I did want Spears."

Parcells was meeting with scouting director Jeff Ireland the morning of the draft. Ireland called Stephen Jones and told him they had a big problem. Jones was understandably confused. He thought they had an agreement that it was Ware at number 11 and Spears or Northwestern defensive tackle Luis Castillo at number 20. Parcells did not want Ware.

"Well, who does he want to pick?" Jones said.

"All I know is he wants to go Spears," Ireland said.

"Jeff, hell, we don't have anybody who has Spears going this high. Especially over a pass rusher," Jones said.

"He wants to meet," Ireland said.

Ireland, Jones, and Parcells got together in Ireland's office. "How you doing?" Jones said.

"Fine," Parcells said.

Parcells had his game face on. He was ready for a confrontation. If it couldn't be Spears, he had been set on Merriman. "I agree we can't do Merriman. I've run my traps and confirmed what everybody else was worried about. We can't take Merriman. I get that. But we're taking Spears. Just so you know, I'm adamant that we take Marcus Spears," Parcells said.

"Bill, we're not going to take Marcus Spears. You've been telling me all along how we got to get somebody who can get pressure on the passer. You sat in there and we all agreed that at the end of the day Spears was the perfect 3-4 end. He wasn't going to be a ten-sack guy. He would be two-gap and hold up against the run. He's not a pressure player. We're not going to take him," Jones said.

219

"We are going to take him. I think he can get pressure," Parcells said.

"Bill, you find me one fucking scout, I mean one scout, who wants to take Spears over Ware. Just go do it. Go find it," Jones said.

"Jeff?" Parcells said.

Ireland sank down in his seat. He didn't want to disrespect Parcells, but he wanted Ware.

"I know Jeff doesn't want to take Spears. It's not fair for Jeff sitting here," Jones said.

"That's bullshit. You and Jerry are just like the fucking Krafts. You say one thing and do another," Parcells said.

"I fucking take offense to that. Go look on your fucking sign that says, 'Just coach the team.' We said all along if it came right down to it that Jerry had the final call on who we were going to pick in this draft," Jones said.

"You set on this? We're not going to take Spears?" Parcells said.

"We'll take Spears if Ware is not there. But if Ware is there, we're taking Ware," Jones said.

"Fuck you," Parcells said.

"Hey, fuck you, too. Let's get everybody in a room and see if we can get the consensus to take Spears. I'm all for it," Jones said.

"I'm out of here. I don't even need to be at the fucking draft today. Don't count on me being there," Parcells said.

"Okay," Jones said.

Parcells stormed out of Ireland's office. He was being a baby. Jones didn't know whether to laugh at the absurdity of his coach threatening to boycott the draft because he was not getting his way or to think this was indeed a crisis. Parcells might not have had final say but he had plenty of say, and Stephen and Jerry valued his input. It was a different dynamic than when Kraft took away his personnel power and sided with his scouts to draft Glenn over Parcells's preferred option of trading down and selecting defensive tackle Tony Brackens. Or when five days after that draft Kraft cut Christian Peter, a fifth-round defensive tackle from Nebraska, after stories came out of how he abused women in college. In addition to being appalled by Peter's history with women, Kraft was not going to have a player on his team that his wife, Myra, would be uncomfortable around. Of course, Parcells upset Myra by once referring to Glenn as "she" when injuries limited his ability to participate in training camp as a rookie.

Glenn actually became one of Parcells's favorite players. He was just showing Glenn tough love to motivate him. He was a difference maker in the Patriots offense and a deep threat for Drew Bledsoe, and Parcells now loved him. One day, Parcells walked over to Glenn and laughed. "Keep doing stuff like that and I'm going to call you Miss America." Parcells was stubborn and set in his ways. But once you became a Parcells Guy, you were in the club no matter what. Before the 2003 season, Parcells was the driving force behind the Cowboys' acquiring Glenn in a trade with the Packers. He was heartbroken when Glenn died in a car accident in Dallas in 2017.

Parcells really liked Stephen and Jerry, so this made it a much different situation than he had in New York and New England. He might not have liked Young, but at least he respected him and was grateful he promoted him from defensive coordinator to head coach in 1983. He respected Kraft as a businessman but not as a football man. Now he had reached the point in his life where he had only so many knock-down, drag-out fights left in him, but his desire for Spears over Ware was worth going to the mat.

After they exchanged their fuck-yous, Stephen Jones sat wondering if his coach was going to attend the draft. Then he did the logical thing. He called his father.

"Well, we got a problem. I don't even know if Bill is going to show up for the draft. He is pissed," Stephen said.

"He will have to be pissed. We are going to take Ware if he is there," Jerry said.

Jerry and Stephen checked one more time to see if they were on the same page of Ware over Spears. They became more entrenched than ever. If Ware was there, he was theirs. They didn't have even one of their scouts recommending Spears over Ware, who had a great workout at the scouting combine in Indianapolis the end of February. They thought it might take a season for Ware to become fully acclimated to playing linebacker and at the higher level of competition, but when the education was complete, there was going to be hell to pay for the quarterbacks he tormented.

"Well, hopefully Bill will show up. But if he doesn't show up, he doesn't show up," Jerry said.

The Cowboys used a conference room across from the scouting office as their draft war room at Valley Ranch. It started filling up with scouts. Twenty minutes remained before the draft began in New York at 11 a.m. Dallas time. The previous two years Parcells had taken his seat to the right of Jerry Jones a full ninety minutes before the first pick. There was an uneasiness in the room. The scouts knew there had been a major disagreement between the coach, whom they trusted and wanted to please, and the owner, who paid the bills.

Stephen, sitting to his father's left, turned to talk to him.

"I don't think he's coming. I really don't think he's going to be here."

The draft was ten minutes away. No Parcells. Finally, he

walked in, set down his binders on the table in front of him, and didn't say a word. "Everybody feels the tension," Stephen said.

Stephen started a conversation about the players on their draft board. "Bill won't even look up," Stephen recalled. "He's over there piddling around. He won't talk to anybody. You could cut the tension with a knife."

Like every team in the league, the Cowboys were watching on television from their war room as the draft day drama played out. Paul Tagliabue walked to center stage in a huge ballroom at the Jacob Javits Convention Center on the west side of Manhattan.

Tagliabue: "With the first pick in the 2005 NFL draft, the San Francisco 49ers select Alex Smith, quarterback, Utah."

As the players got picked off the board, Stephen looked over at Parcells, who was still moping. Jones sensed Ware would be there for the Cowboys. *Boy, here we go*, he thought to himself. Auburn running backs Ronnie Brown, second to the Miami Dolphins, and Cedric Benson, fifth to the Chicago Bears, were taken quickly. The Cowboys wanted defense, so they were happy offensive players were going early. Cornerback Adam "Pacman" Jones was selected sixth by the Tennessee Titans. He would make more news for his legal troubles than his playmaking ability and would later play in nine games for the Cowboys in 2008.

The draft's biggest mystery was in the greenroom where University of California quarterback Aaron Rodgers was still awaiting a phone call from his new team. Until a day or two before the draft, he was in contention to be the number 1 pick by his hometown 49ers, but when they passed on him to select · Smith, it started a free fall. Rodgers would have been an excellent choice for the Cowboys, but they had signed Bledsoe to a three-year contract two months earlier and didn't consider quarterback a priority. Rodgers dropped all the way to the Green Bay Packers at number 24. The Detroit Lions had the tenth pick, one spot before Dallas. Even though the Lions had picked wide receivers Roy Williams and Carlos Rogers in the top ten of the previous two drafts, they went for Southern Cal wide receiver Mike Williams, despite GM Matt Millen wanting Ware. The Cowboys were now on the clock. Only three defensive players had been picked—two cornerbacks and a safety. No defensive ends or linebackers. The entire room signed off on taking Ware except for Parcells. This was a battle he could not win. Parcells and Jones were sitting so close to each other that the coach's left arm was touching Jerry Jones's right. They had not said a word to each other since Parcells had walked into the room hours ago. As the Cowboys were set to turn in their pick, Parcells started writing feverishly on a yellow legal pad in front of him. Jerry had no idea what he was scribbling.

"If said player DeMarcus Ware is drafted by the Dallas Cowboys and said player does not have twenty sacks within the first two years playing for the Dallas Cowboys, then the said owner of the Dallas Cowboys will owe the head coach of the Dallas Cowboys for the next three years five free trips on the owner's G-5 jet anywhere he wants to go."

Parcells signed the paper. He printed Jerry Jones's name on the bottom and put an "X" next to where he wanted him to sign. He pushed the pad in front of Jerry and banged his hand on the table. For the first time in the draft room, Parcells is smirking. Jones read the proposed agreement.

"Okay," Jones said.

He signed the paper but not before he wrote in an addendum to the contract.

"If said player does have twenty sacks, then the said owner of the Dallas Cowboys gets those same trips on his G-5 jet but with the head coach's girlfriend. Coach Parcells won't be on the plane."

He pushed the pad back to Parcells. He left a space for Parcells to sign. Jones knew Parcells's father was a labor lawyer and was amused at how Bill tried to create a legal document. Parcells signed by his name.

"We both fell out," said Jones.

Parcells had not said a word to Jones, but now they were hysterically laughing.

Tagliabue: "With the eleventh pick in the 2005 NFL draft, the Dallas Cowboys select DeMarcus Ware, defensive end, Troy."

Parcells looked up. "Ware is going to be a helluva player," he declared.

Of course, when the Cowboys' turn came up again to make the twentieth pick in the first round, Spears was still on the board. There was no way Jones could not pick Spears. Parcells might have quit on the spot. It turned out to be an amazing draft for Parcells to beef up his front seven: Ware, Spears, Kevin Burnett, Chris Canty, and Jay Ratliff.

Postscript I: Ware had 19.5 sacks in his first two years. Parcells won the bet, but he was gone from Dallas right after the 2006 season before he could collect. Just as well. Parcells hates to fly.

Postscript II: Ware played nine years in Dallas and had a franchise-record 117 sacks and finished with three years in Denver, adding another 21.5 sacks and a Super Bowl title. He is certain to join Jones and Parcells in the Hall of Fame. Spears had 10 sacks in eight seasons with the Cowboys before playing one year in Baltimore where he didn't register a sack.

* * *

The biggest showdown in the history of the Jones family came on May 8, 2014, the day of the draft. Stephen had always been a voice of reason for his father, reeling him back in when he needed a reality check. Jerry likes to think big and wanted to instill in his oldest son that playing it safe only leads to mediocrity.

The entire Jones family loved Tony Romo. "I absolutely think of Tony as a brother," Stephen said.

When Stephen's son, John Stephen, was on his way to winning his first state championship, his parents, grandparents, uncles, aunts, and siblings were there to support him. So was Romo. When John Stephen needed a tutor to work on his mechanics, Romo met him at the Cowboys practice facility.

As much as the Joneses considered Romo part of the family, they knew it was prudent to find and develop his eventual replacement. By the time of the 2014 draft, Romo was thirty-four years old with a long injury history. The Cowboys had been a Romo-centric team from the time Parcells inserted him at halftime against the Giants early in the 2006 season.

Johnny Manziel was a star quarterback at Texas A&M, 180 miles from Dallas in College Station. "Johnny Football" was barely six feet tall but he was bigger than the game. Jerry Jones is a businessman first and a showman second. He didn't create the world-famous Dallas Cowboys Cheerleaders. That was Schramm. He didn't come up with the America's Team nickname, either. But he knew how much each meant to the Cowboys' global recognition. As the days to the 2014 draft dwindled, Jones became obsessed with Manziel. He overlooked the character issues that were knocking him down draft boards. He didn't seem to care much that Manziel would have to transition from the spread offense he ran at A&M to the structured game of the NFL and become a pocket passer. Manziel beat then number 1 Alabama with a vintage performance in 2012 and became a celebrity quarterback. Jones hit it off with Manziel when he had him as a guest in his suite and they spoke for hours when the Cowboys hosted the NCAA Final Four basketball tournament in 2014 a few weeks before the draft. Manziel wanted to be a Cowboy. Jones wanted him to be a Cowboy.

Jones loved him so much he could barely contain his enthusiasm. Heck, if the Cowboys had the number 1 pick in the draft, he might have lobbied for him over Jadeveon Clowney. As it stood, the Cowboys were picking sixteenth, and Stephen Jones, Will McClay—the vice president of player personnel—and the scouts were unanimous: No Johnny Football for us. The Cowboys' priority was defense. They had three players targeted who they figured had a good chance to make it to their pick: UCLA linebacker Anthony Barr, Pitt defensive tackle Aaron Donald, and Ohio State linebacker Ryan Shazier. They were most optimistic that Shazier would get to them. He was a smallish linebacker, and they were certain if only one of the three fell, it would be Shazier and they would be thrilled. If they were all gone, Notre Dame offensive tackle Zack Martin, who was projected to play guard in the NFL, would be more than a consolation prize.

Early in the draft process, Stephen Jones didn't think he would have to fight off his father to avoid Manziel, because the exit polls after the combine indicated he would be off the board considerably earlier than when the Cowboys were picking. They did their due diligence anyway and discussed Manziel at length in their draft meetings. "Jerry was not wanting to hear everything that was said in terms of what our scouts had, in terms of his off the field, other than what was on tape," Stephen said. "Obviously he made great plays, and living right here in Texas, we were very aware of everything in terms of how he played the game and he was a dynamic guy. Johnny Football. Heisman

Trophy winner." Stephen didn't want to discuss the intel yet on Manziel's problems away from the field that was coming up in the research. He tucked it away, figuring the Cowboys would not have to make a decision on Manziel anyway because another team would snatch him off the board. To avoid picking a meaningless fight with Jerry, the rest of the organization was hoping Manziel would indeed be taken before they picked. "Rather than have an all-out shit show, we just kind of put him up there with a mid-first-round grade," Stephen said.

When draft day arrived, Manziel was at Radio City Music Hall in Manhattan with the other players invited by the NFL to attend the biggest off-season event on the league calendar. Manziel's stock was dropping as more information on his drinking and lifestyle became available, and Stephen Jones knew there was no way the Cowboys could take him. Imagine the circus if Johnny Football was playing close to his friends in Texas. Perhaps it would help sell some tickets, but just his presence would be a distraction the Cowboys did not need. The aggressive Dallas media would have Manziel on the ten o'clock news every time he was spotted in a bar. Besides, it would put inordinate pressure on Romo, knowing the fans would be calling for Manziel the first time he threw an interception.

Jerry thought it was a given that if the defensive players were gone and Manziel was still available, then he would be the Cowboys' choice. Just as Jerry surely had "the talk" with his son as he reached his teenage years, the roles were now reversed, and hours before the first pick, Stephen needed to have "the talk" with his father about Manziel that he'd hoped to avoid.

"I'm sure we don't need to go over it," Jerry said.

"Maybe we better," Stephen said.

"I assume, if he's there, we take him if all these defensive guys are gone. You'd take him, wouldn't you?" Jerry said.

"I wouldn't take him," Stephen said.

Jerry owned the team. Stephen knew his father had final say. But Jerry was also smart enough to listen to his son, who was bright enough to graduate Arkansas with a chemical engineering degree while playing varsity football. Offensive coordinator Scott Linehan made it very clear he was going to have to devise and customize an offense strictly for Manziel because the Cowboys could not run the same schemes as they did for Romo. Ideally, teams want to keep as much of their base offense as they could intact if they have to play the backup. That was not going to be possible if Dallas drafted Manziel.

Jerry asked if he was going to be the one person in the room who wanted Manziel if the defensive players were gone.

"I think you're the only one that would take him at that pick," Stephen said.

"None of the offensive guys want him?" Jerry said.

"I don't think so. I don't think so. I know so that they don't want him," Stephen said.

"What about scouts?" Jerry said.

"I know they don't, either," Stephen said.

"I didn't know you felt that strongly about it," Jerry said.

"Well, I do," Stephen said.

Stephen Jones's nightmare scenario played out right in front of him on the big-screen television in the draft room. Barr went ninth to the Vikings. Donald went thirteenth to the Rams. Shazier was his only hope to avoid an all-out war with the father he loved more than anything, but, in all good conscience, he could not let him make a pick with his heart.

The Bears took Virginia Tech cornerback Kyle Fuller with the fourteenth pick. The Steelers were the only team in the way of Dallas getting Shazier. Commissioner Roger Goodell got up from his seat in the NFL waiting area backstage, emerged from behind a curtain, and strolled across the Radio City Music Hall stage made famous by the Rockettes and their famed Christmas show.

"With the fifteenth pick in the 2014 NFL draft, the Pittsburgh Steelers select Ryan Shazier, linebacker, Ohio State," Goodell said.

"Game on," Stephen Jones mumbled under his breath.

The Cowboys were on the clock. The Manziel-to-the-Cowboys rumors had spread throughout the league. "This should be an interesting ten minutes," Green Bay Packers quarterback Aaron Rodgers tweeted.

"I think we need to take Manziel. Let's go around the room," Jerry said.

Johnny Manziel was the top-rated player on the Cowboys' board when it was their turn to pick. By three slots over the next available player, which was Martin.

Jones was now looking intently at his son, McClay, and the scouts. They all had their heads down to avoid eye contact with the boss. Stephen stole a peek to confirm nobody was going to break ranks and cave under the pressure of his billionaire father.

Jerry looked directly at McClay.

He was a four-year starter at defensive back for Rice, then played and coached in the Arena Football League, and coached in the XFL. He was the head coach of the Dallas Desperados of the Arena League, owned by Jerry Jones from 2004 to 2008. Then he worked in the Cowboys' front office before Jones promoted him in 2014 to senior director of player personnel. He put together the Cowboys draft board and ran the draft. This was his first draft, and now the owner was staring right at him, hoping he would side with him.

"What do you think, Will?" Jerry said.

"I just think there's too many issues to take him this high with our first-round pick. And Zack Martin is a player," McClay said.

Jerry went around the room. Nobody spoke up for Manziel. Jerry turned his attention back to Stephen.

"Dad, no one wants to take this guy. He doesn't represent what you want in a quarterback around here. I don't see how we take this guy," Stephen said.

"I want to take him. Scott, how is this thing going to work out?" Jones said, now focusing in on Linehan, desperately trying to find an ally.

Linehan outlined how he would have to redesign the offense. He explained how the players would struggle having to learn two systems.

"Dad, there's no one in this room who wants to take him," Stephen said.

If Stephen thought being alone on Manziel Island would convince his father to back down, he was wrong. What Jerry wanted, Jerry got. He wanted to buy the Cowboys, so he outbid the competition and bought the Cowboys. This was his team. It was his draft room. He'd hired everybody in that room. He wanted Manziel.

The ten minutes the Cowboys were allotted to make their pick was now down to sixty seconds. Every single person in that room wanted Martin to add to an offensive line that already had superstar first-round picks at left tackle in Tyron Smith and center Travis Frederick. Three studs on the o-line would protect Romo, hopefully lengthen his career, and take the pressure off him by opening up the running game for De-Marco Murray.

Chris Hall, the Cowboys' assistant scouting director, had the critical job of updating the draft board with each pick, keeping his eye on the clock, then phoning in the choice to the Cowboys' representative seated at a roped-off area at Radio City. For most teams it was usually the video director, the pilot of their charter flights for road games, or a friend of the owner. The job was easy: Write down the selection, walk it to the podium, and hand it to an NFL staffer at the front of the room.

"Chris makes sure all the trains are running on time," Stephen Jones said.

The Cowboys draft room was about to run off the track. Hall needed the pick or the Cowboys were going to be forced to pass. When that happens, it's embarrassing to the franchise and a sure sign of dysfunction. They spend millions of dollars scouting players at practices and games, then go through the grueling off-season evaluation period that includes the combine, pro day, and private workouts on campus and private visits for their top thirty players at the team facility, and spend months getting the draft board in order so when the pick comes up, it's like picking apples off a tree. Just grab the one in closest reach—the top player on the board. Unless it's Manziel. Teams that wander too far from their board always pay for it in the end. If the Cowboys were forced to pass, the Ravens would be on the clock. The Cowboys could jump in and make their pick at any time, but it would give Baltimore the opportunity to run their pick to the podium and perhaps grab Martin. The clock was now down to seconds in the Cowboys room. Jerry Jones had not yet signed off on Martin. He was still holding out for Manziel. He thought Manziel was special.

"We got to get the deal in," Hall pleaded.

"What do you think? What are you going to do?" Jerry said as he turned to Stephen one last time pleading to hear the words "Johnny Football."

"I think we turn in Zack Martin," Stephen said.

When Stephen leaned to his right and told Jerry one last time that Martin was the pick, Jerry didn't fight him. Stephen took that as a sign of Jerry waving the white flag and signing off on Martin. He didn't wait for a verbal confirmation.

"Turn it in, Chris," Stephen said.

"I didn't say turn it in," Jerry shouted.

"It's already turned in," Hall said.

The Cowboys draft room celebrated when Goodell announced the pick. That was not a slap at the owner; it was the standard reaction in every draft room when the scouts got their man.

"Boy, everybody is happy except Jerry," Stephen said. "Everybody is kind of fired up but a little subdued."

They knew they had overruled the boss. The scouts were getting Martin on the phone so he could speak to Coach Jason Garrett and Jones and be welcomed to the Cowboys' once big and happy family.

Stephen tried to stay low-key out of respect for his father. Then he was startled when Jerry slapped him on the right leg so hard it made a loud cracking noise. Jerry told his son to "come here" so he could lecture him in his ear without the rest of the room hearing his anger.

Jerry to Stephen: "I didn't get to own the Dallas Cowboys, I didn't get to sit in this room, by always making decisions right down the middle of the road. You're never going to do great things in life if you don't take chances. What you did right there is down the middle. You don't do great things by going down the middle."

"Okay," Steve said.

"Okay, we're good. I'm glad we did what we did," Jerry said. Stephen was relieved.

Manziel was picked six spots later by the Cleveland Browns.

He was out of the NFL after just two seasons, a certified bust who couldn't get his personal life straightened out or stay out of the world of TMZ, and drank his way into football oblivion. Martin went on to be a perennial All-Pro. Manziel and Martin each signed contracts in the spring of 2018 that put an exclamation point on Stephen's victory over Jerry in the draft room. Manziel's desperate attempt to salvage his career resulted in him signing with the Hamilton Tiger-Cats of the Canadian Football League for $122,000 in base salary with a $10,000 signing bonus plus incentives. One month later, the Cowboys signed Martin to a six-year $84-million extension that included $40 million guaranteed, the richest contract for a guard in NFL history. Manziel didn't play a regular-season snap and was traded midseason.

"Had Jerry really, really, really wanted to take Manziel in the draft, he would have done it," Stephen said. "I always tell people that no one understands Jerry because everybody thinks he'd just take Manziel because he wanted to. But that's not him. He really does want to build a consensus. Had that been split fifty-fifty, he'd have gone Manziel. When there was no support to take him, he went with what he should do."

Stephen is his father's son. He's a risk taker but in moderation. He is a deal maker but removes the emotion. He is supercompetitive. He sat in the draft room knowing Martin was the right pick but hurting because his father was telling him he would fail in life making safe decisions. Stephen prevented his family from making a disastrous decision. If Manziel could not handle Cleveland, he might have totally imploded in the fishbowl of Dallas, and every one of his missteps would have been a reflection on Jerry Jones.

When the Browns parted with Manziel, the Cowboys never considered bringing him in for a workout. By then, his drinking was out of control and his résumé was further clouded by a domestic violence incident with his girlfriend. The most damaging residual impact could have been to Stephen's psyche after his father called out his ability to make tough decisions.

"He didn't really apologize," Stephen said. "He just said, 'We're good, we're good.'"

His father's comment did connect like a punch to the gut. "It hit home," Stephen said. "I agree with that to some extent, but you can't always do that. Sometimes there is a time to take a risk, but not when there is zero support for the guy."

Even so, that summer Jerry Jones was quoted by ESPN expressing a lifetime's worth of regret for not trusting his instincts and taking Johnny Football. "If we had picked Manziel, he'd guarantee our relevance for ten years," he said. "When we were on the clock, I said if we pick the other guy—any other guy—it would be a ticket to parity, more 8-8 seasons. The only way to break out is take a chance with that first pick, if you want to dramatically improve your team. That's why I wanted Manziel, but I was the only guy who wanted him. I listened to everybody...And I'm not...not...happy."

When you invest $154 million and it turns out to be worth nearly $5 billion, there is a tendency to think you have all the answers. As Jones went from Switzer to Gailey to Campo, it didn't seem totally outrageous to think one day Jones would never be happy unless he coached the Cowboys himself. He earned points by hiring Parcells to get the organization back in the right direction, had it going for a while with Wade Phillips, and has stuck with Garrett much longer than he might have twenty years ago. As he passed his mid-seventies, Jones craved stability. Garrett is a good coach who once was in high demand and elected to stay in Dallas as offensive coordinator when he was a frontrunner in 2008 for jobs in Baltimore and Atlanta. He's not a great coach. He is good enough to win when the talent is superior, as it was in 2014 and 2016, but still hasn't proven he's good enough in January.

Garrett's record as the Cowboys' head coach after the 2017 season was 67-53. After taking over when Phillips was fired halfway through the 2010 season, Garrett made the playoffs twice in his first seven full seasons. He had a winning record three times and won just one playoff game. Even when the NFC East went through a down period, Garrett was unable to take advantage. In the 2011, 2012, and 2013 seasons, the Cowboys finished 8-8 but went into the final game each year in a winner-take-all showdown for the NFC East title. In consecutive years, they lost the final game and the division title to the Giants, Redskins, and Eagles, keeping Dallas out of the playoffs. The Cowboys couldn't sustain success following Garrett's two best seasons. They were 12-4 in 2014 but then 3-13 in 2015, playing most of the season without Romo. They were 13-3 in 2016 but only 9-7 in 2017, with Elliott sitting out six games. "The NFL is competitive. We know the nature of it," Garrett said. "Our division is competitive. What you try to do is work as hard as you can and put the best product out there and compete at everything you do. If it works out, great. If it doesn't work out, you learn from the experience and move on."

Garrett prefers to portray a vanilla personality in his press conferences. He rarely supplies any colorful quotes or provides more than boilerplate answers. He showed a different side in Amazon's *All or Nothing* series chronicling the Cowboys' 2017 season that debuted the following spring. Garrett exhibited both a tough and a nurturing side with his players. He was brutally honest in his Monday staff meetings often attended by Jerry and Stephen Jones. He not only broke but shattered the record for f-bombs set by Rex Ryan in HBO's *Hard Knocks*.

Garrett's seasons have ended in disappointment each year, whether they were losing two heartbreaking playoff games to the Packers or failing to make the playoffs. Each year Garrett is near the top of the list of coaches on the hot seat. By early December of a down year, the rumors start that Jones is ready to fire him. That speculation is always followed by Jones issuing strong words of support. There seems to be a mandate at the beginning of every season that Garrett must get Dallas deep into the playoffs to keep his job. But he is a survivor. Jones likes him and is averse to starting over with a new coach. He is comfortable with Garrett and may think this is as close as he will ever get to adding head coach to his many titles.

If Jones has not come down from his owner's suite to put on the headset by now, it's not going to happen. "I don't think he ever felt he could coach the team," former Cowboys fullback Daryl Johnston said. "The thing about him that people have to understand is that he has made good decisions and poor decisions throughout his tenure as the owner, president, and general manager of the team, but all he wants to do is win. That's all he wants to do. Sometimes it impacts his decision-making process, but we always knew it came from a good spot."

After his four years with Parcells, it's clear Jones has shied away from bringing in another powerful coach. Phillips had already been a head coach in Buffalo and Denver and an interim head coach in New Orleans and Atlanta when Jones hired him. He was just happy to have the job. Phillips is an excellent defensive coach but has been more successful as a coordinator than a head coach. Jones fired him in the middle of his fourth season in 2010 and promoted Garrett, who had been the offensive coordinator. Garrett is second in longevity as the Cowboys' head coach behind Landry. Jones is very comfortable with him and has given him a surprisingly long time to prove he can be successful.

The long gap between the Cowboys' last Super Bowl following the 1995 season to their next one, whenever that might be, has been embarrassing for Jones and the organization. He has built a new stadium and a new training facility, each the most decked out in the NFL, but he has not been able to add a new Lombardi Trophy to the lobby display at The Star.

CHAPTER EIGHT

Who's Got Next?

Jerry Jones was waiting to hear the entire question, but asking it was uncomfortable.

"Who takes over after...?" it started.

"After what?" he said.

"I'm not sure how to say this, but you are almost seventy-six years old, so hopefully you will be around for another fifty years...," the questioner continued.

Jones started laughing.

"Don't be sensitive. We can take it," he said.

"Okay. Who takes over after you die? What is the succession plan?" he was asked.

The Dallas Cowboys would fetch the greatest price in the history of sports if they ever went on the open market. The $4.8 billion value assigned by *Forbes* in the fall of 2017 would be only the starting point in negotiations if a few billionaires looking for a new toy were to become involved in the bidding to create competition. The numbers could get silly.

Except the Cowboys will not be for sale after Jones dies. The plan is for his children, Stephen, Charlotte, and Jerry Jr., to each own one-third of the team. When the last of the three passes, the Cowboys still will not be for sale. The Jones grandchildren will take over. The family business is staying in the family.

Stephen will get the Cowboys' league vote as it pertains to NFL matters. He is the oldest and has been by his father's side from the first day Jerry bought the team in 1989. Stephen was not quite twenty-five years old. He is two years older than Charlotte, who is three years older than Jerry Jr.

"The key answer is I want them all running the organization," Jones said. "Stephen is the oldest. I don't want that to take away from his competence. Stephen is a chemical engineer by education. That's pretty accomplished right there."

That's because he wanted to play football at Arkansas rather than Princeton. As a compromise, Jerry told him he had to take the hardest major in Fayetteville. "He's been here doing this since he's about twenty-four, twenty-five years old," Jones said. "He's got it all. Charlotte has been such a great asset to everything we are about. Jerry is the closest one to me, which may not speak well for him. In terms of his ability, he's imaginative and he knows how to creatively handle and work through challenges."

Team owners are in possession of a valuable piece of property that they are reluctant to give up. When Wellington Mara and Robert Tisch, who each owned 50 percent of the Giants, passed away within weeks of each other in 2005, the team remained in their families. Wellington's son John, the oldest of eleven children, and Tisch's son Steve, the oldest of three, assumed their fathers' positions heading up the families' interests. Original Buffalo Bills owner Ralph Wilson died in 2014, but there was no desire to keep the team in the Wilson family and it was sold to Terry and Kim Pegula over Donald Trump.

Jones not only has made provisions for his family to continue to own the Cowboys, but he intends to keep on running the team himself from his enormous corner office on the second floor of The Star, where his three kids' offices are within shouting distance if he yells real loud. He has been in good health, especially after having his right hip replaced in 2015 and six weeks after having the left one replaced. His hips may have worn down—he did play college football—but doctors tell him the moneymaking part of his body is in tip-top shape.

He went into a prominent Dallas hospital when he was seventy-four to have an MRI and a CAT scan. He checked in under the name Chambers, which was the maiden name of his wife, Gene. The two radiologists didn't recognize him.

"Mr. Chambers," one of the doctors said, "I just wanted to come up here and see you and tell you that I noticed your age on the records here. You have the brain of somebody thirty years younger, as far as looking at the size of it. You have shrinkage in that area as you get older and yours has not done that."

Of course, that came as very good news to Jones. He knew he was smart, but now he also knew that his brain was holding its own as he neared eighty years old.

He will be sticking around the Cowboys if the rest of his body holds up as well as his brain. "I would hope as far as competence is concerned, knocking on wood, and I don't want to get out over my skis, the main thing is I don't want to do anything else," he said.

He loves it. He's passionate about it.

"I haven't worked a day in my life since I bought the Cowboys," he said.

He is thrilled to be working with three children who all strive to make him proud. He has not set up a competition to determine who gets a better seat in his 50-yard-line suite on game day or who gets to run the team if he's out of town for a week or when he dies.

"Dad said a long, long time ago, 'I will tell you, the three of y'all will accomplish more as a team than you ever will individually,'" Jerry Jr. said.

Jerry realizes, however, like any kids they are jockeying for their father's approval.

"Each of them is different in their contribution," Jones said. "They actually are different in their skill levels, but I would completely reject competition between each other but will admit freely they want to please me. They are unquestionably motivated to see me smile."

One day Jerry Jr. was walking out of the brand-new team headquarters with his father to watch the Cowboys practice. "My dad, and granddad on his side, they had an insurance company, and Dad reminds me often as we watch the five-time world champion Dallas Cowboys practice that this sure beats the hell out of selling insurance," Jerry Jr. said. "That's an understatement beyond belief." If one can outdo the others, the Cowboys benefit. "We all have children and we all have been children. The nature of things is you want to be looked at in a positive light with your parents. That's been going on since the beginning of time," Jerry Jr. said. "That is obviously important to our family. Our family is blessed to work together. I would not call it a competitive thing with Charlotte and Stephen. It's that old saying, 'To [whom] much is given, much is expected.'"

They have learned the football and stadium and marketing business together. "Grandpa Jones didn't run a football team," Jerry said. "This has everything to do with how well we work together. They've established their skills. They've established their contributed territories. I didn't know how to do many of the things that I am doing today. They were sitting there at twenty-three and I was a forty-six-year-old. Who do you think had the best ability to wrap their minds and grow with stuff as you found out? The twenty-three-year-old or the forty-six-year-old who would have a drink or two? What we've done is on a parallel path. You talk about marketing. I wasn't doing that. I was drilling oil and gas wells."

Jones's model of making the Cowboys a family-run business is not unique in the NFL. The Rooneys, Maras, and Halases have always involved multiple generations working for their clubs together and then ownership being handed down. Jonathan Kraft is the oldest of Robert Kraft's four sons and is intimately involved in the day-to-day operation as team president. Jones has taken it one step further by not only having each of his three children running important departments, but he has empowered Stephen by putting him in charge of the football operation and handling the salary cap.

Kraft purchased the Patriots in 1994, five years after Jones bought the Cowboys. New England has clearly been better on the field during that time, but the Cowboys still set the standard in moneymaking and brand recognition.

"When I came into the NFL, it was not a welcoming place," Robert Kraft said. "Jerry was one of the most welcoming people. He and Stephen and Jerry Jr. and Charlotte and Mrs. Jones. When we played down there we would go to dinner at their house and that helped us form a close relationship. He was very open and helped us as we tried to come in and figure out what we were doing. Jerry is one of the great salesmen and is very innovative. In the beginning, we learned a lot."

New England was a more challenging market for Kraft than North Texas was for Jones, although neither team had been winning in the years before they took over. The Patriots were the only NFL team that was fourth in popularity in its town. They were behind the Red Sox, Celtics, and Bruins. In Dallas, it was the Cowboys and then, oh yeah, the Mavericks and the

Rangers were around, and soon there would be the Stars. It was all Cowboys, all the time.

"As far as the way they run their operation, we have great respect," Kraft said. "They are very passionate in a very football-oriented base. Being that they are in Texas, which has more football fans per capita than any other part of the country, there is a lot of respect for the game. It's an advantage for them and they have capitalized on it beautifully. If every family would be like the Jones family, we would be even stronger as a league."

* * *

Charlotte Jones was working in Washington for Tommy Robinson, an Arkansas congressman, putting her Stanford education to good use. The Cowboys had drafted Air Force defensive tackle Chad Hennings in the eleventh round in 1988, the year before Jones bought the team.

The Cowboys, of course, had great success drafting military men. They took Navy quarterback Roger Staubach in the tenth round of the 1964 draft, taking advantage of an NFL rule that allowed them to draft him when he still had one year of eligibility remaining. He played his senior year at Navy, and then the Cowboys waited as he served his four-year military commitment. He joined the Cowboys as a twenty-seven-year-old rookie in 1969, and he won two Super Bowls as the starting quarterback before concussions forced him to retire after the 1979 season.

Jones was anxious for Hennings to get to Dallas. Tex Schramm retained his rights by signing him to a multiyear contract with a $25,000 signing bonus. Hennings was a pilot, and as a result his commitment was eight years. Jones called Charlotte for help.

widely circulated. She attempted to emphasize that the Cowboys did not condone domestic violence but felt this gave them an opportunity to show that people can make mistakes and recover.

"That's why this is such an incredible opportunity. That's why I am not afraid of this move. I'm a mom. I've got a daughter. I've got two sons," she said in the video. "This is a serious issue for me, personally. I want my kids to know that domestic violence is not acceptable. But I also want them to know that if they make a mistake, no matter what the issue is, I'm not just going to throw them out. I've got to help them come back and make a better choice."

The Cowboys needed help with their pass rush, and Hardy was an elite pass rusher. They never even worked out running back Ray Rice, who was caught on hotel surveillance tape hitting his girlfriend, then was suspended by the NFL and cut by the Ravens. Why no Rice? Because they did not need a running back in decline. If a player has the skill set to help a franchise, they will overlook his warts and claim they believe in second chances.

Hardy had been found guilty by a judge of beating his girlfriend, but he exercised his right to request a jury trial. The case was dropped when the woman would not cooperate with the prosecution and she instead accepted an out-of-court settlement. Hardy signed a one-year, $11 million deal with the Cowboys. He was suspended ten games by Goodell for conduct detrimental to the league, but he appealed and it was reduced to four games. Hardy never came out publicly and expressed remorse or apologized. He became a distraction and exhibited disruptive behavior with the Cowboys, so he was not brought back in 2016. He registered six sacks in twelve games, and that was the end of his football career.

Hardy turned out to be the wrong guy for the Cowboys to bet on.

"I think from his track record, he was," Charlotte Jones admitted two years later. "I don't think I knew that going in. The world that we are in and the visibility of what we do brings a whole other layer of complexity onto just a challenging issue. We are family here, so I treat them like that and I take that chance with them. Then hopefully they want to take the chance with us. Sometimes, that doesn't work, though. That was an example of it not working."

Just four months after the 2015 season and the failed Hardy deal, the Cowboys drafted Ohio State running back Ezekiel Elliott in the first round with the fourth overall pick. A few weeks before training camp, he allegedly was involved in an altercation with his girlfriend in Columbus, Ohio, that haunted Elliott and the Cowboys for nearly two full seasons. After a thirteen-month investigation, Elliott was suspended six games by Goodell for the start of the 2017 season. Elliott fought the punishment and traded court victories with the NFL until he finally gave up and was forced to sit out the six games at the most important part of the season. Elliott's absence ruined Dallas's chances to make the playoffs.

The Cowboys didn't know Hardy before they signed him. They did the usual extensive work on Elliott before the draft that teams do with all prospects. The incident happened less than three months after they drafted him. Elliott was never charged with a crime, and the NFL's leading investigator cast doubt on the credibility of the girlfriend and recommended Elliott not be suspended. The Cowboys never wavered in their support of him.

"His situation is incredibly unfortunate," Charlotte said. "Heading into the league so young, they are my son's age.

That hits home with me. Are we making the right decision? Are we in the right company? Do you have the right influences around you? And in his case, not being in the right company is not an excuse, but it certainly makes this challenging for you. You have to be even that more cautious about your behavior and respectful about your behavior than you ever were before. This is what happens when you put a star on the side of your helmet."

The Cowboys' unconditional defense of Elliott became a lightning-rod issue after details of physical force allegedly used by him on his girlfriend were released from the NFL's investigation in Goodell's letter to Elliott. The NFL detailed stomach-churning evidence. The league felt it was burned by following law enforcement in the Rice case in 2014 and insisted it would not be guided by that again.

"I think Zeke is a good guy," Charlotte Jones insisted. "He wants to make people proud. He wants to make himself proud, his mother proud, and his fans proud. He's far from perfect. But I do know that he's bound and determined to get a new start and do things better going forward."

The NFL's letter to Elliott was damning, once again putting Charlotte Jones in an awkward position. If she defended Elliott, she was not defending women. If she was critical of Elliott, then it would hurt the brand she was trying to promote. The letter detailed injuries Elliott's girlfriend, Tiffany Thompson, sustained on July 17, 2016, on her arms, neck, and shoulder as a result of Elliott using physical force. The letter said that two days later he inflicted injuries to her face, arm, wrist, and hands. Then two days after that, she sustained injuries to her face, neck, arms, knee, and hips as a result of physical force used by Elliott. The letter was accompanied by photographic evidence.

"That is not the guy I know," Charlotte Jones said.

* * *

The Jones family can't get enough of each other.

They work at the office together. They go to training camp together. They go to the games together. Jerry's four grandsons rode in the car with Grandpa at the Hall of Fame parade. "Absolutely the most precious pictures," Grandpa said.

The Joneses even take time off together. "Our family vacations become board meetings," Charlotte said.

The Cowboys play at home every Thanksgiving. The entire family has a holiday meal with the Salvation Army at the game. It is the charity of choice for the Jones family, and Charlotte was the first female in 125 years to be named national chairman of the Salvation Army Advisory Board.

The next day, the family travels out of town together. They used to go duck hunting in Stuttgart, Arkansas, where they owned a lodge. Or it was off to their home in Destin, Florida. They fixed up Jerry's parents' old house on a ranch in Springfield, Missouri, and that's been the recent destination on the day after Thanksgiving. In the off-season, they've all gone to Europe together. Leading up to a bye weekend a few years ago, Gene Jones called her daughter to find out what they were doing. "I don't know if I'm going to tell you," Charlotte replied.

She was kidding. "We have such a close family," she said.

The Cowboys were in Washington for their game in 1989. It was the only game they would win the entire season. Stephen was working for the Cowboys. Charlotte was working for Robinson. And Jerry Jr. was in college at Georgetown. The night before the game, the entire family went out to dinner at Sfuzzi in Union Station. Actor Burt Lancaster was in the restaurant.

"Oh my gosh," Gene Jones said.

She was taken aback. "My mother was a huge Burt Lancaster fan," Charlotte said.

The Joneses were not well known at the time. All Jerry was known for was firing Tom Landry. "We were nobody," Charlotte said. "We were these people from Arkansas that had just bought this team. We were nobody in this restaurant."

Gene Jones was starstruck.

"I know you love him," said Shy Anderson, who was then Charlotte's boyfriend and is now her husband. "I'm going to see if I can get his autograph on the menu."

Anderson walked over to Lancaster's table, whose group had finished eating.

"Excuse me, my mother-in-law is a huge fan. Do you mind signing?" Anderson said.

"How dare you come up to me? This is my private time," Lancaster shot back.

He berated Anderson and made a scene. Anderson sheepishly walked away and came back to the table. The whole family saw what happened.

"Didn't get it," he said. "Didn't work very well."

The Jones family sat in shock. How rude.

"Let that be a lesson to everybody here," Jerry said.

"I'll never be a fan of his," Gene said.

From that point forward, Gene Jones couldn't stand the mention of Burt Lancaster's name. As the Cowboys' success made the family more visible, they were encouraged by Jerry to remember the empty feeling they had when Lancaster turned down the autograph request, and never to act that way if a fan should ask them to sign a menu or a football or a program.

Even so, one time Jerry was grumpy and having a bad day when he told a fan he didn't have time for an autograph. "Remember Burt," his family told him.

He stopped and reached over to sign. "Have a great day," he said.

That story has never been forgotten. "We've had the Burt story for the last twenty-nine years to realize that the day no one comes up to ask you for a picture or your autograph will be your darkest day," Charlotte said.

She was still in Washington when her father was closing the deal to buy the Cowboys. The transaction was announced; Landry had been fired and Schramm and Brandt would soon follow; and the family had taken over the offices at Valley Ranch, but the contract still had a few outstanding issues that needed to be resolved.

"Jerry, you know you don't have a deal yet," Jones's attorney, Dick Cass, told him. "The paperwork is not done. You haven't resolved all these points."

It was six months after Jones had taken over, and the season was about to start. Jones told Bright that they needed to agree on a bunch of final clauses. Bright resisted and told Jones they'd already shaken hands.

"There is no more negotiating," Bright said. "I will go to the next person in line and sell the team to somebody else."

That would have been an embarrassment to the NFL for letting Jones make the changes without the deal having closed, and it would have been humiliating to Jones. Bright never intended to reopen the bidding but suggested to Jones a bizarre way to resolve the final points that were worth several million dollars. Jones did not have a lot of loose change lying around.

"I'll tell you what. We'll flip a coin," Bright said.

"Flip a coin?" Jones said.

He was not happy.

He agreed to the coin flip. Bright removed a coin from his pocket and tossed it in the air. Bright called heads. Of course, it came up heads.

"Sorry, Jerry, I win," Bright said.

"What do you mean, 'sorry'? I own the Dallas Cowboys," Jones said.

Jones never asked to see the coin. Bright teased him that he trusted him. Was it a two-sided coin with heads on each side? Bright sent the coin to Jones as a keepsake. It was embedded in a frame and Jones never found out if it was legitimate.

"It's one of those things that you never want to look," Charlotte said. "You never want to know."

No big deal. What's a couple of million dollars when it cost $8 million to throw the most elaborate Hall of Fame party in NFL history?

Jerry Jones hit the biggest oil gusher of his wildcatting career when he bought the Cowboys and still gets weepy when he remembers how he risked it all. Imagine the tears when the Cowboys finally win another Super Bowl.

ACKNOWLEDGMENTS

It carried the same significance as being the White House correspondent for the *New York Times* or covering the Pentagon for the *Washington Post*.

That was the pressure, status, and exhilaration of covering the Cowboys for the *Dallas Morning News*. It was the most fun I ever had in the media business. That includes appearing weekly as the inside information reporter on HBO's *Inside the NFL* when it was the best football show on television, and writing my NFL column for nearly three decades for the New York *Daily News* in the greatest city in the world.

The Cowboys were special when I worked for the *Morning News* from 1981 to 1989, and they are still special today. They've always been special. That's why it was such an enjoyable journey researching this book. There were so many great stories to tell over three distinct eras of America's Team: the Landry Years, the Jerry-Jimmy Years, and the Jerry-Without-Jimmy Years.

One thing I regret was never covering the Cowboys in the Super Bowl when I was with the *Morning News*. That was back when newspapers were thriving and spent money. The *Morning*

News was the paper of record for the Cowboys. They were the most important story in Dallas, which made them the most important beat at the *Morning News*.

I settled for covering the Cowboys in a couple of NFC Championship Games and two sales of the team. Along the way, I spent eight seasons around one of the greatest and most iconic coaches in NFL history and was there when he was fired. I sat in the second row in the team meeting at Valley Ranch for the contentious Saturday Night Massacre press conference, when Jerry Jones bought the team and officially announced he was firing Tom Landry and hiring Jimmy Johnson. I was in Anaheim the night there was a death threat on Landry's life during a game against the Rams, and he went into the locker room to be fitted for a bulletproof vest and he came back to the sidelines and no player or coach would stand near him.

Even after I left Dallas and moved back home to New York and covered the Giants in four Super Bowls—they won three of them—and the Jets—of course, in none of them—I still loved writing about the Cowboys. I did get to cover them in three Super Bowls when I was at the *Daily News*, but it wasn't the same as if I was still at the *Morning News*. Even so, I was in their locker room working for the *Daily News* a few days before a big game against the Giants in 1993 when Johnson asked me to come into his office. Unsolicited, he went into a rant about how the Giants were a bunch of whiners. That made the *Daily News* back page. The Cowboys sell. They always sell.

* * *

The first stop writing this book was midtown Manhattan.

Late in the 2016 season I spent two hours with Jones at the St. Regis Hotel. I met with Tony Romo at a CBS luncheon a few weeks before his first game in 2017 and then spoke to him again months later.

I came to Dallas in October 2017 and had an amazing week of visits with Charlotte Jones Anderson and Stephen Jones. I teased Stephen about sending his son to the Manning Passing Academy in Louisiana and having him learn from Eli Manning, the enemy, but then again, Dak Prescott was once a camper and a counselor at the camp. The next day I sat down with Jason Witten at the Cowboys facility (retirement was not on his mind at the time), spent time at Tony Dorsett's house, visited with Stephen Jones again, then spent the late afternoon with Michael Irvin. When you are with Irvin, there is always adventure.

As soon as I arrived at his home in Plano, he said, "Let's go."

"Huh? Where?" I said.

One of his relatives had been involved in a car accident, and she needed him to talk with the police. Irvin hopped on the Dallas North Tollway, pulled over to the shoulder, did what he had to do, spoke to the police, and we were on the way back to his house. Irvin has such a big family that I'm not sure how he juggles all his obligations and responsibilities.

He is also one of my favorite Cowboys. On the day he was drafted by the Cowboys in 1988, there were rumors that the Packers, picking seventh, might select Irvin. He wanted no part of playing in Green Bay. He was used to South Florida weather. The Cowboys ranked Irvin the best player in the draft but felt confident they could get him at number 11. Dallas was where Irvin wanted to be.

Now the Packers were on the clock and Irvin was nervous. He has sixteen brothers and sisters, and his house was packed with family and friends waiting for the call from his new team. Irvin stood up in the living room of his mother's house in Fort

Lauderdale and made an announcement as the clock was ticking on the Packers.

"If the phone rings, nobody pick it up," he screamed.

He was hoping if the Packers wanted him and nobody answered the phone, they would not take him.

The phone did not ring. Green Bay selected wide receiver Sterling Sharpe, and four picks later the Cowboys took Irvin.

The entire Jones family was very giving of their time for this project. When I got together with Charlotte and Stephen at The Star Jerry was not available on that trip and I spent the rest of the season trying to carve out time to meet with him. Then the Ezekiel Elliott situation wouldn't end, Jones got himself in the middle of the National Anthem protests by NFL players, and then he pushed back strongly against Roger Goodell's new contract. Each time I tried to set up a meeting with Jones, he was embroiled in another mess.

Finally, on January 26, as I was literally walking into the team meeting room at the Giants headquarters for the introduction of Pat Shurmur as their new head coach, my cell phone rang. It was Jones's superefficient longtime assistant, Marylyn Love.

"Can you hold for Jerry?" she said.

Bad timing. Damn.

I asked Jerry if I could call him a little later. He asked me if the next day would be better, since he knew I would be busy. The next day was a Saturday. Jerry gave me his home number and asked me to call him at noon. At 11:45 my phone rang. It was Marylyn. I felt for sure something had come up and Jerry had to postpone.

"Jerry is ready. He would like to know if you could call him now," she said.

Two hours later, I thanked him for his time. I asked about six questions. Well, maybe ten. Jerry likes to talk and I like to listen. I had my tape recorder going and my feet up on my desk. I hope he was just as comfortable. The two hours went fast. A few weeks later, I was able to speak with Jerry Jr., and he provided much of the detail for the "Cowboys, Inc." chapter.

The saddest part of this book for me was reporting the chapter on the friendship of Ron Springs, Tony Dorsett, Robert Newhouse, and Dennis Thurman. Thurman, Springs, and Dorsett were my guys when I covered the team. Newhouse was a little older and more cautious as he tried to hang on for a few more years. It's still startling to me that these four guys who were so tight they were truly like brothers didn't get to see each other grow old. Springs and Newhouse died much too young. Dorsett has serious memory issues. Thurman, the last of the four, is aging well. He has been out of coaching since the end of the 2016 season.

Everson Walls, by the way, was the best friend a football writer could ever have, as he provided me insight and information that led to many headlines. He had a carefree attitude, which helped him play cornerback. He could get beat for 30 yards on one play, immediately eliminate it from his mind, and come up with an interception on the next play. He had no issues with telling me what was happening with the Cowboys behind the scenes. Of course, I agreed not to use his name. Fair trade-off.

Walls was so underpaid by the Cowboys I felt bad for him. So I started to write about how the Cowboys were taking advantage of this great kid from Dallas, a free agent who led the league in interceptions as a rookie, and were really screwing him when they should have been taking care of him. Walls was so appreciative that I listened to his story and presented his point of view that we became lifelong friends. The media in Dallas had been so promanagement that once the players saw I was willing to give them a forum to air their gripes, they lined up to speak with me.

Now it can be told: One off-season in the early '80s, the NFLPA created a pamphlet listing all the players' salaries. It was mailed to every player in the league. Walls called me at the *Morning News* and said, "Guess what just came in the mail."

Walls had it and I wanted it. He lived in North Dallas and was leaving for the airport in forty-five minutes.

This was way before you could Google any player and find out his salary. The pamphlet was gold.

"If you can get here before I leave, it's yours. If not, I will give it to you when I get back in a couple of days," Walls said.

A couple of days?

"I'll be right over," I said.

I ran out of the *Morning News* office. The drive with no traffic was usually thirty minutes. My route took me past the Texas School Book Depository, down the street in front of the grassy knoll, and to the Dallas North Tollway. I got there in thirty-five minutes. Walls was standing on the front step of his house with an envelope in his hand.

"Enjoy," he said as he handed it to me.

"Have a great trip," I said. "Hope you're going somewhere fun."

The list was alphabetical. I compiled all the Cowboys' salaries. We ran the entire list in the next day's newspaper in a two-page spread. It looked like the listings of the New York Stock Exchange. The next day I had writers from all over the country asking me to read them their team's salaries. Can't you get it from one of your players? I asked. Nope, they said. Back then, there was only one Everson Walls, and there has not been another one like him.

Postscript: Giving me the NFLPA list was one sign of his

generosity. What he did for Springs, giving him one of his kidneys, was an act of heroism. I always thanked Walls privately every time he helped me break a story, but now, all these years later, I want to thank him publicly. I only wish Springs was around longer. I know Everson Walls feels the same.

I also want to thank Rich Dalrymple, the Cowboys' senior vice president of public relations and communications, who was helpful in setting up many of the interviews. Jerry can be slippery and hard to pin down, but Rich knows his every move. I want to thank the Jones family, Jimmy Johnson, Bill Parcells, and all the players who were so accommodating. I had never spent time with Witten before I spoke with him for the book. Now I know why he wins all these humanitarian awards.

Some friends asked why we chose to call the book *How 'Bout Them Cowboys?* After all, it's about much more than the line Johnson made famous in San Francisco after the 1992 NFC Championship Game. "How 'bout them cowboys?" has come to transcend Jimmy's speech. It encompasses what the Cowboys are all about.

A little background: In the week leading up to the Cowboys' victory over the 49ers at Candlestick Park, CBS producer Bob Stenner called Dalrymple and asked, if Dallas won, could the network bring its cameras into the locker room to televise the celebration? Dalrymple worked with Johnson at the University of Miami and Johnson considered him a confidant. He knew Jimmy as well as anybody. As a result, he knew better than to ask Johnson about the cameras knowing he was so focused on winning the game that he would likely toss him out of his office accompanied by a few choice words.

Dalrymple never did ask Johnson leading up to the game. He never did give Stenner an answer. After the Cowboys won, the cameraman for CBS sideline reporter Lesley Visser approached

Dalrymple as they were walking up the tunnel to the Cowboys' locker room.

"Can we bring in the cameras?" he asked.

Dalrymple caught up to Johnson as they neared the locker room and finally asked him. Johnson was so overcome with excitement he pretty much would have agreed to just about anything. He said yes to the cameras. So, with a national audience looking in, Johnson stood on a podium in the middle of the locker room and shouted, "How 'bout them Cowboys!" If he had not let the cameras in, nobody would have heard the line and I would have needed another title for my book.

It was great to work again with my favorite editor, Sean Desmond, who also happens to be a huge Cowboys fan. One day, I've told him, the Cowboys will win the Super Bowl again. Just don't know when. If only Romo hadn't fumbled that snap in 2006. Sean's assistant, Rachel Kambury, was invaluable. So was Cindy Birne, my publicist extraordinaire in Dallas.

As always, my most important support group was there pushing me to the finish line: my wife, Allison, and college-graduate kids, Michelle, Emily, and Andrew, who was my researcher and fact-checker. I'm so proud of all of you.

How 'bout them Cowboys?

INDEX

ABOUT THE AUTHOR

Gary Myers has covered the NFL since 1978 and is the former NFL columnist for the *Dallas Morning News*, where he also covered the Cowboys, and the New York *Daily News*. He has authored four books: *The Catch*, a look at the iconic 1981 NFC Championship Game between the Cowboys and 49ers; *Coaching Confidential*, which details the pressures of being an NFL head coach; the *New York Times* bestseller *Brady vs Manning*, an inside look at the greatest rivalry in NFL history; and *My First Coach*, which explores the relationship between quarterbacks and their fathers. Myers was the inside information reporter on HBO's *Inside the NFL* and co-host of the YES Network's *This Week in Football*. He is a voter for the Pro Football Hall of Fame and a former adjunct professor at his alma mater, Syracuse University.